MW01088568

THE DARK SIDE OF THE WORKPLACE

The workplace can be a hotbed of difficulty and incivility—from rumors spread about an individual, to the agonies of stress, to physical attacks and even death. Evidence suggests that not only does incivility have significant implications for employees, organizations and society, it is also on the rise. In recent years we have experienced increased acts of incivility in the workplace, social media and government positions.

There is a direct correlation between uncivil behavior and financial outcomes for organizations. It is estimated that stress related to uncivil actions in the workplace costs organizations approximately $300 billion annually. The cost of personal implications for employees is often too high to calculate as individuals experience loss of reputation and significant psychological and physical distress. With the increased use of social media, individuals are experiencing incivility that crosses the boundary between their personal and professional lives.

This book delves into the darker side of the workplace, discussing bullying, toxic work environments, corporate psychopaths, the struggles of stress, and more. It combines recent research and case studies to provide an understanding of these behaviors, and offers practical solutions on how to cultivate a healthy working environment.

Annette B. Roter is an Assistant Professor at Viterbo University in La Crosse, Wisconsin, USA. Her research focuses on dysfunctional behaviors in the workplace. In 2017 she published *Understanding and Recognizing Dysfunctional Leadership: The Impact of Dysfunctional Leadership on Organizations and Followers*, published by Routledge. She has published several articles on the topic.

THE DARK SIDE OF THE WORKPLACE

Managing Incivility

Annette B. Roter

Routledge
Taylor & Francis Group

LONDON AND NEW YORK

First published 2019
by Routledge
2 Park Square, Milton Park, Abingdon, Oxon OX14 4RN

and by Routledge
711 Third Avenue, New York, NY 10017

Routledge is an imprint of the Taylor & Francis Group, an informa business

© 2019 Annette B. Roter

The right of Annette B. Roter to be identified as author of this work has been asserted by her in accordance with sections 77 and 78 of the Copyright, Designs and Patents Act 1988.

All rights reserved. No part of this book may be reprinted or reproduced or utilised in any form or by any electronic, mechanical, or other means, now known or hereafter invented, including photocopying and recording, or in any information storage or retrieval system, without permission in writing from the publishers.

Trademark notice: Product or corporate names may be trademarks or registered trademarks, and are used only for identification and explanation without intent to infringe.

British Library Cataloguing-in-Publication Data
A catalogue record for this book is available from the British Library

Library of Congress Cataloging-in-Publication Data
Names: Roter, Annette B., 1967– author.
Title: The dark side of the workplace : managing incivility / Annette Roter.
Description: 1 Edition. | New York : Routledge, 2019. |
Includes bibliographical references and index.
Identifiers: LCCN 2018027847 | ISBN 9781138559295 (hardback : alk. paper) |
ISBN 9781138559301 (pbk. : alk. paper) | ISBN 9780203712900 (ebook)
Subjects: LCSH: Work environment. | Violence in the workplace.
Classification: LCC HD7261 .R588 2018 | DDC 658.3/12—dc23
LC record available at https://lccn.loc.gov/2018027847

ISBN: 978-1-138-55929-5 (hbk)
ISBN: 978-1-138-55930-1 (pbk)
ISBN: 978-0-203-71290-0 (ebk)

Typeset in Bembo
by Out of House Publishing

To Clemens and Rosemarie Roter

CONTENTS

Acknowledgements   *x*

1   Introduction   1
    My experiences with the dark side   1
    Understanding the dark side of the workplace   5
    Aggression   6
    Labeling behaviors   6
    Causes of dark side behaviors   8
    Walking the fine line   9
    Incivility in society   10
    Work and life integration   11
    Importance of the topic   12
    Layout of the book   13

2   Incivility   16
    Civility and incivility defined   16
    Incivility in society   18
    Societal incivility and technology   20
    The rise of incivility: increase in incivility or just awareness?   21
    Incivility in the workplace   22
    Categories of workplace incivility   23
    Workplace incivility behavior   24
    How incivility in the workplace plays out   25
    Causes of incivility in the workplace   26
    Types of incivility in the workplace   27
    Organizational impact of incivility   32

Incivility and organizational culture 33
Reactions to workplace incivility 33
When incivility turns dysfunctional 33

3 Dysfunction in the workplace 36
Dysfunctional co-workers 36
Bullies 36
The paranoid 50
Narcissists/egotists 51
Backstabbers 58
Master manipulators 59
Emotionally abusive co-workers 61
Conclusion 63

4 Deviant behaviors in the workplace 66
Corporate deviances 66
Behaviors associated with deviance 68
Identifying deviant behaviors 68
What triggers employee deviance? 69
Types of deviant behavior in the workplace 70
Thieves 70
Psychopaths 70
Harassment 80
Challenges linked to sexual harassment 87
Evil in the workplace 89
Counter-productive workplace behaviors 89
Workplace violence 92
What can organizations do to prevent deviant behavior? 95
Conclusion 96

5 Impact of dark side behaviors on the workplace 99
Introduction 99
Impact on individuals 100
Organizational impact 107
Conclusion 113

6 Ways to address the dark side 114
Addressing dark behaviors in the organization 114
Confronting the dark side 118
Interventions 120
What managers can do to address these behaviors 121
Addressing team-level dysfunction 123

Culture of the organization 124
Organizational investigations 125
Removing retaliation in the workplace 126
Individuals dealing with dysfunction and incivility 126
Dealing with an uncivil or dysfunctional leader 133
How individuals can address dark behaviors 134
Individual action as a bystander 135
Individual ways to address dysfunctional behavior 136

7 The phenomenon comes to life 138
The crossover between incivilities in society and in the workplace 138
The passive-aggressive 141
The victim 144
The gossip 149
The harasser 150
The self-promoter 155
The narcissist and the bully all in one 158
The "queen bee" syndrome 164
Conclusion 168

Index 169

ACKNOWLEDGEMENTS

With every project there are so many people to acknowledge. Thank you to Ms. Lisa Kilmer for the time spent editing and providing assistance during this project. Your support and friendship through the years has come to mean a great deal to me. Peter Clark for time spent on pulling research for me; I appreciate all that you do for me, and a promising young researcher you have become.

Acknowledgements go to my family for their love and support. To my mother, Rosemarie Roter, thank you for all that you do, including the support you give to me each and every day. I promise to slow down one day…I'm just not sure when! To Petra and Greg, thank you for your support and encouragement. To my father, Clemens Roter, who would have gotten a kick out of this—I just wish you were here to see it. To my friends, thank you for your support, encouragement and for cheering me on—you all mean the world to me. To Ron, thank you for your advice, counsel and encouragement. To Eric, you brought this all to fruition and got me going; I thank you so very much. Also to my students, past, present and future, you all make it so worth it.

Acknowledgement goes to my research participants and the individuals who have come forward to share their stories. Thank you for sharing your experiences, pain and suffering, along with your successes in conquering the dark side. Through sharing your experiences I hope we can help others get through these experiences. Thank you! To the people in my life that have shown me their dark sides, thank you. Because of you I am a better, stronger and more confident person.

1

INTRODUCTION

My experiences with the dark side

Before we begin to explore the topic of the dark side of the workplace, it is best to understand where I as the author come from regarding this topic. Understanding my experience with the dark side and my fascination with it provides context for the topic. Sharing these experiences demonstrates that we all experience this type of behavior at some point during our careers. It may be as the target or as a bystander. No one is immune.

My first dark side experience changed my perspective of the workplace. In this position, I put my training to use to follow all the proper protocols, but I was not prepared for the backlash or the negative behaviors that occurred. In school, I was prepared to follow the laws, guidelines, and to do the right things. What I learned was how to deal with the dark side that I faced. Let me share this experience.

My first few years of employment with this organization were enjoyable. I found the culture extremely positive, healthy and focused on the well-being of the employees in the organization. It was an incredible place to work. At the helm of the organization was the president, a man who was the epitome of leadership. This leader was fully engaged in the organization and the employees, and he walked the floors every morning, visiting everyone with a kind word. Every year on the Christmas Eve and Christmas Day morning shifts, the president dressed as Santa Claus and wished a merry Christmas to everyone who had to work on the manu-facturing line. He handed out gifts personalized for each person; something they either needed or would like. For example, one year an employee got a new fishing reel he had been wanting, while another got a movie collection they enjoyed. In other cases, an employee might be struggling with financial issues and would there-fore receive a gift of money. After walking the manufacturing floor handing out gifts, the president arranged for a dinner to be served to the employees who were working. Volunteers from the leadership team helped to serve the dinner. This was a time when people actually volunteered to work, allowing those who had families to have time off. Every holiday was marked with some sort of celebration. The employees realized that, while they were working during these holidays, the president made time during his days off to celebrate and recognize them. Employees loved this leader and would do anything for him and the organization.

A few years later, another company acquired the organization. The acquisition resulted in a shift in leadership. As part of the acquisition, the company named a new president who was supposed to bring in innovative ideas and take the organization to a new level. The new president was the direct opposite of what the employees and the culture of the organization had been founded on. He was cold and he refused to relocate to the headquarters location, which was in the Midwest; he was from the West Coast. As part of his compensation package, an agreement was made that he could create offices on the West Coast, but once a month he would need to meet in the Midwest. He had agreed to this arrangement, but one of the stipulations in his contract was that he travel in a private plane to the offices. When traveling overseas he expected to fly business or first class.

When the new president came in, he would only visit for short stays, which might mean an overnight trip, or on rare occasions he would come in for three days. When he got to the corporate location, he came up the back stairway and went straight into his suite of offices, shut the door and closed the shades. Only a select few individuals came to meet with him. If the shades were closed, that was the signal to the employees that he was in town, and the atmosphere of the corporate office was filled with tension. When the shades were open, the atmosphere was calm and relaxed. He did not connect with the people of the headquarters office, let alone with the manufacturing employees. As he became acclimated to his position, he brought in his own people for his leadership team.

At the time, I worked in Human Resources. The vice president of HR at the time was Bill, a very caring man who was extremely knowledgeable about the HR industry. He was sought after within the industry for his expertise and he was invited to consult with other organizations. Bill was seen walking the floors with the former president, connecting with employees. The new president chose to replace Bill with Kent, who had worked as the personal assistant to the new president. One day Bill was there, and then the next his office was cleared out and he was replaced by Kent. Kent was a friend of the new president, a yes-man who agreed with every decision he made, and he carried out the personal agenda of the president, whether right or wrong. Ethics was something that did not concern the new leadership team and many of the acts that took place straddled the lines of ethics. They dangerously skirted around ethical issues and their behavior disturbed many, but nothing was said until a rumor surfaced about Kent and his assistant regarding sexual harassment. Since the report was about the VP of HR, it was filtered up the ranks to the president, who suggested it go to HR and Legal of the parent company that had acquired the organization. Prior to the complaint being escalated, the president called Kent, informed him of what was happening and gave Kent time to prepare his story. A full investigation took place but Kent strongly denied the accusations and was protected by the president.

Approximately seven individuals were included in the investigation. Each of the individuals who came forward faced retaliation at some point. The first person terminated was Susan, who was let go immediately, taking the blame for spreading false rumors about Kent. Her office was cleared out in the evening when no one was around. The employee who had filed the report and made the complaint to the president followed proper procedures as outlined by company policy. She was not the person who was harassed, but she followed proper procedures by filing the complaint. However, she experienced retaliation for a year. Regardless of the fact that proper protocol was followed, Kent stated that he was disappointed that this person had not spoken to him first to tell him about the complaint. He stated that he could have addressed the problem without an investigation that wasted everyone's time and money. He also questioned this person's loyalty to him and the organization.

During the next year, Kent made life miserable for all those involved in the investigation and constantly claimed his innocence. Eventually, all seven of the employees involved in the claim were let go from the organization for various reasons. Many of the reasons for termination were not clear. The organization blamed a lack of fitness, even if the employee had been there for over 20 years. A year later the HR person who had filed the report, the person whose loyalty Kent had questioned, was let go. Their past performance reviews were positive, but the reason given for termination was lack of loyalty. The organization provided a generous severance package in lieu of the person filing any lawsuits. That person was me.

I took the severance package, landed a new job shortly after and decided to move forward. Three months after my termination, Kent divorced his wife and began to date the same assistant who was at the center of the rumors. Eventually the relationship ended and the assistant filed a complaint of sexual harassment against Kent. Rumors began to fly around the corporate office, as well as around the offices of the parent company. Eventually it was realized that Kent was a liability to the president and the organization, and Kent was let go. In the meantime, several individuals lost their jobs in retaliation; the organization was in disarray and losing money. It had morphed from a positive, well-functioning organization into one of clear dysfunction, unethical behavior, retaliation and fear.

My next run-in with dysfunction in the workplace came in 2008. It was the year that my father passed away from a long and grueling battle with Stage 4 lung cancer. Before he died, I worked for a leader considered to be strong and positive, Betty. Betty knew I was struggling with balancing work, a PhD program and going back and forth to help my mother care for my father. She accommodated my schedule and helped me balance my workload. Betty grew her people, and to this day I feel privileged to have worked with her.

Three weeks after my father passed, the 2008 recession hit. I found myself unemployed, emotionally and physically exhausted. No one was hiring during this time, so finding a job was a challenge. I found a position with a non-profit that seemed like the perfect fit and one I looked forward to joining. I packed up my life, relocated for this new position and got ready for a new chapter.

The new position was exciting for about the first month. After that, I found myself in what I referred to as the depths of hell, working for an organization that oozed dysfunction and a variety of different dark side behaviors, from incivility to blatantly deviant behaviors. Employees within this department experienced everything from emotional to physical abuse. While I was familiar with emotional abuse within organizations, the thought of physical attacks was unheard of to me. However, physical attacks including throwing objects at people, pushing and grabbing were common. The emotional abuse was devious and damaging. It was during this time that I was working on my comprehensive exams and dissertation. I decided to change my research focus so that I could understand this phenomenon. While I was certainly not new to these behaviors, I was left wondering what was going on and while I was frustrated, I was also intrigued to research the topic.

For the next ten years, this became my life: researching and exploring the topic of dysfunction in the workplace; trying to understand how and why people act the way that they do in the workplace; and examining dysfunctional behaviors in society and trying to understand the correlations between incivility in society and in the workplace.

What I have found in my own personal experiences and research is that the phenomenon is widespread. Cultures can become very dark for both the organization and the employees. On a personal level, my experiences affected my relationships in my personal life. Physically, they influenced me negatively as well, but I was able to recoup.

One organization that I have researched is in the midst of dysfunction. A new leadership team has left the employees of the organization in the whirlwind of incivility and dysfunctional behaviors. The organizational grapevine uses social media to share issues occurring on a daily basis. This technology has become an outlet for employees to vent and share their experiences. Individuals hide behind anonymous profiles to protect themselves from being identified. No one will come forward to address the toxic environment for fear of losing their jobs or experiencing some form of retaliation from individuals within the organization. When terminations are shared on social media, the feeds are filled with postings such as, "Who will be voted off the island next?" (from the TV show *Survivor*), or messages to people still with the organization such as, "May the odds be forever in your favor" (*The Hunger Games*), wishing the "survivors" the chance to see another day. A handful of individuals have challenged the environment, and those individuals are swiftly "encouraged to leave" before they are blacklisted. Others just keep a low profile, counting the days to when they can retire.

Because of the stress within the organization, the culture is one wherein incivility and dysfunction are the norm. Complaints of harassment and discrimination go unaddressed. Kindness is now replaced with rudeness, contempt and anger as people struggle with the oppressive environment. Meanwhile, employees are looking for other jobs and have become disengaged. They are keen to exit the organization as soon as they can. Other employees are isolated and work in constant fear. Not only is there a fear that they cannot trust leadership, but also that they are unable to trust their co-workers.

Understanding the dark side of the workplace

Understanding the dark side of the workplace can be difficult and confusing. As employees, we have expectations of going to work, doing the job we have been paid to do and having relationships that are respectful and cordial. However, we deal on a daily basis with an array of different personalities and dynamics. A majority of the time the dynamics are civil and respectful, yet there can be dynamics that are negative. When negative behaviors happen in the workplace, we can sometimes understand the negative personality that we are dealing with. It may be a one-time event because a person is stressed and lashes out in frustration, but it passes when they apologize and the relationship moves forward. At other times it may be periodic episodes of rudeness and occasionally it can be a relentless onslaught of behaviors that continue on a weekly basis, lasting weeks, months and even years.

To understand the dark side of the workplace, it is important to define what this phenomenon is. To start with, the definition of the dark side is broad. There are a myriad of behaviors that encompass this type of behavior. This spectrum can range from rude comments, to dysfunctional behaviors, to violence and other deviant behaviors in the workplace. For the purpose of this book, I have chosen to examine the dark side of the workplace in the context of behaviors motivated by an employee or group of employees that ultimately have negative consequences for another individual or group of individuals within the organization, or for the organization itself (Paetzold, O'Leary-Kelly & Griffin, 2007). These types of negative behaviors are motivated by something that addresses the need of an individual or individuals. There might be intention from the individual to be seen, noticed or recognized, albeit in a negative way, or it might fulfill a psychological component for them. These behaviors have some sort of intention behind them for the perpetrator's personal gain. As a result, we will explore the full spectrum of behavior to understand the dynamics involved and to provide individuals with a context for the various behaviors they may experience in the workplace.

If we look at the behaviors on a spectrum, we can classify the behaviors into three categories: non-deviant, dysfunctional and deviant. Non-deviant behaviors are the mildest form. Non-deviant behaviors are passive behaviors that are often referred to as incivility or uncivil acts. These behaviors include rudeness, gossip and indirect behaviors—for example, rolling the eyes when someone is talking, or not saying good morning to someone when they come into the office. Often perpetrators may not even be aware of how these behaviors affect a person in a negative way. These behaviors may or may not be intentional: the perpetrator could be too busy to say hello (i.e. non-intentional), or the perpetrator may just not like the other person and purposely avoid them (i.e. intentional). The recipient of the behavior can either let the behavior go or it can negatively affect them.

Dysfunctional behavior is behavior wherein the intensity is escalated to a level that is repetitive and causes intentional harm to an individual—for example, a person who constantly humiliates their target in front of others in the workplace, or a person who specifically looks to cause discomfort to another person. Most of the time when these behaviors happen, the person is aware of what they are doing and it is meant to promote their own personal goals for their own gain.

The next level is deviant behaviors in the workplace; these are actions that are extreme. This behavior is focused on intentionally harming the organization and/ or the employees. In these cases, the behavior is harmful to safety, security and even life. These are extreme cases of exerting power and aggression over others.

Aggression

In the all of the cases of dark behaviors, there is a level of aggression linked to the behavior. Aggression is a form of behavior that is directed towards another person with the goal of harming or injuring them, so that they are motivated to avoid such treatment (Baron, 1977). Workplace aggression is viewed as any form of negative behavior directed by an individual or individuals with the goal of harming one or more people in the workplace or the entire organization. Buss (1961) focused on three separate types of aggression in the workplace. These include:

1. **Physical-verbal:** Harm through actions or words.
2. **Active-passive:** Can be produced by either acting or failing to act. For example, an individual needs resources to do their job, but another purposely withholds these resources to block them from properly performing their work.
3. **Direct-indirect:** Harm occurs by actions directed at the intended victim or by actions that harm individuals indirectly.

Table 1.1 provides further insights into Buss's (1961) work on aggressive behavior.

Labeling behaviors

The works of Buss (1961) focused on different categories of aggressive behaviors. Through the years, further scholarly research has continued to provide context around dark side workplace behaviors by continuous explorations of the topic. The research demonstrates that there is an abundance of labels for dark side behaviors in the workplace, ranging in severity and context. The following list provides further examples of the various terms for dark side behaviors in the workplace.

TABLE 1.1 Buss's major categories of aggression (Paetzold et al., 2007)

Type of aggression	Examples
Physical-active-direct	Punching, kicking, stabbing, shooting another person
Physical-active-indirect	Sabotaging a piece of equipment so that another person will be hurt when using it; hiring a paid assassin to kill another person
Physical-passive-direct	Physically preventing another person from obtaining a desired goal or performing a desired act (i.e. failing to move out of a person's way when asked to do so)
Physical-passive-indirect	Refusing to perform necessary tasks (i.e. refusing to provide information or help needed to another co-worker)
Verbal-active-direct	Insulting or using derogatory terms about another person
Verbal-active-indirect	Spreading malicious rumors or gossip about another person
Verbal-passive-direct	Refusing to speak to another person or refusing to answer questions posed to another person
Verbal-passive-indirect	Failing to speak up in defense of another when he or she is unfairly criticized

Blue-collar crime: Theft, property destruction, record fabrication, fighting, gambling.

Dysfunctional work behavior: Intentional, unhealthy behavior that causes harm to another.

Employee deviance: Unauthorized, intended acts that damage property, production or reputation.

Employee misconduct: Misuse of resources from absenteeism, to theft, to accepting bribes.

Non-performance work: Not performing work that is required, while also performing other acts that are not desirable, or completing work that is non-work related (e.g. finishing homework during work hours, or working on a sideline business while working for another organization).

Occupational aggressive crime deviance: Negative, illegal, injurious, and devious behavior conducted in the workplace. Usually acts that are considered illegal.

Organizational retaliated behaviors: Deliberate organizational behavior perceived as unfair, based on perceptions by disgruntled employees.

Political behavior: Behavior that serves the specific needs of an individual or group of individuals; non-sanctioned or illegitimate behavior aimed at people both inside and outside the organization.

> **Unconventional work practices:** Odd and unusual behavior which is often associated with illegal or disruptive behaviors.
>
> **Unethical workplace behavior:** Behavior that deliberately and obviously infringes upon the accepted norms of ethical and moral codes within the organization or society.

Through the research, there have been several attempts to categorize these behaviors, yet researchers struggle with properly identifying and classifying them. It is clear that, regardless of the term used, the impact and costs of these behaviors are high for individuals as well as for the organization. These costs can range from psychological, to physical, to organizational impacts. From an organizational stand-point, organizations spend billions of dollars every year trying to address, prevent, reduce or terminate individuals in order to stop these behaviors from happening in the workplace.

Causes of dark side behaviors

Darkness in the workplace incorporates behaviors which may start out as mild, such as petty gossip, rudeness or theft of food from the break room. These behaviors can quickly escalate into dysfunctional behaviors such as bullying, aggression and emotional abuse. In rare cases, dark behaviors include deviance in the workplace, including physical attacks, theft, sabotage and, on rare occasions, homicide.

Demands and technology

Reasons for increased levels of incivility and dysfunction in the workplace include a rapidly changing global economy, demands for quick decisions, highly stress-filled positions, employees being required to be available 24 hours a day, seven days a week, and an overall lack of resources and employees being stretched too thin. In addition, we have become a society that relies on technology for our communication and to provide us with information on demand. Technology is a valuable tool for communication, allowing us to stay in constant contact, but there are downsides to it. Where once face-to-face conversations required people to sit down, talk things out and address issues, emails and texting have replaced personal interactions. As we have learned, with technology, much can be lost in translation. Hastily sent emails can cause misunderstandings or emotional reactions without intentional harm. It is easy to ignore a text or email. Responding with short emails that do not address the misunderstandings or emotional reactions can lead to potential escalation of conflict if not addressed.

Leadership expectations

In some cases, leadership believes they are required to be hard-nosed and uncaring, which can create cultures that drive negativity to followers of the organization. Leaders can demand respect instead of earning it, and step on people on the way up the corporate ladder, all in the name of competition. Organizations may create a culture that demands thick-skinned individuals, and where good people are viewed as weak. Individuals may have negative views related to empathy as a weakness. These individuals do not think that the needs of the employee should be addressed; instead these individuals view their egos as needing to be addressed.

Evidence suggests that all of these behaviors have significant implications for employees, organizations and even society as a whole. In recent years, we have experienced increased acts of darkness in the workplace at all levels, including front-line workers, managers, C-suite executives and high-ranking governmental figures (Stincelli, 2017). As a result, it is inevitable that individuals will eventually be exposed to some level of darkness in the workplace.

Walking the fine line

Dysfunction and incivility, like beauty and art, are in the eye of the beholder. What one person may view as acceptable behavior, others may view as unacceptable, offensive and destructive. The problem with uncivil, dysfunctional and mild deviant behaviors is the understanding and interpretation of these events. These behaviors are interpreted through the eyes of the receiver, and many different factors contribute to this interpretation, including culture, gender, generation, organizational norms, values and the industry in which the behaviors occur. The following provides examples of how interpretations can be clouded.

> **Generation:** A common complaint in the workplace is the understanding of generations. One might hear, "My generation always worked hard and we had to pay our dues. This new generation is so lazy and entitled. They don't want to wait their turn and expect everything just to be handed to them." Alternatively, "This older generation just won't change and they are so difficult to work with. I just wish they would retire already." These over-generalizations may be viewed as true by an individual of the same generation as the person making the comment and may be ignored by those of another generation. For a younger or older generation, these comments might be viewed as offensive and insulting.

> **Gender:** A woman working in a predominately male industry may be exposed to different types of discussions in the workplace. It can be very common to have lunchroom conversations that discuss off-color topics or use derogatory comments. The use of swearing may be common during meetings, both informal and formal. The culture may condone this type of behavior as men just being men. For a female, the discussions may be offensive and uncomfortable. In other cases, the female may just accept the behavior and not be offended.

Incivility in society

For many, there exists a belief that incivility and dysfunction are found in all areas of our lives and are integrated into both our personal and work lives. As a society, we have become emboldened to speak our minds; we feel that we can act out whenever necessary and these bold and brazen behaviors make us heroes in the eyes of others. An example of incivility that has turned into dysfunctional and deviant behavior is road rage. In recent years, there has been an increase in the severity of road rage, which started with honking horns, hand gestures and screaming, and now includes causing property damage and physical damage to others (Møller & Haustein, 2018). Years ago, when people were cut off on the road, we would beep, maybe yell and then move on. We let it go, for the most part. Since then, road rage has escalated to the point where normal people act out their aggression in ways they normally would not. Being angered because someone is traveling the speed limit and not going fast enough for the person behind them can cause that person to react. It begins with flashing lights, hand gestures and screaming insults, and progresses to following the person to confront them. These behaviors can quickly escalate out of control. More and more cases of road rage are demonstrating deviant behaviors, such as throwing objects, stalking, purposely causing accidents, or hit-and-runs, and drawing guns on individuals. People are killed because of acts of road rage through unintentional or intentional aggression. Road rage is just one example of how behaviors can start with uncivil acts and quickly escalate to deviant behaviors.

There are some that believe there has been an increase in incivility in society: simple gestures such as people not holding doors open for one another; making unkind comments or shaming individuals because of their gender, sexuality, social status or physical attributes; people talking on cell phones without realizing that their voices can be heard throughout the restaurant or coffee shop; blocking the aisles of grocery stores while talking on the phone; or using the express checkout line for more than ten items. While these examples might seem like minor issues, they can cause individuals frustration and stress.

Since the recent US elections, we have witnessed a perceived increase in uncivil behaviors, with one political side lashing out at the other, and vice versa, because they do not agree with each other's points of view. Political parties have become polarized. Helping to fuel this conflict is the use of social media. We have become even more emboldened to act out towards one another through avenues such as Facebook and Twitter, which provide a platform for participants to voice their opinions with a level of anonymity. Instead of having civilized debates and discussions, individuals will often lash out at one another using social media and often not even know whom they are attacking.

Social media only allows us to see what the participant wants us to see. We have the ability to create fake profiles that allow individuals to "troll" other people's pages and to attack them. Our knowledge of others is limited to what they share, so we do not know much about the individual other than what we create in our own minds. However, this does not stop us from passing judgement on them because they do not agree with our points of view. Whether these viewpoints are political, personal, religious or sexual, people may share their opinions on social media, but they risk being shamed, attacked or harassed by other individuals who do not know them. Lashing out at others has become an acceptable approach of incivility. We read news announcements and make our own judgements about the facts. In some cases, we do not give individuals due process and do not assume they are innocent before proven guilty. We have become judge and jury on the topics that go against our point of view.

We witnessed this several times a week during the 2016 US presidential race when Donald Trump used this form of incivility and dysfunction as part of his campaign strategy: calling for other candidates to be locked up, blaming others for things that went wrong and lashing out at people who challenged him. As a result, this behavior was accepted and he was elected president. Some saw this happening and believed that it was an acceptable form of interaction for their personal and professional lives.

An example of the perception of dark side behavior relates to political components. For years, we have experienced political campaigns that are filled with everything from mudslinging, to character assassinations, to attacking the morals and values of individuals. Instead of focusing on the issues that need to be addressed, we focus on which of the candidates is most trustworthy of our vote. We can see this example play out in the United States, as we are exposed to a political system and a leader that individuals love and whose words and actions they believe in, while others despise his agenda and what he stands for. However, the reactions to comments and actions are based on the perception of the person experiencing the exchange. These philosophies have been with man since the dawn of time. There have been scores of leaders who have been viewed as strong champions of change, challenging the status quo. While some may admire these characteristics of leadership, others may view these same behaviors as the narcissistic, destructive acts of individuals out for their own personal agenda, harming everyone who stands in their way. Which person is right?

Work and life integration

So, what does societal incivility have to do with workplace incivility? As discussed, we have become emboldened and brazen in our actions around incivility and dysfunctional behaviors within society, and as such there is bound to be a crossover of uncivil societal behaviors into our professional lives. Some would argue that it is far-fetched to connect incivility and dysfunction in society to the workplace, and vice versa. On the contrary, I would argue that there is a very clear link between the two. Let us go back to the example of political discussions.

An individual posts something on their social media page about a political candidate. A co-worker reads this post and disagrees with the comment made about the candidate. They post something to disagree with the individual and they both start to share negative posts with one another. Either they then go to work and continue to exchange dialogue, or they have mixed feelings to a point that they ignore each other. The individuals' personal lives have now been integrated into the workplace. This is inevitable, as we have become more connected through technology. No longer are we looking to find work–life balance; we are struggling with how to balance the integration of our personal lives with our professional lives.

Importance of the topic

For organizations today, it is important to understand the impact that dark behaviors have on organizations, the culture and individuals within the organization. These types of behaviors violate organizational norms and healthy relationships between employees. Employees exposed to these types of behaviors suffer on a daily basis. These feelings may manifest themselves in physical or emotional distress, and result in similar negative behaviors such as retaliation, sabotage and other negative actions. For organizations, practitioners and employees it is critical to understand how these behaviors affect the bottom line and culture of the organization, as well as the employees as a whole. This book will address these topics in further detail in upcoming chapters.

Impact of dark behaviors in the workplace

When examining the costs of uncivil, dysfunctional and deviant behaviors in the workplace, we see these behaviors impacting the target, bystanders, other employees, the customer and the organization, including the culture of the organization. Targets of dysfunctional behavior experience feelings of despair, isolation, desperation, shame, depression and anxiety. Because of these psychological feelings, employees may manifest these behaviors in their work through low self-esteem, poor performance and reduction in creativity, along with lack of engagement.

Employees look for ways to cope with these feelings, and they may act out in a variety of ways. For example, employees might react with revenge, disengage from their work, and in some cases leave the organization. Other ways that employees might cope is by turning these behaviors inward and causing personal harm through increased use of recreational drugs and alcohol, over- or under-eating, or unhealthy, self-abusive behaviors. There have been reported claims in regards to individuals looking for extreme ways to cope, including contemplating and or committing suicide as a form of escape from the situation (Eliason, Streed & Henne, 2018). As the negative feelings associated with psychological distress coupled with negative coping mechanisms continue to manifest, they may present themselves in the form of physical symptoms affecting the health and well-being of the employee. Physical symptoms include headaches, cardiac issues, hypertension, diabetes and other physical ailments. In addition, employees can also suffer from post-traumatic stress disorder long after being removed from the situation. While believing that simply removing themselves from the situation will solve the problem, targets can live for years with emotional scars from the events. In many cases, targets choose to suffer in silence or they may share these events with friends and family, who often feel helpless and unable to help the target. Strains in relationships occur over time and cause further issues and concerns related to the dynamics in the target's personal life.

Bystanders or other employees who witness these behaviors happening often struggle with how to cope with the situation. They may be pulled into the uncivil, dysfunctional or deviant behavior without even being aware that their behavior is wrong. In other cases, they may be pulled in for fear of retaliation against themselves. Bystanders who are not pulled into the issues, but instead witness the events, can find themselves struggling with how to stop the behavior or help the target. Many bystanders will suffer from survivor's guilt as they struggle with the question, "Why them?" Other employees or bystanders can also be there to pick up the slack for the target, who is unable to come to work because of illness or because they are unable to face the dysfunction. Bystanders and employees may become disengaged with the organization and wonder why nothing is being done to address the problems, or they may become angry that the target is not pulling their weight as the bystander is taking on extra work.

Finally, the organization can face a myriad of issues related to dark behaviors. These issues may include erosion of the organizational culture, increased staff turnover and lack of employee engagement, as well as decreased productivity, creativity and innovation, just to name a few. In addition, the organizational bottom line can be impacted through an increase in healthcare premiums, overtime costs, lost opportunity costs, staff turnover, sabotage and other costs associated with these negative behaviors.

Layout of the book

As we move forward into the topic, it is important to understand the layout of this book. The book has been laid out based on the spectrum of dark side workplace behaviors already discussed. For the purpose of this book, we will look at the three levels of dark side behaviors that fall outside normal and acceptable workplace behaviors. We will examine each of these behaviors in depth, from mild negative intentions such as uncivil actions, dysfunctional behaviors, to deviant behaviors. In order to understand the different levels of darkness in the workplace, we will explore each of the levels one by one. The following lays out each of the chapters to understand the context of the behaviors and how they are inter-related.

- **Chapter 2: Incivility.** This chapter will focus on understanding the history of incivility and addressing these behaviors in society and the workplace. With the dynamics of individuals and each person's individualized behaviors, there will always be challenges in regards to how people interact with one another. There are different categories of incivility, ranging from minor incivility such as rude comments that are intentional but cause a person to be uncomfortable, to non-verbal gestures and random comments, to petty gossip. Chapter 2 will explore these types of behavior in further detail. We will look at the connection between incivility in society and in the workplace, as these behaviors are often inter-related.

- **Chapter 3: Dysfunction in the workplace.** This chapter will focus on moderate dysfunctional behaviors, which include mild to moderate forms of emotional manipulation. We look at different dysfunctional behaviors related to bullies and the different types of bullies we may encounter. Next, we will explore the paranoid, the narcissists/egotists, the backstabbers and the emotionally abusive tactics related to dysfunctional behaviors. We will spend a great deal of time on this chapter, as this is the area that individuals tend to struggle with the most, and it is probably the most difficult to understand or categorize.
- **Chapter 4: Deviant behaviors in the workplace.** This chapter will explore deviant behaviors in the workplace, focusing on behaviors that cause extreme physical and emotional distress to the target. We will explore the topics of corporate deviance, theft and sabotage. Then we will explore corporate psychopaths, forms of harassment, evil in the workplace and workplace violence.
- **Chapter 5: Impact of these behaviors in the workplace.** This chapter will explore the impact that these behaviors as a whole have on the individuals who are identified as the target of these behaviors. We will explore issues regarding the target's physical and emotional distress, along with the coping mechanisms used to address these issues. In addition, this chapter will explore the cost of these behaviors to organizations and how these behaviors affect organizations.
- **Chapter 6: Ways to address the dark side.** In this chapter we will explore the ways in which individuals can address these behaviors on an individual basis. This chapter is designed to help practitioners, leaders and organizations identify interventions that can be implemented in the workplace. These interventions are designed to aid in addressing these behaviors and building a healthy, productive culture that promotes innovation and creativity.
- **Chapter 7: The phenomenon comes to life.** Finally, in this last chapter we will explore years of research and examples from research participants who have experienced various forms of darkness in the workplace. Each of these stories will help to bring the phenomenon to life so that individuals will have the ability to provide context around their experiences of various situations. For the purpose of this chapter, and to protect the identity of the individuals, names and organizations have been changed; however, the actual incidents are real and have been shared through hours of interviews. Some of the stories have had additional insights added in order to enhance the phenomenon, but the actual events are true. These stories were chosen to provide the reader with the ability to indirectly experience the phenomenon of dark side behaviors in the workplace.

References

Baron, R.A. 1977. The prevention and control of human *aggression:* In: *Human aggression: Perspectives in social psychology (A series of texts and monographs)*. Boston, MA: Springer.

Buss, A. 1961. *The psychology of aggression*. New York and London: Wiley & Sons, Inc.

Eliason, M.J., Streed Jr, C., & Henne, M. 2018. Coping with stress as an LGBTQ+ health care professional. *Journal of Homosexuality*, 65(5), 561–578.

Møller, M. & Haustein, S. 2018. Road anger expression: Changes over time and attributed reasons. *Accident Analysis & Prevention*, 119, 29–36.

Paetzold, R., O'Leary-Kelly, A., & Griffin, R. 2007. Workplace violence, employer liability, and implications for organizational research. *Journal of Management Inquiry*, 16(4), 362–370.

Stincelli, E. 2007. *The dysfunction of toxic leadership*, IRIS.

2

INCIVILITY

Incivility has become the buzzword of our time. Within the last several years incivility has been used to describe behavior that is considered demeaning, rude and demoralizing to another person. Within organizations incivility slowly creeps in, spreads and permeates through all layers of the organization. Employees act out in subtle ways by making snide comments, not helping others to complete their work, using sarcasm and conflicting body language and barking demands at others. While some will act out verbally, others are more quiet, acting out in different ways such as minor sabotage, body language and gestures.

Porath (2016) found that uncivil behaviors range from nasty comments, to intentional sabotage, to undermining, to checking emails and texting during meetings. Early research from Porath (2016) found that, in 1998, 50% of workers experienced some form of incivility within the workplace at least once a month. Fast-forward to 2011, and 50% of workers reported experiencing incivility in the workplace at least once per week. Five years later, in 2016, the number rose to 62% experiencing incivility at least once a week. 99% of workers reported that they had witnessed uncivil behaviors. Porath (2016) noted that uncivil behaviors will ebb and flow based on levels of stress, cultural turbulence, uncertainty, complexity and volatile work environments. These types of behaviors can be found in all areas of our lives, including societal environments and especially in our work lives.

Civility and incivility defined

The term "civility"

In order to understand the topic of incivility, it is important to provide a baseline understanding of civility. Understanding civility provides a lens to recognize and measure behaviors that go against the norm. The following provides us an understanding of the term "civility", identifying its origins and interpretations.

The term "civility" has been with us throughout history and can be traced back to the Romans, where the term *civis* was used to define citizens and *civitas* referred to citizenship (Simpson, 1960, 109). Eventually, the term "civility" was used as a connection back to the term "civilization". Modern England and Western Europe use the terms "civil" and "civility" to indicate behaviors of proper conduct (Gillingham, 2002, 267)

Civility is considered a social norm or a standard of behavior, meaning that, as individuals, we have a common and shared belief about how we should act and about proper behavior in society or the workplace (Fehr & Fischbacher, 2004, 185). This is the behavior that we come to expect of others (Sinopoli, 1995, 613). The goal of mankind is to act in a way that is based on socially accepted norms and standards of behavior that are laid out by society as well as in the workplace. In a civilized society, we act in an ethical and respectful way.

Many scholars agree that civility allows individuals to share ideas and concepts in a respectful manner. Carter (1998, 338) explained civility as "an attitude of respect, even love for fellow citizens". Other scholars define civility as treating others with dignity; individuals act in a reasonable way and are courteous to others. Even in cases of disagreement there is an expectation and level of respect. For some, civility is as simple as living by the Golden Rule: to treat others as you want to be treated.

The term "incivility"

The term "incivility" is derived from the Latin term *et non est civis*, meaning "not of a citizen". Later, the term "barbaric" was used in response to challenges related to behaviors faced by the discovery of "inhabitants of the New World and then applied to the contrast between English Civility and Irish Barbarity" (Gillingham, 2002, 269).

Incivility is not a new concept. In the sixteenth century, Erasmus became fed up with watching the undisciplined children of his time and he went on to publish the book *De Civilitate Morum Puerilium Libellus* (*A Handbook of Good Manners for Children*). Topics covered in the book included table manners, how to dress and how to address one's elders. The book was extremely popular; over 130 editions were printed over the course of 300 years and translated into 22 languages. Erasmus believed that manners were critical to the proper upbringing of children in order for them to become vital participants in society. Later, Erasmus's book was used as a foundational piece for the education of children. Fast-forward almost 500 years and Erasmus's book is still available for purchase at many different bookstores.

There are challenges when we look for clear-cut definitions of civility and incivility. As countries become multi-national and continue to diversify, it has become a challenge for individuals to come up with a precise definition of these terms. What one culture or individual believes is civil behavior, others may view as uncivil. For example, a joke that one person finds funny, another may find offensive. The perception of behavior is situational and it is a challenge to clearly provide boundaries and guidelines on the topic.

Incivility in society

To understand incivility in the workplace, it is important to understand the role of incivility in society as it permeates into our workplaces, as discussed in Chapter 1. Research by communications consultant Shandwick, Tate and KRC Research (2016) found that individuals perceive that civility has been steadily declining over the years. The majority of individuals cite the causes of this decline as the use of social media, technology, politicians and the fault of governments. An example of uncivil behavior in society is political smear campaigns targeted at tearing down the opposing side and portraying information that is negative about them. Voters are left to determine which candidate is the best based not on issues but on character and perceptions of character. Meanwhile, within society we experience personal insults, public shaming, interrupted conversations, cyberbullying and trolling. We see this behavior portrayed in our media outlets such as television, movies and network news.

Research by Shandwick, Tate and KRC Research (2016) shows that Americans feel as though incivility has consequences and tends to be directed towards certain individuals and groups. There is a direct link between incivility in society and violent behavior, online bullying, discrimination/unfair treatment, humiliation, harassment, intimidation and threats. Table 2.1 provides insights into the groups that are most frequently the targets of incivility.

Further research has discovered concerns related to the erosion of civility. The following poll results demonstrate thoughts regarding incivility and Americans (Shandwick, Tate & KRC Research, 2016).

- 6.7 is the average number of times Americans encounter incivility in a seven-day week (of this number, 3.3 are online and 3.4 are face-to-face interactions).
- 84% have personally experienced incivility.
- 59% have quit paying attention to politics because of incivility.
- 53% have stopped buying from companies because of uncivil representatives.
- 34% have experienced incivility at work.
- 25% have experienced cyberbullying or incivility online (up nearly three times since 2011).
- 22% of parents have transferred children to different schools because of incivility.
- 75% of Americans believe that incivility has reached crisis levels.

TABLE 2.1 Societal targets of incivility (Shandwick, Tate & KRC Research, 2016)

Societal targets of incivility

Group	Percentage
African Americans	77
Immigrants	73
Women	72
Lower income	72
Homeless	71
Muslims	71
LGBTQ	70
Hispanic/Latino	69
Police officers	66
People with physical disabilities	65
People with intellectual disabilities	64
Refugees	64
Working class	62
Native Americans	60
Caucasians	58
Jewish	58
Blue collar	58
Mid-income	56
Asian American	55
Christians	54
Men	53
Military veterans	52
Evangelical Christians	50
Atheist/Agnostic	48
White collar	44
Upper income	39

- Nine in ten Americans say that incivility leads to intimidation and threats (89%), harassment (89%), discrimination (88%), violence (88%) and cyberbullying (87%).
- More than one in two blame politicians (75%), the internet/social media (69%) and the news media (59%) for the erosion of civility.
- 79% say that uncivil comments by political leaders encourage greater incivility in society.
- 78% feel that excessive media coverage of uncivil comments by politicians encourages more incivility in society.
- 59% expect civility to worsen over the next few years, while only 22% expect it to improve.
- 75% of the public says incivility is leading to political gridlock.
- 60% say incivility has led them to become disengaged in political debates or conversations.

Places where people experience incivility:

- 56% while driving.
- 47% shopping.
- 34% at work.
- 25% online.
- 25% at school.
- 25% in the neighborhoods they live in.
- 22% at social events.
- 22% on public transportation.
- 13% at political rallies.
- 8% in places of worship.

Finally, approximately six in ten (69%) Americans acknowledge that they have engaged in uncivil behavior (Shandwick, Tate & KRC Research, 2016).

Societal incivility and technology

One of the largest arenas for incivility is the world of cyberspace. A Pew Research study found that 70% of 18–24 year olds stated that they have been victims of online harassment, and 26% of women in that range have experienced online stalking (Lenhart, 2007). A 2014 study published in the *Journal of Personality and Individual Differences* (Buckels, Trapnell & Paulhus, 2014) found that approximately 5% of internet users identified themselves as cyber trolls (individuals who purposely stalk others on the internet), and scored high in dark personality traits such as narcissism, psychopathy and sadism. These individuals found that they were able to exercise these dark personality traits through the cloak of secrecy that the internet allows. In real-life interactions, they may not demonstrate these characteristics and may mask these behaviors in normal face-to-face interactions. However, the internet allows them a level of confidence to exercise these behaviors without being caught. Phillips (2016) describes internet trolling as follows: trolls' behavior is portrayed as aberrational and the opposite of how normal people converse with each other; however, most individuals involved in trolling are normal people, who do things that seem fun at the time but that have huge implications in the long run.

Cell phones are another culprit related to incivility. In the past it was common to shut down cell phones in restaurants, places of worship, work and other public places. However, people no longer feel the need to shut down their phones. It is common for people to pick up a call in a restaurant, movie theater, grocery store and become wrapped up in their own world, not recognizing others around them and the disturbance they might be causing. Individuals become oblivious to their surroundings and others around them.

In most cases, people now expect uncivil behavior in every aspect of their lives. Common courtesy and respect is taking a backseat to disrespect and rudeness. As one can see, the impact of incivility in society has increased. Many believe that it is at crisis level and that this negative behavior is not going to change anytime in the future, unless it is addressed at the upper levels of leadership within our countries, which are believed to be at the root of the problem. Incivility is rapidly rising across the globe and understanding ways to address these behaviors can be challenging for all involved. With societal changes occurring related to civility and the impact of incivility in society, there is bound to be an intersection between incivilities, how we act in society and how we interact in the workplace. The following sections focus on this intersection and how incivility in society relates back to the workplace.

The rise of incivility: increase in incivility or just awareness?

One could argue that there appears to be an increase in uncivil behaviors in society, but others argue that there is not an increase in these types of behavior and that these behaviors have always existed. Instead, some believe that there is an increase in awareness and knowledge that the behavior is happening. Just as Erasmus in 1530 identified that there were issues with the upbringing of children and manners during his time, we experience these same difficulties today but in different contexts. With the increase of social media, recording devices on our phones and 24-hour connectivity which allows us to be in constant contact with one another, there may be an increase in awareness of the topic. We are able to document and share with vast audiences what we witness on a daily basis, whether it is an interaction between two people arguing or the recording of events as they take place. As a result, we have more outlets through which to share these acts. Our sharing includes family members, friends and eventually the globe, as in some cases this information goes viral. We have seen viral videos of babies and puppies doing cute things, and we have witnessed viral videos of people at their worst. Videos have gone viral that shame others, including body shaming, cyberbullying, incidents of police brutality and the attacking of individuals for their beliefs, values, norms and how they choose to live their lives. We have come to believe that if we don't agree, we can take a picture or post something on social media. Not fully knowing the situation or the person, we easily pass judgement on others and/or a situation. As a result, passing judgement has become a component of our social fabric.

Through the internet, individuals have access to biased media outlets, fake news, political blogs and individual posts. These outlets are used to elicit a response from their audience in order to increase viewership, thus increasing revenue through advertising and building a following. For many the response can be visceral and emotional. Research analyzing online discussions from a newspaper website found that roughly one in five comments included some form of incivility, with direct insults of another person being far and away the most common variety (Coe, Kenski & Rains, 2014, 673). With the increased number of social media platforms available, individuals now have more avenues for conversation. Meanwhile, incivility continues to become more noticeable and awareness continues to grow.

In addition to the increase in awareness, our ability to dialogue with people we know and strangers can result in additional conflict. As the research mentioned previously shows, there is a clear increase in perceived incivility and in people having difficulties navigating through conflict as it relates to these forms of technology. There was a time when there was a grey area in regards to debates, but recently sides seem to have become either black or white, leaving little room for civil debate to unfold. With the recent 2016 elections in the United States, we can see the division within the United States as the political sides lashed out at one another. Research related to the 2016 election found that 72% of Americans considered presidential candidate Donald Trump's actions uncivil. Of the 72%, approximately 53% stated that they had voted for him, accepting this behavior (Pew Research, 2016). We have become more aware of uncivil behaviors through televised political ads focused on mudslinging, malicious rumors and character assassinations. During this election period, each side would state that they would take the high road when others went low with their comments. At the end of the day, both sides went low in their behavior, and on January 20, 2017, Donald Trump was elected as the 45th President of the United States. His presidency has been anything but smooth: it has been plagued by the commentary of news networks, two-sided media coverage and social media outlets fueling the fires. Meanwhile, the president is known for tweeting his disdain and his controversial opinions, with little regard for whom his comments may offend. Some view this type of leadership as refreshing, while others are turned off by these tactics. In either case, is this the new way of interacting in politics?

At the end of the day, we do have more outlets through which to share the uncivil acts of others. We have an increased knowledge of these types of behaviors. When the leader of one of the most powerful countries in the world is able to get elected based on a platform of incivility, it would seem natural for others to believe that this type of behavior is acceptable.

Incivility in the workplace

Incivility exists in organizations throughout the world. This type of behavior can take many different forms. Andersson and Pearson (1999) first defined incivility as "low intensity deviant behavior with ambiguous intent to harm an individual, in violation of workplace norms or mutual respect". Caza and Cortina (2007) provided a simplified definition of incivility in the workplace as a low-intensity deviant behavior with or without intent to harm. Andersson and Pearson (1999, 457) characterized uncivil behaviors as rudeness and a lack of regard for the other person. Exposure to workplace incivility can result in a negative impact on employees in terms of mood, cognitive distraction, fear, perceived injustice, damaged social identity and anger (Barling, Rogers & Kelloway, 2001; Cortina et al., 2002; van Jaarsveld, Walker & Skarlicki, 2010). These types of reactions can negatively impact the health and psychological well-being of employees.

Incivility can be difficult to deal with in any context, but in the workplace it can have several implications for a person's livelihood and basic needs. This type of behavior can take many different forms within organizations. Uncivil behavior can be unintentional or there can be a motive behind it. Incivility is typically a mild form of aggression. These types of behaviors in the workplace can include sending demeaning messages, treating someone as incompetent or like a child, excluding someone from meetings, not greeting someone when passing them in the hallway, cutting off a person who is talking, or simply missing the trash can when throwing something away and leaving it for someone else to clean up (Pearson, Andersson & Porath, 2000). Other examples of uncivil behavior in the workplace include slamming doors, whispered or sidebar conversations, texting or taking phone calls during meetings and a simple disregard for other people's time. For many, this type of incivility is all too familiar. We have all dealt with that individual who is texting, checking emails or taking phone calls during meetings. At first these behaviors are subtle, and most of the time people are not even aware of how these behaviors are perceived. At first, these behaviors don't bother us, but if they are repeated they can start to annoy individuals. These behaviors are usually not meant in malice or anger. However, it is easy to see how these behaviors can seem benign at first and then eventually spiral out of control, and turn into a larger problem if not dealt with properly. These types of behaviors can negatively influence individuals and may lead to escalation of negative behaviors, which will be discussed in later chapters. For many in the workplace, incivility is the less obvious behavior which it can be easy to overlook or dismiss. But make no mistake: this type of behavior can negatively affect morale and employee engagement.

Categories of workplace incivility

There are many different types of incivility in the workplace; the following will look at different categories related to incivility in the workplace.

Interpersonal incivility: An example of this type of incivility is when an individual is walking down a hallway and another employee says hello, but that person looks away and does not respond. Alternatively, a person could be walking into a building and they do not wait to hold the door open for another individual. In these two examples, the behavior may or may not be intentional; more than likely it is not. It is important to recognize the intent of the person who we perceive as acting out. The person exhibiting the behavior might not have seen the other person, they might have thought the other person had the door, their mind might have been focused on something else, or they might have said hello and the other person did not hear them. These factors would indicate that the actions were not intentional. However, the person might not have said hello because they didn't want to engage in conversation with the other person, or they purposely did not want to hold the door open for them. Then the behavior would be intentional and related to interpersonal conflict.

Cyber incivility: Rudeness that manifests itself over electronic media can be as simple as not replying to an email or text message, especially when someone is waiting for a response. Again, no response could mean that the person is busy, sick or simply didn't see the email, or that they are waiting for someone else to get information to them before they can reply. All of these examples indicate that the lack of response is not personal. However, if the person intentionally withholds their response knowing that this will cause another person harm, anxiety or psychological distress, this is considered intentional incivility. Another action related to perceived cyber incivility is the tone of an email. Emails that are short and to the point may be perceived by one person as a quick response or by another as abrupt and rude.

Victimless incivility: In this case, there is not an intended target for the uncivil behavior. For example, it could be as simple as taking the last supply of something and not letting people know they are out; a person could drink the last of the coffee and not make another pot. Similarly, the person could not refill the copy machine when it runs out of paper, or walk away from the copier when there is a paper jam. In these cases, there is no one person singled out as the target of the incivility. Instead the target is a random person: the next person to use the copy machine or to get a cup of coffee (Sliter, 2013).

Workplace incivility behavior

Uncivil acts are similar to aggravations or agitations. What distinguishes this type of behavior is the term "ambiguous intent". There are different levels of uncivil behaviors and different degrees of intent. Martin and Hine (2005) stated that subtle incivility is considered annoying but not physical in any form. The following provides examples of subtle or slight behaviors:

- **Asking for input but ignoring it:** For instance, when a person asks for feedback or calls a meeting for insights but has already made up their mind on what to do. They have no intention of using anyone's input and believe that they are including others for the sake of courtesy. In reality, the person is wasting everyone's time and causing aggravation.
- **Forgetting to share credit:** It is quite common to hear, "I feel like I am forgetting to recognize someone." Ignoring other individual's efforts on a project and taking personal credit for the work done by other team members.
- **Looks:** Giving someone a dirty look or a condescending sneer, glaring at someone, smirking or rolling the eyes. Looking over a person's shoulder when they are talking, to see who might be more important to talk to. An individual constantly looking at their watch when they are talking to someone, as though they have someplace else to be.
- **Interruptions:** An individual interrupting others or talking over people to make their point. The person constantly interrupts individuals or walks into a co-worker's office when they are on the phone or meeting with

someone. An individual walking up to a group having a conversation and starting another conversation, or providing input that is not related to the conversation.

- **Not listening:** A person being distracted by technology, multitasking during a conversation or being on their cell phone during a meeting. Not actively engaging in listening to a conversation, for example by texting or checking Facebook or emails.
- **Standing over someone:** Standing over the shoulder of someone when they are trying to work, or hovering over another person while they are busy and focused on something else.
- **Speaking down to others:** Talking down to a person and acting as though what that person has to say does not matter. Speaking to others as though they are a small child or slowly enunciating words to make another person feel incompetent.
- **Teasing:** Subtle teasing (e.g. about the way a person looks, acts or does their job) that seems harmless but still causes hurt and uncomfortable feelings.

These examples can be viewed as subtle levels of uncivil behavior. All of these examples can be seen as aggravations or irritations to another person, but the behavior is not physically harmful. While this behavior can seem harmless at first, if it continues it can turn into dysfunctional types of behavior (see Chapter 3). Subtle behaviors can escalate into overt behaviors and these behaviors can quickly turn dysfunctional. The following overt uncivil behaviors start to blur the lines between incivility and dysfunctional behaviors.

- Constant disruption of meetings through interruptions, cutting in and overpowering others.
- Not talking to or sharing information with another person. This behavior becomes overt when the behavior begins to interfere with the work and productivity of others.
- Overruling decisions without reason, such as when decisions are made in a vacuum, or decisions made by the team are overruled by one person without reason or cause. The team feels as though their contributions do not matter.
- Signing people up for inappropriate websites in order to bog them down or to cause embarrassment to the recipient.
- Spreading hurtful or malicious gossip or rumors that can impact a person's reputation or livelihood.

How incivility in the workplace plays out

The following demonstrates the evolution of incivility in the workplace. In this example, we can see subtle forms of uncivil behaviors that morph into overt behaviors which eventually blur the lines between incivility and dysfunctional behaviors.

Example: You are walking into the workplace with your hands full. A co-worker walks past you, and grabs the door, and you believe that they are holding the door open for you. You smile, relieved, but they let the door close in front of you. You struggle to balance everything to open the door. You make your way into the office and make eye contact with the front office receptionist, offering a smile and saying good morning to her. She looks down and does not say anything to you. You get to your office, drop the items and head to the break room for a much-needed cup of coffee, but you notice that someone has drained the coffee pot and not bothered to start a fresh pot. You start a new pot and wait while it is brewing. Mike from Accounts comes in and starts talking about the weekend and what the week ahead holds. You are in the middle of telling him about an important meeting you have with a new customer this week, when Sally comes in and interrupts your conversation to ask Mike what he thought about the umpire's call at their children's softball game. Mike asks Sally if she noticed that Barb and Brian from Accounts were sitting at opposite ends of the bleacher and says that he heard that they were getting a divorce. Sally responds that she heard that as well and adds that Brian has been drinking again and they have been talking about separating for a number of months. You stand back, realizing that you have become invisible. Sally reaches over to the coffee machine and starts to pour a cup of coffee from the fresh pot you just made. She spills some coffee on the counter but does not bother to wipe it up. She says goodbye to Mike and never acknowledges that you were in the room with them. Mike then says he is hungry, so he goes into the refrigerator and helps himself to someone else's yogurt. He smiles and winks at you, saying that since there is not a name on the container it should be okay to take it; surely they will not mind. He goes to his desk.

In this example, we see several acts of incivility taking place. Some of the behaviors can be considered low-intensity behaviors that are not intended to harm anyone. However, other behaviors teeter on the verge of dysfunction and could cause harm to another individual, especially related to reputation. We can agree that all of the behaviors are violations of social norms, workplace etiquette and basic respect and courtesy. The interpretation of these behaviors is associated with the perception of the person targeted. For example, a person who helps themselves to someone else's lunch in the break room could be considered rude, while others might say that this behavior could be viewed as stealing and is unethical. Still others might view this behavior as okay if the person was hungry and did not have the money to buy food for themselves.

Causes of incivility in the workplace

There are a myriad of reasons why people act out in the workplace. Increased diversity and a global culture have caused misunderstandings and misinterpretations of intentions. Workplace demands have increased as employees are asked to do more with less, and to focus on ensuring that the customer's needs are met and organizational initiatives are addressed while also being fiscally responsible. A shrinking market of skilled labor is placing further demands on employees who are stretched too thin. These factors coupled with unique work-group and individual dynamics have put employees on edge. Workplaces are rife with competition; constant change, volatility in governments and economics, and uncertainty are other issues facing organizations. As a result, employees are exhausted and burned out. A study conducted by van Jaarsveld et al. (2010) found a connection between job demands and emotional exhaustion as mediators in employee incivility. This supports the research conducted by Hockey (1993), who stated that when employee job demands are high, their ability to execute their role diminishes. The research from van Jaarsveld et al. (2010) also indicates that, when emotionally exhausted, employees tend to lack the cognitive resources necessary to act in a civil manner to others, including other employees and customers.

Types of incivility in the workplace

We have discussed the different levels of workplace incivility up to this point; however, we have not fully discussed the different ways in which incivility plays out in an organization. The following discusses several different ways in which incivility can be demonstrated in the workplace.

Rumor mills and gossip

Workplace gossip can be defined as a form of negative, informal communication among colleagues, focusing on forms of slander and/or false information. This communication centers around the private, personal and sensitive information of others in the workplace. Gossip typically has an element of truth along with speculations of truth. Peter Vajda (2007) identified workplace gossip as a form of violence, referring to it as a verbal attack against another. This form of attack is viewed as a passive-aggressive form of behavior resulting in interpersonal conflict in the workplace.

Gossip seems to start out as a harmless act. Conversations that start with "Have you heard?" or that discuss someone's personal life, relationship status or workplace interactions are viewed by some as idle chitchat. However, what seems like an innocent discussion can become destructive to workplace relationships. The types of individuals who exhibit these behaviors are referred to as "gossipmongers" or as people who participate in rumors with the intention of causing drama, harm and destruction. They will do this by spreading lies and half-truths that are designed to intentionally destroy individuals and reputations.

Consequences

So how does one tell if a conversation is harmless or destructive? It is important to analyze the conversation and ask whether these actions can affect someone in a negative manner or cause them harm in any way. Does it or could it cause division within the work group or harm the reputation of another? Does it fuel negativity? Is there a potential for an emotional reaction? Can it increase conflict in the workplace, damage reputations, erode trust, impacting team and individual work? Does it create a toxic or hostile work environment? Answering yes to any of these questions indicates that this is a harmful conversation that can quickly cross the line. When these conversations become negative and destructive, we find the following consequences for relationships, individuals and the organization.

Loss of productivity: Employees engaged in talking and gossiping about another are not focused on the work at hand. When the person is the topic of the gossip, they may spend a great deal of time focused on defending themselves or worrying about what is being said. Therefore the focus on work is lost; time at work is spent talking about non-work-related issues, clarifying misinformation or trying to stop the spread of the gossip or rumors.

Loss of trust and hurt feelings: When something is shared in what one believes is confidence, it can be difficult to find that the information has been shared with others and the level of trust is eroded. When gossip or rumors spread, levels of trust minimize quickly. Feelings become hurt when someone believes that the person they once trusted is in reality not someone they can trust at all.

Change in the perception of others: If rumors are spread, we tend to believe what is being said until it is proven otherwise. As a result, the perception of the person being gossiped about is changed. When a new perception kicks in, it becomes one's reality. Once a person's reality alters, it can become what one believes to be true. This altered reality can become difficult to change.

Increase in staff turnover: When gossip and rumor mills become the norm within an organization, there may be an increase in turnover. The people targeted will try to fix the situation, or find that they cannot change the perception and look to leave the organization. Others find that gossip and rumors are the norm within the organization. They may find this behavior unprofessional and eventually try to find work elsewhere.

Inappropriate conversations: When gossiping, conversations can become inappropriate as others become engaged in trying to embellish the conversation and add more to the dialogue that can be hurtful or inappropriate. These inappropriate conversations can border on the brink of creating a hostile work environment.

Participants in gossip

Who are the people that engage in gossip? First, there are the individuals who find themselves involved in the gossip who set these negative conversations in motion. In some cases, they may share stories or secrets innocently with someone they trust. That person may then share that same information with others and before long the gossip and rumors take off. Then there are the individuals who engage in the conversation, who add to the story or embellish the truth. There are others who do not engage in the conversation by adding information, but they are an active audience for the narrator to share stories about others. All of these participants are active in the role of gossiping. By listening to an individual spreading falsehoods or stories about another, we are providing a platform for the behavior to fester and grow.

Individuals who like to gossip are actually fueling their own ego. They feel that they have something vital to offer and seek an audience who will listen to their stories and provide them the attention they are seeking. When they share information with others, they feel as though they are in the know and have exclusive information about individuals or about what is happening within the organization. Having an audience helps to fill that need for recognition. In many cases, they will seek out people who they know will listen to them, who are interested in the information that they have to share, or who are not busy and are open to hearing what is being said.

Organizational gossip

Gossip is not just limited to individuals but can focus on the organization itself or on its customers. An example of speculation related to an organization is employees talking about the organization's reports of poor earnings or a decline in revenue. Employees begin to talk about the problem and then speculation begins in regards to what the organization will do (e.g. eliminating hours or cutting positions) and who will be more likely to lose their jobs because of cuts. In this example, the speculation is related to fear of the unknown or lack of communication on the part of the organization to properly address alternatives to the situation. A potential result of this type of gossip is employees leaving the organization to protect themselves.

Reactions to gossip

When employees recognize an individual as a gossiper, they will tend to react in several different ways: they may avoid that person, participate in the gossip or manipulate the gossiper to their advantage. For example, individuals who want to get a message out to others may use the gossiper or "grapevine" to plant the seed. An employee who wants the leadership to know something but does not want to share that information directly with them may use the rumor mill, knowing that the message will get to the powers that be.

Some people may view gossip positively if it portrays another in a positive light. This type of gossip is viewed as harmless—for example, "Did you hear that James is up for a promotion? This is such great news since there's no one more deserving than him and he does such a great job at everything he works on." This type of gossip might seem harmless, but if James is not aware of the promotion and things change then it could become negative.

Passive-aggressive behavior

Passive-aggressive behaviors in the workplace are challenging to address and to deal with. They do not like direct conflict and will avoid it at all costs. They will bottle up their resentment and pass it on to others while completely avoiding the need to address the conflict directly. Because of their ability to manipulate situations, they will cause their target to feel as though they are one who is causing problems. Targets can feel as though they are on a rollercoaster ride, not knowing where they stand with this individual. To observers, the target looks like the problem. Passive-aggressive individuals might have used this tactic for many years and have been able to perfect their behavior, while their targets may be new to it. When the passive-aggressive individual is confronted during conflict they will act innocent or give a blank stare, saying they do not understand what the problem is. They then will go in for the attack, leaving their targets little opportunity to defend themselves. The passive-aggressive individual does not want to speak about their feelings. They will not admit to having a bad day, to having been hurt or to having had something done to them. Instead, they will immediately move into protection mode. They will not say they are upset but will instead say things like, "I'm fine" or "it's okay", which usually means they are not. These tactics let people think everything is okay, but in reality they are just buying time to plot their revenge or attack. Passive-aggressive individuals do not have the skills to address conflict in a healthy manner. As a result, they use the tactics they are most comfortable with.

Tactics: Signs of a passive-aggressive individual

As mentioned, it can be challenging to identify a passive-aggressive individual. An aggressive individual is easy to identify, as they will lash out verbally or physically when they are upset. We see this behavior and recognize what it is; there is no misunderstanding it. However, a passive-aggressive person will lash out in subtle and indirect ways. For example, a highly competent passive-aggressive individual will "forget" to invite you to an important meeting, or the passive-aggressive person will put other people's needs before yours in order to make life inconvenient for you.

Passive-aggressive individuals may or may not know that what they are doing is negative. For some passive-aggressive individuals, this behavior has become a way of life for them; they have allowed themselves to recognize it as acceptable. For most passive-aggressive individuals, the behavior is deliberate and will make them inefficient in their work, avoid responsibility and refuse to state their needs or concerns directly. Rather they will do so indirectly.

The following outlines the tactics that passive-aggressive individuals like to use.

Dishonesty: These individuals will not speak honestly or candidly about their feelings. They will not admit that they have been hurt or offended and they do not speak up about what is bothering them. Instead, when they are upset or offended, they will become immediately offensive. Their typical response will not be an honest one and they will sugarcoat their feelings until they can bring them up when the target least expects it.

Isolation or exclusion: They might send emails informing people of their plans or sharing information. The passive-aggressive will conveniently overlook others and not include them in communications, meetings or necessary information. Social events are also used as a tactic to isolate targets: the passive-aggressive will invite a group of individuals to lunch but not their target. When the target asks why they have been excluded, the passive-aggressive will look dumbfounded and say, for example, "I know I sent you that email," or "I just assumed you were too busy," or "It was just a simple mistake." This will send the target off to search for the email that was never sent. If the target asks for a copy of the email, the passive-aggressive will say, "Oh, I already deleted it. I am so sorry, I can't resend it to you."

Control: They will deliberately arrive late to meetings or social gatherings they do not want to attend. Sometimes this is an unconscious behavior, and other times they know that others will wait for them and this demonstrates their control over the situation and the individuals involved. They will come across as busy and preoccupied during meetings, demonstrating that they are bored or feel as though their time is much more important than the topic being discussed. While the passive-aggressive individual avoids conflict or addressing the elephant in the room, they are demonstrating that they are in control of the situation and, in a sense, have the upper hand.

Kindness that cuts: The passive-aggressive individual will never give their targets any type of praise or recognition. If they do use praise, the praise will link back to the passive-aggressive in some form. When they give compliments, these will come across as backhanded and will make the target feel uncomfortable; for example, "That blouse looks great on you. Usually that color doesn't look good on people with your coloring," or, "That project was good. I once did a similar project but of course it was much larger in scale and promoted me to the position that I have now," or, "You did a good job on the assignment. I'm just surprised they didn't push back on the statements you made." Passive-aggressive individuals typically try to avoid conflict, but with these backhanded compliments they are really fueling the conflict and hoping to escalate it. It is like poking a sleeping bear; eventually the bear will awake and lash out. That is what the passive-aggressive individual wants: for their target to lash out so that they can come across as the victim, and the target is viewed as the one furthering the conflict.

Silence: Passive-aggressive individuals love to use silence and pouting when they do not get their way. They think they are avoiding conflict, but with their silence and pouting they are ultimately making matters worse. People are left wondering what is wrong and what they did, but when they ask, the individual will respond, "Nothing. Everything is just fine," and yet the silence and pouting will continue.

The passive-aggressive will snap out of the silence when they are ready, when they feel they have punished their target long enough, when they have received enough attention or when no one is acknowledging their behavior. Then, just as quickly as they went into silence, they will become involved and engaged again, leaving their target wondering where they stand with this individual.

Wishful thinking: Often the passive-aggressive will make a wish out loud and then declare that it will never happen; for example, "I wish someone would take my Saturday shift, but I guess that's not going to happen." They will get their need out then downplay it to make others feel as though they need to step in and help. They want to appear too humble to ask for help. For example, instead of simply saying that they would like a report to be finished on Wednesday, they might say, "It would be great if that report would be done on Wednesday but that is asking for a lot. I guess Friday will have to do." They will throw out this request to see if someone will take the bait; when no one latches on to the clue, they will move into silence until people figure out what the problem is. Sometimes individuals will catch on and honor the passive request. However, when the request is not honored, the passive-aggressive will continue with their behavior until they are ready to move on, but they will bring it up at a later date.

Leaving tasks undone: Passive-aggressive individuals like to leave tasks almost completed—for example, the report that is almost done or the project that is near completion but for some reason never gets finished. This signifies resentment for the task, the person assigning the task and the task being assigned to the passive-aggressive individual. They do not want to see the project through and so, eventually, someone else will feel the need to step in to say something or finish the project.

Organizational impact of incivility

Research from Porath and Pearson (2009) found that two major components exist in regards to incivility in the workplace: 1) it is expensive and 2) most organizations do little to address or change these behaviors.

As we have discussed in this chapter, rudeness is abundant in our workplaces as well as in society. When employees do not feel valued, they tend to become less creative, less engaged and eventually look for work elsewhere. They check out of the organization either physically or emotionally. The individuals who leave the organization are usually better off. Individuals who stay with the organization typically become immune to the behavior and eventually start to reflect these behaviors onto others in the organization. We often hear this in the cases of organizations where new people go through orientation or, in some cases, "hazing rituals". The bad treatment that was experienced by tenured employees is now handed down to new employees. This type of ritual creates a cycle which continues to spread negative behaviors. Let's explore further the impact of incivility on the organization and its culture.

Incivility and organizational culture

Research has found that incivility relates closely to the culture of the organization versus the focus on one individual (Leiter, 2013). This type of behavior, if left unchecked, can become part of the norm for the organization, part of its cultural fabric, especially in politically charged and stress-filled environments. When leadership participates in uncivil behaviors, they are indirectly promoting this type of behavior. For example, within organizations, leadership may walk away from the gossip or participate in it. When leadership participates this may damage individuals, erode trust and cultivate a toxic environment. It also sends a message to the followers that this type of behavior is condoned and encouraged.

Reactions to workplace incivility

When people are exposed to workplace incivility, the reaction tends to be negative in some way. Employees can deliberately slow down their work efforts or shut down; quality declines and employees become less creative when they feel disrespected.

Research from Johnson and Indvik (2001) has found that individuals who are exposed to incivility in the workplace are mentally fatigued. Because these behaviors are usually difficult to understand and define, employees are left to figure out these ambiguous behaviors by themselves. Because of the fatigue and stress that targets face, they may in turn lash out and become uncivil to others in the workplace in order to release some of the tension and stress they are feeling. Johnson and Indvik's study found that when employees are mentally fatigued it is more difficult for them to control their negative reactions and emotions, resulting in frequent forms of incivility on their part. Their initial intention may not be to hurt or lash out at others, but they may lack the ability to suppress their negative reactions (Johnson & Indvik, 2001).

Customer reactions

Customers can also react negatively to employees or organizations that demonstrate incivility to either their employees or their customers. Customers become less likely to engage with an organization when they perceive that employees are directly or indirectly rude to the customer or to other employees in the organization. Just from witnessing an act of incivility towards another employee, customers tend to generalize that behavior as being part of the culture of the organization and/or brand (Porath & Pearson, 2009). As a result, they believe that they too will be treated poorly and thus will be less likely to frequent that business.

When incivility turns dysfunctional

Research shows that incivility closely relates to and overlaps with dysfunctional and deviant behaviors, including workplace abuse such as harassment, anti-social behavior, sabotage and bullying. What separates incivility, dysfunctional and deviant behaviors is the level of intensity (Hershcovis, 2011). Regardless of the intensity, Hershcovis (2011) found that incivility often leads to dysfunctional, or even deviant, behavior in the workplace and is a precursor to more serious aggression. In the following chapters, we will explore the next level of dysfunctional and deviant behaviors, when incivility goes bad.

References

Andersson, L.M. & Pearson, C.M. 1999. Tit for tat? The spiraling effect of incivility in the workplace. *Academy of Management Review*, 24, 452–471.

Barling, J., Rogers, A.G., & Kelloway, K.E. 2001. Behind closed doors: In-home workers' experience of sexual harassment and workplace violence. *Journal of Occupational Health Psychology*, 6, 255–269.

Buckels, E.E., Trapnell, P.D., & Paulhus, D.L. 2014. Trolls just want to have fun. *Personality and Individual Differences*, 67, 97–102.

Carter, S. 1998. *Civility: Manners, morals, and the etiquette of democracy*. New York: Basic Books.

Caza, B. & Cortina, L. 2007. From insult to injury: Explaining the impact of incivility. *Basic and Applied Psychology*. 29(4), 335–350.

Coe, K., Kenski, K., & Rains, S. 2014. Online and uncivil? Patterns and determinants of incivility in newspaper website comments. *Journal of Communications*, 64(4), 658–679.

Cortina, L., Lonsway, K., Magley, V., Freeman, L., Collinsworth, L., Hunter, M., & Fitzgerald, L. 2002. What's gender got to do with it? Incivility in the federal courts. *Law and Social Inquiry*, 27, 235–270.

Fehr, E. & Fischbacher, U. 2004. Third-party punishment and social norms. *Evaluation and Human Behavior* 25(2) 63–87.

Gillingham, J. 2002. From civilitas to civility: Codes of manners in medieval and early modern England. *Transactions of the Royal Historical Society (Sixth Series)*, 12, 267–289.

Hershcovis, S. 2011. Incivility, social undermining, bullying…oh my! A call to reconcile constructs within workplace aggression. *Journal of Organizational Behavior*, 32(3), 499–519.

Hockey, G.R.J. 1993. Cognitive–energetical control mechanisms in the management of work demands and psychological health. In A. Baddely & L. Weiskrantz (Eds.), *Attention: Selection, awareness, and control*. Oxford: Clarendon Press, 328–345.

Johnson, P. & Indvik, J. 2001. Rudeness at work: Impulse over restraint. *Public Personnel Management*, 30(4), 457.

Leiter, M. 2013. *Analyzing and theorizing the dynamics of the workplace incivility crisis*. Dordrecht: Springer.

Lenhart, A. 2007. Cyberbullying. www.pewinternet.org/Reports/2007/Cyberbullying.aspx.

Martin, R. & Hine, D. 2005. Development and validation of the uncivil workplace behavior questionnaire. *Journal of Occupational Health Psychology*, 10(4), 477–490.

Pearson, C.M., Andersson, L.M., & Porath, C.L. 2000. Assessing and attacking workplace incivility. *Organizational Dynamics*, 29, 123–137.

Pew Research. 2016. *Low marks for major players in 2016 election. Including the winner: Half of the voters are happy Trump won; Democrats take a hard line*. www.people-press.org/2016/11/21/low-marks-for-major-players-in-2016-election-including-the-winner.

Phillips, W. 2016. *This is why we can't have nice things: Mapping the relationship between online trolling and mainstream culture*. Cambridge, MA: MIT Press.

Porath, C. 2016. An antidote to incivility. *Harvard Business Review*. 94(4), 89

Porath, C.M. & Pearson, C.L. 2009. *The cost of bad behavior: How incivility is damaging your business and what to do about.* New York: Penguin.

Shandwick, Tate, & KRC Research. 2016. *Civility in America VII: The state of civility executive summary.*

Simpson, D. 1960. *Cassell's New Latin dictionary.* New York: Funk and Wagnalls.

Sinopoli, R. 1995. Thick-skinned liberalism: Redefining civility. *American Political Science Review,* 89(3), 612–620.

Vajda, P. 2007. Dealing with workplace gossip. *Management Issues.* www.management-issues.com.

van Jaarsveld, D., Walker, D., & Skarlicki, D. 2010. The role of job demands and emotional exhaustion in the relationship between customer and employee incivility. *Journal of Management* 36(6), 1486–1505.

3

DYSFUNCTION IN THE WORKPLACE

As we discussed in previous chapters, the lines between incivility and dysfunction are blurred. In the previous chapter we discussed the role of incivility in the workplace. One can see how rude behavior can quickly escalate into dysfunctional behavior. The difference between incivility and dysfunction is that dysfunction focuses on doing intentional harm to another. Often, incivility does not relate back to intentional harm.

Dysfunctional co-workers

There are several different levels of dysfunctional behavior in the workplace. The goal of this section is to focus on the most common forms. For many individuals it is difficult to label the behavior that they are experiencing, and in many cases they will call it incivility or bullying. In society, we have come to rely heavily on the term "bullying" for mistreatment, but leaning on the most commonly used terms can further muddy the waters. We will discuss bullying, which has its own distinctive characteristics and nuances. Providing an idea and understanding of these behaviors helps to give individuals context for the behavior that they are experiencing. Therefore, in later chapters, we will explore how to handle and address these specific behaviors from an individual and organizational standpoint.

Bullies

The first dysfunction that we will examine is bullying. This section will provide depth and insights into this type of behavior. I have chosen to explore this topic in detail because of the frequency with which the term "bullying" is used both inside and outside the workplace. In recent years, society has used the term "bullying" to label behaviors that are actually incivility. Individuals who are rude or making snide comments are referred to as "bullies"—however, that is often not the case, as we will examine shortly. It is important to understand the specific behaviors associated with bullying, along with the classifications of these behaviors.

Bullies in the workplace

Bullies are nothing new. We grew up with them on the playground and in high school; we found them in the cliques of mean girls or the people who liked to pick fights with others. They were the ones who focused on verbal and non-verbal abuse that included pushing, intimidation and humiliation to get the attention or the rec-ognition they so desperately wanted or needed. Some individuals found that these tactics worked, whether they were targets of the bullies or the bully themselves, and they adapted these behaviors later in their adult lives.

Typically, this type of dysfunction is utilized when the target has something that the bully wants or has personality characteristics that the bully does not possess. In most cases, the target of bullying is either smarter, more well liked or someone that the bully perceives as being weak and an easy target. In order to demonstrate their strength and domination over others, the bully utilizes tactics to demoralize or diminish others. The bully in the workplace is no different from the bully of our youth, only now they are older and much more difficult to deal with.

Workplace bullying is a major concern within organizations today. Research conducted by Namie and Namie (2009) found that, in the United States, over 50% of workers have reported being exposed to bullying in the workplace. In a majority of cases, organizations will recognize bullying as simply two or more individuals in the workplace who just cannot get along. In other cases, bullying behavior is more difficult to recognize. Because of the lack of understanding about bullying, there has been some confusion about what bullying is and what it isn't. For example, some research has characterized the targets of bullying as people who are weak, who lack proper social skills or social networks (Einarsen & Skogstad, 1996; Harvey et al., 2006; Mikkelsen & Einarsen, 2002; Tepper et al., 2006). Other researchers argue that the targets of bullying are the direct opposite: someone that the bully has identified as being strong and a threat to the bully's personal well-being, or someone who may cause others to question the competence and abilities of the bully. During the last several years, the term "bullying" has become popular in our culture. When someone does not get along with someone else, they are typically labeled a bully. For example, the manager who delivers a less-than-stellar performance review is quickly labeled a bully for being unfair. Because of a lack of clear understanding about and misrepresentation of bullying, the concept is often confusing.

Bullying defined

Bullying in the workplace has gained quite a bit of attention in society as well as in the workplace. As a result, it has become the focal point of scholarly research in recent years. But, while it has gained more attention, researchers still struggle to identify one clear definition of bullying.

If we look at the history of research linked to bullying we find that the first study connected to workplace bullying was conducted in the 1990s by Leymann (1990). The term "mobbing" was created to identify situations in which with multiple individuals focused negative behaviors on a single person. It was in the 1990s when Andrea Adams used the term "workplace bullying". She defined workplace bullying as any act that threatens the livelihood and credibility of an individual or individuals (Adams, 2014). Since then there have been different terms used for workplace bullying, including harassment, victimization, psychological terror, aggression, emotional abuse and generalized terms of abuse (Einarsen et al., 2003; Keashly & Jagatic, 2003).

When we look at the definitions of bullying, a range of behaviors is identified. The following provides an outline of these in chronological order, to demonstrate the evolution of the definition of workplace bullying:

- Olweus (1993) penned the first definition of workplace bullying as behavior that is systematic, repeated and intentional and which includes one or more individuals, with the behavior directed towards another individual.
- In 1997, Einarsen and Raknes (1997) expanded upon the definition as intentional, repeated actions that occur frequently over an extended period of time, of at least six months, by a person or persons against an individual, in the form of verbal abuse, behavior that humiliates, threatens or sabotages an individual's work, production or status and where there is a perceived imbalance of power.
- Later, Keashly (1998) provided the following definition: Hostile verbal and non-verbal, non-physical behaviors directed at a person or persons such that the target's sense of him or herself as a competent person and/or employee is negatively affected.
- Fields (1999) defined bullying as a compulsive need to displace aggression achieved by the expression of inadequacy (social, interpersonal, behavioral and professional) by projection of that inadequacy onto others through control and subjugation (criticism, exclusion, isolation). Bullying is sustained by abdication of responsibility (denial, counter-accusations and pretense of victimhood) and perpetrated by a climate of fear, ignorance, indifference, silence, denial, disbelief, deception, evasion of accountability, tolerance and reward for the bully.
- Einarsen (1999) expanded upon the definition of workplace bullying as repeated events and actions that are intended to offend, humiliate, harass, socially isolate or cause the victim stress, negatively impacting an employee's work and demonstrating hostile or aggressive behaviors.
- Yamada (2000, 480) provided the following definition of bullying: "the intentional infliction of a hostile work environment upon an employee by others

in the workplace typically through a combination of verbal and non-verbal behaviors".

- Einarsen (2000) added to his definition the requirement that bullying behaviors occur repeatedly and regularly over a period of time. In this definition, the target is forced into an inferior position through isolation or menial work that diminishes their capabilities.
- Later, in 2009, Namie and Namie, founders of the Workplace Bullying Institute, continued to build upon the definition by adding that bullying is repeated, health-harming mistreatment of a person by one or more workers, taking the form of verbal abuse, conduct or behaviors that are threatening, intimidating, humiliating, sabotaging or any combination of these.
- Barrow (2009) added that workplace bullying is repetitive, abusive behavior that devalues and harms other people on the job.
- Bond, Tuckey and Dollard (2010, 37) stated that "workplace bullying is a serious and chronic workplace stressor that negatively impacts individuals and organizations".

Clearly there is a level of complexity when trying to narrow down a single definition of what bullying is and what it is not. But there are common themes that emerge from these definitions. The primary themes are psychological abuse inflicted on targets over a period of time and repetitive in nature. Workplace bullying relies on hostile actions and words and is characterized as harassment of another. The intention of these actions is to degrade, humiliate and isolate the target. The bully identifies the target and systematically bullies that person, forcing them to become submissive, or to move on to another position or leave the organization. The bully may have one or more targets. What is important to recognize within all these definitions is the common theme regarding the construct of repeated and systematic behavior. This relates to situations in which an employee is persistently exposed to negative and aggressive behaviors at work, primarily of a psychological nature, with the ultimate goal being to humiliate, intimidate, punish or frighten the target. Classification of bullying is that it must be repetitive and happen regularly over a period of time, usually six months. What is important to understand about bullying is that it is an imbalance of power where the bully gets some sort of benefit from weakening their target, thus gaining power and/or control over another.

In the workplace, we can find bullying at all levels of an organization. Typically, though, we will find bullying in leadership roles because they are positions of power. In any case, bullying is persistent exposure of the target to interpersonal aggression and mistreatment by another colleague or superior, with devastating effects on both the target and the organization. In addition, bullying is not just limited to one individual but can include groups of individuals, such as targeted groups including organizational units (Einarsen et al., 2003; Rayner & Keashly, 2005; Hutchinson et al., 2006; Einarsen et al., 2009).

What bullying is not

Before we proceed further in the discussion of bullying, it is important to reflect on the definitions of bullying. Three identifiable and distinctive bullying behaviors in the workplace are:

1. Repetitive behavior that occurs a minimum of twice a week.
2. Long-term behavior that continues for a minimum of six months.
3. Behaviors that occur in situations where the person who is targeted finds it difficult to defend themselves or stop the abuse (Felblinger, 2009).

A simplified definition of bullying is repetitive behavior meant to inflict harm on others. People who are rude, uncivil or lacking in clear manners are not bullies. For example, the person who does not hold the door open is not a bully but is rude and inconsiderate. The supervisor who provides a poor performance evaluation may appear to the person receiving the review to be a bully if the person does not agree with that review. The office co-workers who do not like or talk to one another are not bullies. However, it is also important to note that while these behaviors are not considered bullying, they can quickly turn that way. If the manager who gives a less-than-stellar performance review follows up with an action plan that is difficult to accomplish, or starts to negate the employee's work performance over a period of time, then there is an established behavior of bullying. It is important not to use the term "bullying" for behaviors not considered bullying. When this happens, it clouds the understanding of the term and makes it difficult to address the behavior. Since we have defined what bullying is and is not, it is now important to drill even deeper into this topic.

The bully

One major misconception regarding bullying is that many believe the bully is powerful and controlling. For targets of bullies it is important to understand that, at the time, the bully appears to be powerful and in control because they wish to portray themselves in that manner. If the bully comes across as having control, it is easy for their target to become submissive to what the bully wants. In essence, the target gives control over to the bully, which is easy to do when intimidated, humiliated or isolated.

In other cases, the bully comes across as an extremely self-confident individual. The key thing to remember about a bully is that they are often very insecure and possess low levels of self-esteem. It is when they are controlling the situation or their target that they gain power and thus a boost to their self-esteem. The boost is short-lived and then they go back to their target to build themselves back up. The bully saps self-confidence from others in order to restore their own.

The bully needs to control all situations and all the individuals involved. Their behavior will shift based on the circumstances and the people they are with. If the circumstances require them to be charming, they will become the most charming individual but can just as quickly turn and become hostile. They are looking to protect their self-image, self-esteem and the perceptions others have of them. The bully can target anyone who threatens any of these components; no one is off limits. If the threat is a co-worker or a leader, the bully will adjust their behavior to target that individual.

Bullies typically lack social insights into their behaviors (Namie & Namie, 2009). Their lives are often out of control. They crave power and control in order to gain order in their own lives. When a bully targets a competent individual, the bully has recognized that the target has characteristics that they themselves lack. As a result, they will focus on whittling away at the self-confidence of their target. They will do this through insults, criticism and public humiliation. The target is thrown off because once they were known for their competence and now someone is questioning their abilities. The target will become sensitive and extra vigilant in their work efforts, which can mean they become less confident and begin to make mistakes. All the while, the bully waits for these mistakes so that they can pounce and use them against their target. The cycle continues and it spirals out of control for the target.

The bully's other tactic is to divert any negative attention away from themselves. They want to fly under the radar so that others cannot see their mistakes or incompetence. All negative attention focuses on the target or targets. The ultimate goal of the bully is for the target to become submissive or to exit the situation by leaving the organization, or transferring to another area where the bully is not connected. Once their target is out of the picture, they move on to someone new. The bully will continue this behavior until it is addressed. Unfortunately, though, the behavior often goes ignored and unaddressed.

Tactics that bullies like to use

Bullies use an arsenal of tactics as their weapons; we have discussed some of them above. Bullies will use tactics that they are most comfortable with and they may use a variety of different approaches until they find the combination that works to control their target. The following highlights some of these tactics in further detail.

Exclusion and isolation: Exclusion and isolation are used to gain control and power over the target. The bully will use this approach either socially or professionally by excluding the target from key events. In a professional setting, the bully will purposely omit the target from meetings that affect their work or separate the target from the information and resources that they need in order to perform. When the target brings information forward, these ideas are minimized or diminished. During meetings, they will be unable to provide input into the direction of their own work projects, or those of the team or the organization. Targets learn about decisions being made that will influence their work through rumors or others who are willing to share this information with the target. By hoarding or withholding vital information, the target is left in the dark and is unable to do their job effectively.

In addition to professional isolation, the bully uses social isolation. When the target is socially isolated, they do not have social contact with others and they are unable to share what is happening. Social isolation is used so that others will realize the target is on the outs. The bully will either cause others to want to withdraw from the target or will "strongly encourage" them not to include the target for fear of becoming a target as well. As a result, the target suffers alone and does not have social support to help them cope with the situation. Individuals who have experienced isolation often refer to being an outcast, a pariah or being put in cold storage.

Hostile work environment: The bully creates a work environment that is uncomfortable and hostile. The target experiences gossip, public humiliation, isolation and lack of information and feedback. The bully creates an environment that is challenging and difficult for the target to do their work in. Each day becomes emotionally and physically draining. Because of this environment, the target starts to withdraw, either physically or emotionally. Absenteeism increases; job engagement and satisfaction decline.

Invasion of personal space: The bully loves to make their target uncomfortable and they will do this by standing over their target, leaning in or sitting close just so that the person will feel uncomfortable. When the bully enters the personal space of their target, they are demonstrating physical signs of dominance. The target feels uncomfortable and intimidated. In one study, a research participant stated that her bully always came so close that she could feel his spit when he spoke. She would back up, only to have him move forward until she was pinned up against the wall with no place to go. She said she felt violated and dirty (Roter, 2016).

Unfair or destructive criticism/feedback: The bully does not like to provide positive feedback. By sharing positive feedback, they are validating the work of their target and highlighting their talents, which is the opposite to the agenda of the bully. Instead the bully uses destructive feedback. They typically criticize the work of their target and give feedback that is negative and never positive. The bully's vocabulary includes words such as "incompetent", "crazy", "lazy" and "inadequate". These words attack the self-esteem and confidence of the target. When first used, the target will typically be in shock and find it surreal that these words have been used against them. They might just shrug it off at first, since they might never have experienced this type of negative feedback before, but eventually the behavior will disturb the individual. When giving negative feedback, the bully will not provide any tips to improve performance. The more the bully uses this approach, the more the target begins to believe the negative feedback, especially if the bully is in a position of power or of a higher status.

Name-calling: As mentioned previously, the bully will typically rely on derogatory terms. Their vocabulary is full of hurtful and negative words that are used to diminish their targets. Once they discover the words or phrases that they know hit a nerve or cause negative effects in their target, they will repeat them. They also like to come up with derogatory nicknames for their targets and will share these nicknames with co-workers, in a joking manner at first, but eventually the nickname will stick and become part of the work group's language.

Pointing the finger: Bullies never take responsibility or any form of accountability for negative actions. This is common in most of the dysfunctional and deviant behaviors we will discuss. When something goes wrong, they will look for someone to blame. Once they find their scapegoat, they will latch on to that person. By blaming others, the attention diverts from the bully to their target. Once they have diverted the attention they will continue to go after their target. In some cases, they will create false claims against their target. This tactic is used to keep the attention focused on the target and away from the bully's incompetence and inadequacies. In some cases, the bully will make mistakes on purpose, blame others for the mistakes and then go on to fix the problem. They do this in order to position themselves as the competent hero who has saved the day, while others are labeled incompetent.

Unreasonable demands: The bully makes unreasonable demands knowing that there is no way their target can complete them. Sometimes the target will have to over-extend themselves in order to meet the demands. An example is asking for a report at the end of the workday just as the target is ready to leave. The bully will state that the report is due first thing in the morning. When the target says that they have to go and asks if it can be done in the morning, the bully will tell them "no". In other cases, the demands will come in on the weekend, late at night or during the target's vacation. In one interview I conducted, a target shared that their bully demanded last-minute "emergency" reports while on vacation. When asked if someone else could do it, the answer was no. The target felt as though they had to complete the reports and deliver, and so the individual worked throughout their vacation. Upon their return they found out that the reports were never utilized.

Shifting the responsibility: In other cases, the bully will not follow through on their own work and will pass it on to an already thinly spread target. When the bully is the leader they might give out work that is menial or above the target's skills. If it is menial work, the bully may micromanage the target so that they become frustrated; if it is above their skill set, the bully will become hands off and not provide any guidance or instruction. Unreasonable demands are meant for the target to fail and for the bully to point out the failure to others and to openly criticize the target.

Inconsistent application of rules and policies: For bullies, rules and policies do not apply. They are meant for others. In the mind of the bully, rules and regulations are designed to hold their targets accountable. Typically, bullies will come in late, not adhere to policies and expect to be held to different standards than others. When the bully is a leader, they will be inconsistent with the implementation of rules and policies with others in the department. If they like certain employees, these employees will be exempt from rules and regulations, while the target will be held to the strictest adherence. Bullies use rules and policies for their own benefit and will bend and manipulate these rules to their advantage.

Threatening job or personal security: Holding job or personal security over someone's head is a tactic utilized to create fear in the target. The bully relies on threats implying attacks on personal and/or professional security to throw the confidence of their target. These tactics are designed to throw the target off balance. By attacking the basic need of security, the bully is able to capture the attention of the target and get them to become submissive.

Spreading rumors or gossip: In the incivility chapter, we discussed the role rumors and gossip play in incivility. This area can quickly blur into dysfunction. The bully will use rumors and gossip for malicious intent. Information learned about their target is used as a tactic to discredit them. Rumors and gossip go from idle comments to escalated, malicious and slanderous ones. The bully begins to embellish and twist information in order to ruin the reputation or credibility of their target. The bully is constantly looking for information that can be used against their target and they will use it repetitively. If the information is not enough to take down their target, they will focus on adding falsehoods to the stories in order to make them interesting to others, hoping they will provide further insights that can be used against the target. By making the gossip interesting, the bully knows that the rumor will take off. Nothing is off limits for the bully when it comes to rumors and gossip. Whatever information the bully has on the target will be used against them, whether it is true or not.

Verbal and non-verbal threats: Threats made by a bully include taking work away, not promoting an individual, threatening job status, sharing untruths and isolating and excluding the basic needs of the employee. Non-verbal cues include eye rolling, turning away, mocking, staring or glaring, smirking or shaking the head. All of these tactics make the target feel uncomfortable and off balance.

Physical threats: On very rare occasions, there may be physical abuse. Physical abuse may include intimidating behaviors such as physically blocking a person, finger pointing, invading personal space, shoving, touching, hitting and throwing objects. In the workplace, physical assault may occur from a bully, though this is rare. They prefer to use verbal and emotional assaults against their target.

Demeaning individuals based on race, age, gender, sexuality, weight or disability: The bully may focus on the target's personal and physical characteristics—for example, by demeaning the person for being a certain age, such as being too young or too old to do the work. Other characteristics the bully may focus on include sexuality, disability, weight, physical characteristics and gender. In another bullying incident reported to me, the bully commented about how overweight his team was getting and that he was going to stop bringing donuts to meetings. The following week he brought fruit and donuts. He handed out donuts to people he deemed were not overweight and gave fruit to the people he thought were.

He also verbally called these people out, saying that they needed to lose weight. This behavior continued with other meals, including serving salad to overweight members of the team and rich pasta dishes to people he considered to be a healthy weight, including himself. When told that this behavior was demeaning, he played it down, saying that he was just looking out for the health of his team (Roter, 2016).

Derailment: Derailment refers to sabotaging a person's job or career. This can include a range of behaviors, from placing obstacles in the way of the employee to prevent them from completing tasks, to ending a person's career. The bully derails an employee by making it impossible for them to get projects or tasks completed on time or in budget. The bully will hold back direction, resources or the means of removing obstacles for the target. They also become obstacles themselves. They will ask others to do the same towards the target as well. The bully will cause interruption in the employee's work, resulting in accusations and humiliation as leadership, the bully and their co-workers accuse the target of being lazy, incompetent or stupid. Another form of sabotage includes the derailment of a person's career. For example, if a person wants to participate in prime projects that might highlight their skills or talents, the bully will start a campaign to block the employee from the project. They might use false allegations and the office grapevine to spread malicious rumors or block their target from being successful.

All of the above tactics are used to establish a pattern of aggressive behavior that is designed to inflict psychological harm on the target. The goal of these tactics is to degrade, isolate and humiliate the target. The bully may use one or several different tactics in order to inflict harm on an individual.

Types of bullies

Just as there are different tactics used by bullies, there are also several different types of bullies that we can run across in the workplace. While their behaviors and actions differ slightly, the intent remains the same: to degrade and then control the target. The following discusses the most common types of bullies and how they may manifest themselves. At times we might run across one type or a combination of different types depending on the individual and the situation.

Public bully, or direct bully: This type of bully uses a direct approach and is public with their actions. The public or direct bully uses public forums to inflict humiliation. Their behavior will include screaming, throwing tantrums, invading personal space, public threats and public non-verbal gestures. Their goal is to be the center of attention, flexing their dominance and control in public. When this type of behavior happens in the workplace, the target often feels as though they are being treated like a child. For fear of public outbursts, the target does everything to avoid the bully. During public encounters such as meetings, the target moves into self-protection mode, becoming quiet and withdrawn. The public bully likes this and will continue to lash out and escalate their tactics. Constant humiliation causes the target to completely shut down and fear is instilled into them. They never know when the next attack will occur. They begin to doubt their abilities, depression starts to creep in and these feelings now invade all aspects of their lives (Roter, 2017). Bystanders who witness these attacks will often give this type of bully the floor, which escalates their behaviors. Grandstanding and public displays of power motivate this type of bully.

Silent bully, or indirect bully: This type of bully is the direct opposite of the public bully and prefers to attack behind closed doors and under the radar. They bully in private, with a select few people who are connected to the bully and feed into their negativity. They act this way so others won't witness their actions. In public, their persona will be one of kindness and charm, and people will genuinely like this person. Privately, they will be the direct opposite. They will attack their targets, ensuring that there are no witnesses other than their trusted group of people they know will give them a forum. Word will begin to circulate in the form of rumors, gossip, slander and twisted stories. When the target learns of what is happening and comes forward to share their side of the story, others will not believe their accusations against the bully. People cannot believe that the private bully would act this way, since they are such a great person.

The nuance in regards to the private bully is that they use the information they get from their target, then twist and turn the information. There will be a slight element of truth to what they say, but the majority of the information will be exaggerated and altered. The target will not know they are being attacked until they start to hear the stories being circulated. A friend may come to the target to share the news and let them know what is being said. Because there is an element of truth, the target will have to sort through what is true and what is false. The story will have made its rounds through several different individuals, who may have added their own knowledge or insights into the story. At this point, it will be difficult to pinpoint the source of the rumors. The rumor mill and the grapevine are the best means of communication for a silent bully. They will let the information loose, sit back and watch what happens.

Another tactic that the silent bully likes to engage in is sabotage. They will spend time identifying ways to sabotage their targets and do so silently, through falsified reports, blocked resources, giving wrong information to the target or isolating them so that they are unable to perform their work. The sabotage is quiet and again the target often does not realize what has happened until it is too late (Roter, 2017).

Critical bully: The critical bully is never happy and their mode of attack is to find fault and blame. These individuals tend to be negative by nature. In their mind, everything that happens is the fault of someone else. They believe they are the victim and will lash out at everyone who may be responsible for their problems. They like to nitpick and will find fault where there is none. These are the types of individuals that will use performance management systems to share negative feedback. They will never offer positive or constructive feedback in order to help an individual grow. The critical bully enjoys piling pressure and stress onto their target so that they will make mistakes that can be criticized. To cause stress they will create unreasonable expectations and demands which are impossible to achieve. When these demands are not met, the critic will point out any mistakes, faults or missed deadlines. The critical bully utilizes exaggerated body language and tone of voice to communicate criticism. This will usually come in the form of heavy sighing, eye rolling or shaking of the head. Typically the critical bully has learned this type of behavior from someone in their past; it might have been a former leader, co-worker, family member or friend. Life events have also added to the negativity that they experience and in turn they blame others for their circumstances; in a sense they play the role of the victim (Roter, 2017).

Friendly bully: The friendly bully is the person who will be the first to introduce themselves and make every effort to befriend their target, but who will capitalize on the friendship to get the target to let their guard down and to access information to use against others. Through friendship, the target will become vulnerable and begin to share information, whether personal or business-related. For this type of bully, information and knowledge are power. Information can be used against the target when they least expect it. The friendly bully takes tidbits of information, coupled with gossip from others, and uses it to their advantage. When interacting with others the friendly bully is thinking about how they can use the information they are gaining. In the meantime, the target believes that they have a genuine friendship with the bully, but in reality they are just a pawn for the bully to further their own agenda.

The friendly bully will utilize tactics that are the direct opposite of the critical bully's. As they are building a "friendship" they will compliment and build up their target. They will focus on providing their target with a false sense of security and trust. In addition, the friendly bully is looking to cause conflict and turmoil with others. They will pit others against each other and take on the role of puppet master, controlling and manipulating situations and interactions. They will sit on the sidelines and watch as the conflict begins to unfold in front of everyone, but they will keep themselves out of the line of fire. They will step in if they think that their "friendship" can help to solve the problem or address the conflict. Eventually, the target will realize that the bully is "two faced", but by that time it will be too late. The friendly bully will say they are just the "messenger".

The friendly bully is also busy aligning themselves with upper leadership and presenting themselves in a positive light. They will agree with whatever leadership says. In meetings, they are the ones who will nod in encouragement and agree with everything that leadership says. They are focused on ensuring that leadership thinks they are a true team player, friendly to new hires, cooperative, competent and agreeable. When the target complains about the friendly bully, others will not believe them and will not see any problems with that person—after all, they are nothing but kind, a team player, a good employee and a loyal friend. Instead the target comes across as the one with a problem and at this point the target appears to be less than trustworthy. How can anyone say anything negative about this kind, loyal, team-playing person? After all, aren't you the one who shared information with this person? Aren't you the one who broke the trust of others by sharing personal information? They won't see that the friendly bully is doing anything wrong.

In public the friendly bully will keep up the persona that they are a true friend and will talk up the target and praise them. When the target calls the friendly bully out for their behavior, they will remain cool and collected while the target becomes angry. The target will look emotional and erratic, as though they are the bully. The friendly bully will stand quietly with tears in their eyes and wearing a look of bewilderment. They will play the role of victim, saying that they don't understand and that they thought they were friends with the target; they have been nothing but kind, caring and considerate. Others they will ultimately sympathize with the friendly bully and will treat the target as the villain or the bully (Roter, 2017).

Hoarder bully: The hoarder bully holds onto information in order to control situations. The hoarder bully maintains power by gaining information and resources which they will hold tight. They will hoard years of information, knowledge, processes and procedures, meaning they are able to control who has access to the knowledge and who gets the information. On a personal level, they tie their self-esteem to their knowledge and the resources they control. The hoarder bully will hold on to the information and will control when and how much information they want to share, and with whom. The target is at the whim of the hoarder bully. The hoarder bully does not want others to succeed, and by hoarding information they become known as the "go-to person". While information is a major source of control for the hoarder, they will also hoard the resources they are in charge of—for example:

- Budgetary items.
- Knowledge of institutional processes and procedures.
- Scheduling and timing of resources.
- Staffing.
- Recognition and praise.

When the hoarder bully feels threatened by another individual they will cut the target out of anything that they control. This will include communication channels such as meetings, emails and reports, and other resources needed to be successful. They become the keeper of the information, knowledge and resources. The hoarder bully will be well connected to the rumor mill and will use it as a channel for getting out information that they can control.

There are several tactics that the hoarder bully will use to control a situation. One is silent treatment: they are very good at ignoring requests made by the target and isolating these individuals in order to prevent them from getting the information they need or request. Targets will discover that they do not know what is happening in their department or with their own work. In the meantime, the hoarder bully will begin to make decisions that negatively impact their target. They will create new rules, processes and procedures without discussing these changes. By changing and bypassing current rules and regulations, the bully is able to tighten their control while leaving others guessing. They will ignore the input from others and are likely to put up resistance and obstacles to others in order to block them from moving forward with decisions. Targets typically feel isolated and diminished. Eventually the target realizes that they can't get their work done unless they have the cooperation of the hoarder bully. Then they can give in to the hoarder bully, try to circumvent them or if they experience too much resistance, leave the organization.

The hoarder bully views their target as a threat to their existence. For example, the bully may have been with the organization for a number of years when a younger employee comes in who the hoarder views as a threat to their job. So as not to put their position in jeopardy, they will hold information tightly in order for the person to fail, or to rely on the hoarder. By holding information close, they have the ultimate control. The target is at the mercy of the hoarder bully. This bully works hard to preserve their job and status while being viewed as invaluable to the organization and upper leadership. They create the persona that they are the subject-matter expert and the person with the informal power within the organization. In many cases, they are able to weave this lie so that leadership feels as though they are being held hostage by the hoarder bully. Ultimately the hoarder bully will leave the organization when they think they are ready. Leadership won't touch them because they fear losing the valuable knowledge the bully is controlling. When the bully leaves the organization, they still won't give up the information. They want the organization and others to continue to rely on them (Roter, 2017).

Opportunistic bully: These bullies focus on ways to move themselves forward. They are constantly looking for opportunities to seize positioning power. In the workplace they are cut-throat and look at everything and everyone as a competition. They are known for walking over others to get what they want. The opportunistic bully will use every opportunity to advance their personal agenda, and they will identify individuals, opportunities and situations that can benefit them. Once they identify their target, they will use methods of manipulation to gain the upper hand in the situation, including lying, cheating, using superficial charm and other manipulation tactics. They are comfortable creating obstacles to block others from moving ahead and they are constantly looking for ways to align themselves with senior leadership or finding a member of the leadership team to sponsor them. Typically this sponsor will see nothing wrong with the opportunistic bully and will often view them as ambitious, a go-getter, extremely competent and often a lot like the corporate sponsor. In the eyes of the sponsor, the opportunistic bully can do no wrong and is considered a superstar.

The opportunistic bully will have two personas. The persona in the workplace is usually cut-throat, but outside the workplace the bully will come across as kind and caring. They will sign up and volunteer for opportunities that will help them to network with key individuals. They are often very active in civic, educational and spiritual environments and very giving of their time. They will come across as a person that is devoted, generous and caring. This persona makes it difficult for targets to say anything bad about this person. Targets will share with friends and significant others just how difficult it is to work with this person, then when they run into them in public their persona will be completely different. People will say that they are shocked, after meeting them, by how wonderful they are, and they won't be able to articulate what the target has been complaining about. They are not at all the monster that has been portrayed. In public this person will have positioned themselves as a volunteer at their kids' school or sports team, as supportive civic members, giving of their time and talents. They do this to build up their public image and to ensure that they are viewed positively for any opportunities that may come up. In addition, they know that their positive deeds will come back to the organization, which in turn will negate any negative impact that they may have on their targets (Roter, 2017).

We have taken the time to explore the different tactics and types of bullies in the workplace. Bullying tends to be the most common form of dysfunctional behavior that will be experienced in the workplace, and therefore it was important to discuss this topic in detail and depth to provide an understanding of the different nuances related to bullying in the workplace. Next we will explore other types of dysfunctional behaviors in the workplace.

The paranoid

Paranoia is a behavior wherein an individual seems mistrustful of others. This can be due to a lack of trust which may or may not be justified. For example, if someone has done something unfair to another person, that person may be less inclined to trust the person who has upset them and may be paranoid regarding their intentions. At other times paranoia is a manifestation of a personality disorder that has built up for many years and it can be so extreme that it can cause the person to become disassociated from reality. This type of behavior is what psychologists refer to as paranoid schizophrenia, which is often treated with extensive therapy and drugs. This type of paranoia is less common in the workplace, though it can be experienced. For the sake of this section we will not delve into paranoid schizophrenia, as it is a medical and psychological issue that must be addressed by professionals in the field. Instead, we will examine the topic of paranoia as a dysfunction and how this behavior can play out in the workplace.

Paranoia is typically linked to individuals with a high sense of suspicion, a tendency to blame others, strong levels of mistrust, sensitivity to any form of negative feedback and feelings of being singled out or persecuted by others. Their fears are typically irrational; however, their beliefs can become so entrenched that they become their reality. They also tend to expect the worst from others. These negative feelings become self-fulling prophecies. For example, if a person fears that they will be fired they might obsess about this, act out and as a result lose their job, all because of their initial fears. This then reinforces their beliefs that others are out to get them.

When this happens, they blame others in order to protect themselves. In their mind it was not their fault and they blame what has happened on someone being out to get them. The paranoia becomes a cycle that they experience.

The paranoid individual will come across as normal, performing their work and basically keeping to themselves, but when their fears are manifested, usually because of stress, they will become angry, demanding and difficult to work with. As a mode of protection, paranoid individuals will begin to withdraw physically and emotionally from teams and work groups. They will create barriers between those who they don't trust and themselves. People who have trust issues often find it difficult to work in teams, to collaborate or to cooperate with others. In our team-based work environments, this type of dysfunction can be extremely detrimental and can prevent teams from functioning in a healthy manner.

Contributing factors that may increase paranoia include stressful interactions, uncertainty or organizations going through large-scale change initiatives. Paranoia is often ripe in environments where employees are exposed to constant layoffs and highly competitive environments. Paranoia is like a spark that can spread through an organization, rapidly becoming a firestorm. One person with paranoia will share their reality and fears with others who may believe these fears. Others can then display the same levels of paranoia, creating a culture of distrust.

Work environments that are naturally unhealthy may not foster trust and collaboration. These types of dysfunctional organizations may cause people to become paranoid for all the right reasons. People who are new to the environment, who are not aware of the dysfunction, may question why a person or several individuals are acting the way they are. Since they do not know all the history or nuance that has created the dysfunctional work environment, they are left wondering and feeling paranoid about what is happening. In other organizational cultures, a state of fear is part of the culture and work environment.

Individuals may find themselves being overly suspicious in the workplace. They may question the motives of others, of leadership or of the organization. We have all experienced levels of suspicion in the workplace. For example, we might experience suspicion about a person or situation, which could be considered a level of paranoia. Paranoia can mean feeling persecuted without any form of justification and based on perceptions. Feelings of paranoia can stem from off-the-cuff conversations that spark fear in an individual. These feelings can be short-lived, but if they are stoked they can become someone's reality. For some individuals, paranoia can be manifested from years and years of their own reality.

Narcissists/egotists

Maccoby (2016) has shared that psychoanalysts do not usually get close enough to narcissistic employees or leaders to fully investigate them. As a result, research related to this type of dysfunction in the workplace can be challenging since these individuals typically do not recognize that they are narcissists. Because this type of behavior is an enigma, the narcissistic personality continues to be one of the most researched of the dysfunctional behaviors. Early research conducted by Freud (1914) discovered that narcissism was related to a psychological element that was part of who the person was. Later research found that there are two sides to narcissism: a positive and a negative component. For the purpose of this book we will explore the negative component of narcissism.

Narcissism defined

The definition of narcissism is ever evolving. Scholars have referred to narcissism as an "unhealthy self-absorption", a "personal form of admiration", or a "perverse self-love" (Ellis, 1927; Kets de Vries, 2001; King, Rosenthal & Pittinsky, 2007). Other definitions include individuals who are extremely troubled or uncomfortable with themselves, which results in feelings of deprivation, anger and emptiness. Morin (2013) described narcissism as attention-seeking individuals with an inflated sense of entitlement coupled with a denial of their own weaknesses. They demand constant attention from people around them as they see the world as revolving around them. In their perception, no one exists but themselves. Paulhus and Williams (2002) defined narcissism as a personality trait that encompasses grandiosity, arrogance, self-absorption, dominance, superiority, entitlement and frailty of their own self-esteem. Through a review of the various themes related to narcissism, the common ones are individuals who are self-centered, demonstrating over-confidence in their abilities, attention-seeking behavior and feelings of entitlement.

It is important to recognize the differences between narcissism and individuals who have high levels of self-esteem. Individuals with high self-esteem are confident in their abilities but possess a caring component which is lacking in narcissistic individuals. The narcissist is typically indifferent towards the needs and well-being of others. They possess low levels of self-esteem which are masked through charm; they appear confident and develop a façade. The façade is so realistic that the narcissist starts to believe it and creates an inflated sense of themselves and their abilities. In addition to elevating their façade, they will seek the admiration of others and positions of status, power and prestige in order to fuel their façade.

Corporate narcissism

Narcissism is found at all levels, within organizations, governments or for-profit and non-profits corporations. For the sake of this section, we will discuss the corporate narcissist. The corporate narcissist will appear to be committed to the strategy and direction of the organization. However, their only commitment is to their own goals and personal agenda. What makes the corporate narcissist compelling is that they will demonstrate high levels of ambition, the ability to attract followers who will buy into their message and the uncanny ability to create a compelling vision. From this description one would think that the narcissist would make a strong leader or employee, but that is not true. On the contrary, they lack the traits of effective and successful employees. The narcissist is too self-absorbed, lacks listening skills, does not take criticism well and possesses low levels of emotional intelligence. However, because of their ability to sell themselves they are able to package their skills quite effectively and move up through the organization very quickly. They make the ideal employee in some organizations as they appear to be highly motivated, energetic and have a winning mindset.

Types of narcissists

There are several different categories of narcissist which we will discuss. Understanding the types of narcissist helps to provide a framework to identify the type of narcissist that is being experienced. The following provides a description of the different types of narcissist that may be encountered in the workplace.

Productive narcissist: We all possess some form of narcissism. For the majority of individuals their level of narcissism is a healthy manifestation that they have the ability to control. We are able to recognize our strengths and weaknesses and embrace these for what they are. The productive narcissist is not blinded by their abilities and are aware of their narcissism in a healthy way.

Extreme narcissist: We are all familiar with this type of narcissist, and for the most part this section focuses on the extreme narcissist as they are the over-the-top types. It is the person who is self-serving, self-promoting, grandiose and exaggerated in their vision. They truly love themselves and think that they are the best and no one else can compete at their level. In their minds everything they do is perfect, exceptional and no one can touch their abilities. When something goes wrong it is the fault of someone else, never themselves. We often see these types of individuals in politics and upper-level positions. However, we will encounter them at all levels trying to flex their muscle and to get people to like them.

Quiet narcissist: This is the type of individual who flies under the radar. They act confident and seem secure. They keep to themselves and only speak up when it is for their own benefit. Behind the scenes they are talented at planting seeds of doubt into other people's minds; they are able to create self-doubt, self-loathing and depression in their targets. If we look at this type of narcissist, we find that they are similar to the bully as they focus on destroying others in order to build themselves up and to be viewed as successful. The quiet narcissist puts people into categories based on what they perceive as that person's weaknesses, and they will use these categories to benefit themselves. They will make subtle comments or jokes that will cause individuals to question themselves. At first it starts off as subtle joking, and since it comes from someone we know and usually respect, we let it slide. The quiet narcissist might make fun of the target or provide a stinging put-down that begins to cause self-doubt. All the time that they are causing self-doubt, they are promoting themselves and their abilities. The quiet narcissist will utilize passive-aggressive behaviors to cause individuals to feel as though something is not right. For example, they might come up behind a person using the copy machine and refill the paper before they have the chance to do it themselves. The narcissist might then say, in a passive-aggressive manner, "I'm used to following behind you and cleaning up your messes. If it wasn't for me, nothing here would ever get done." The quiet narcissist will point out simple mistakes. They will say things such as, "I don't agree with your point," but when asked why they don't agree they will just respond, "I think you are wrong." The other person will move into a defensive mode to defend their viewpoint, but afterwards the narcissist will say again, "I don't agree." The person might then walk away and wonder why they don't agree, and want to go back to find out what the problem is, to prove their point of view or to get concrete reasons as to why there might be a problem. This tactic is used to cause the other person to break down and to create frustration in the person trying to defend their point. Meanwhile, the quiet narcissist will sit back and watch things unfold as the other person becomes frustrated, sharing more information to prove their point. All the while, the quiet narcissist is gaining insights, information and data that they will use to position themselves in a positive way, such as for their own benefit or to obtain their personal agenda. Essentially, their target will have done their research for them, and the narcissist will go back to leadership and put forward the same point as their target with the data that has been provided. The target will argue that this is what they've been trying to say all along, but it will be too late and the quiet narcissist will have won the battle. They will come across as the subject-matter expert and believe in their own abilities.

Characteristics of the narcissist

The narcissist employee is a gifted communicator with a commanding presence. Individuals are drawn to them and can be pulled into their presence, which is often a façade. While some people are blinded and enamored by the narcissist, others quickly identify that there is a problem with this person. The narcissist might come across as too good to be true, and that is usually the case. Their façade is fine-tuned and perfected over time and with experience. It may take some time, but eventually their façade will begin to crack. This typically happens when they are faced with high-stress situations and they have a difficult time balancing their lies and tactics. When the façade begins to crumble, narcissists increase their focus on themselves, highlighting their own talents, who they know and what great work they do. The key to surviving a narcissist is to identify their tactics and approaches. If individuals can spot a narcissist early they have a chance to protect themselves. The following details the characteristics of the narcissist and how they use them in order to position themselves.

Lack of empathy: Empathy is the ability to recognize and appreciate the feelings of others. Narcissists are unable to understand empathy because their focus is on one person: themselves. They are constantly seeking self affirmation from others which helps to build up their self-esteem. They are deaf to the feelings, words and behaviors of others. The narcissist is focused on their own issues and not on others', so they have a difficult time relating to or empathizing with others.

One-sided decision making: The narcissist typically only sees one perspective: their own. They lack the ability to understand the diverse perspective and advantages that others might bring to the table, which hinders their ability to make decisions effectively. When decisions are made by the narcissist they are usually one-sided, and any feedback that differs from their agenda is ignored. When the decision is successful the narcissist will take full credit. On the flip side, if the decision is wrong then the narcissist is quick to blame others.

Visioning: The narcissist has grand visions of what things should look like and these visions are used to build their confidence (Rosenthal & Pittinsky, 2006, 622–623). Because they have an exaggerated sense of their own abilities, they believe they can do anything and they trust that these visions can and will become reality. Because of their conviction and false sense of confidence, others are drawn to them. These followers become diehards and will stick with the narcissist through thick or thin. Others will follow them until they see through the façade or get wise to the tactics.

Self-focus: Every interaction that the narcissist engages in will be centered upon themselves. If at any point the conversation drifts away from them, they will become visually frustrated and irritated. The narcissist will offer up non-verbal cues, including rolling of the eyes, deep sighing, fidgeting and distracted looks that indicate they want to exit the conversation. They will do everything to navigate the conversation back to themselves. At first this navigation will be subtle, but it can become more aggressive and involve interrupting or making inappropriate comments that will stun others into silence, allowing the narcissist to jump in and refocus the conversation. Keep in mind that the narcissist needs to dominate every scenario.

Inability to maintain relationships: Since most of the narcissist's time is spent focused on themselves, they have a difficult time maintaining relationships. During the beginning stages of a relationship, the narcissist will appear to be engaged, but that is only to position themselves for their own advantage. Eventually, the focus will fade and divert to the narcissist. The narcissist will only focus on others if they feel that it will suit their purpose and personal agenda. Once the person has served their purpose they will be discarded quickly. Relationships, in the eyes of the narcissist, are a means of promoting their own needs. People grow tired of catering to or stroking the ego of the narcissist and tire of the attention being one-sided. Narcissists have an uncanny ability to recognize when people are on to their tactics and will typically cut the relationship off before the other person can do so.

Challenging: The narcissist demands constant praise and will surround themselves with people who demonstrate admiration, adoration and worship for the narcissist. Once the narcissist is challenged by someone or feels that another does not appreciate them for who they are, the narcissist will lash out. They don't like to be challenged. Challenging their power makes them feel out of control. Once the perception of power is disputed, they may feel as though their self-esteem is also challenged. They will do whatever they can to turn the tables on the person challenging them. This is usually done by making life difficult for the challenger. The severity of the attack will depend on the threat perceived by the narcissist.

Minions: The narcissist will typically have a cadre of followers who adore them. These individuals follow the narcissist in order to get some false validation as to their own self-worth. The narcissist does not view them as a threat and recognizes their ability to help the narcissist with promoting their agenda. These individuals will do anything to stay in the good graces of the narcissist and will serve them as needed. In some cases, the narcissist will use them as spies, or to refuel their own self-esteem, to be hostile towards others, to implement the dirty work or to provide a semblance of a relationship or friendship to the narcissist. One thing that a narcissist demands is loyalty from their inner circle. Their minions will be extremely loyal to, and do whatever is needed to stay in the good graces of, the narcissist because they know the wrath of betrayal. As quickly as a narcissist will attach themselves to their followers, they will just as quickly end the relationship.

Positioning: The narcissist is skilled at positioning themselves to be in the line of sight of the powers that be. One reason that narcissists typically move into leadership positions is because they are successful at positioning themselves and networking with all the right people. They will place themselves with higher-ups in order to promote their agenda, to move into high profile positions or to be assigned the prime projects. The narcissist will always demonstrate their value to the organization and make others feel as though the organization would fail without them. They market themselves as the perfect employee to members of upper leadership. Being in the spotlight, self-promoting and being a chameleon are all ways in which the narcissist will get others to see them. Another method of self-positioning that the narcissist loves to implement is creating drama. They will do this through gossip, rumors and sabotage, and as others scramble or fight one another, the narcissist will come in and save the day. They will have a solution for the problem they created.

Taking credit: The narcissist enjoys taking credit for the work of others. Ideas generated by the narcissist are typically someone else's (Thomas, 2010). They will draw upon the successes of others, then repackage and twist these successes so that they appear to be their own ideas. When a team is successful, the narcissist will not give credit to the team but will shine the spotlight on themselves. They may mention the team, but they will be subtle in pointing out what they themselves did to make the project a success. They may point out that it was their vision or leadership that made the team successful. It is important to note that the narcissist is quick to take credit and has no problem pointing fingers at others and blaming them when things go wrong.

Not playing well with others: We pointed out already that the narcissist likes to be the center of attention, is unable to empathize with others and is not good at relationships. As one can imagine, the narcissist is also not the best team player. Firstly, the narcissist will ensure that the team is focused on them. When working on a project, the narcissist will identify things that can escalate their agenda or help them to position themselves. In a team environment, they will come across as disruptive, combative, negative and resentful of people in leadership-focused roles. They will monopolize team time to focus on things important to them, looking for ways to show themselves in a positive light. To leadership, they will come across as an asset to the team and will sell the efforts of the team as their own ideas. Another tactic that the narcissist likes to deploy is creating internal conflict within the team. Conflict is used for their benefit. By pitting people against one another, the team will become distracted and not focus on the narcissist. In other cases, the narcissist will become the buffer in the conflict and act as the individual who saves the team.

Emotionally challenged: Emotions make the narcissist uncomfortable as they view emotions as a sign of weakness. For a narcissist, emotions are tools used to advance their agenda. For example, they will use happiness to lure people in, and once that happiness has been established the narcissist will slowly chip away at it in order to weaken others. When called out for something, the narcissist will play the victim and lean upon sadness or seek pity so that others will feel sorry for them. One emotion that a narcissist is comfortable showing is anger. They will use anger, but only in a strategic way. Their anger is typically controlled and is not shown in an outward manner. They will contain their anger until the right moment, when people least expect it. Then they will use that anger and energy to regain control over the situation or person. Their anger will never be seen as irrational and it will be very controlled. The anger will be displayed in forms of malicious and/or vindictive behavior that are focused and strategic (Thomas, 2010).

Unable to thank others: The narcissist is unable to say thank you. Whatever assistance individuals provide is for the servicing of the narcissist's needs. The narcissist views people as objects and thus cannot understand that they have emotions. The only time they will demonstrate gratitude is in a public forum which requires them to look good. At that time, their praise will come across as gushing, over the top and insincere.

Distrusting of others: Narcissists do not trust others; they are constantly waiting for people to figure them out. They are suspicious and wonder what other people are thinking and what their agenda is. Since their world is built on lies and façades, they are always on their toes. Glad (2002) stated that the narcissist will create enemies where none exist. If they feel that something is off, they will turn the tables. Eventually they will turn on even their most loyal followers. The narcissist is always one step ahead of their competition. They are always plotting and scheming in order to advance themselves.

Based on the information that we have discussed in this section, we find that the narcissist is the most difficult of the dysfunctions to address. Because these individuals are so absorbed in themselves, they don't recognize their own dysfunction. As they continue to build upon their narcissism, they become more enmeshed in their own abilities and talents. Eventually, they get to a point where they can't be touched. They won't believe people who challenge their narcissism because this will only attack their self-esteem, so it is best for them to ignore the feedback.

Backstabbers

Backstabbers have always been in the workplace and they will always be part of the fiber of organizations. These individuals are extremely ambitious, with high goals for achievement, but they are usually not politically astute. By making others appear small or humiliating them, the backstabber believes they will be able to achieve their goals much faster. Any person viewed as competition is a threat and the backstabber will focus on making that person professionally vulnerable. Their actions are usually private or carried out behind the back of their target. They will be kind to the target, but behind the scenes they will do whatever is required to win. The actions of the backstabber are well planned and very calculating. What separates backstabbers from other dysfunctions is that they know exactly what they are doing. They are cunning, crafty and calculating. They will stop at nothing to make someone look bad in the eyes of others, including higher-ups. People who are targets of the backstabber often use the term "threw me under the bus". Often the target does not see it happening until it is too late and can't be stopped.

The backstabber's own performance can be brought into question by others. Most of their career is spent being questioned about their abilities. At some point, they will have learned that the best way to divert attention away from them is to make someone else look bad. This relates back to accountability: before blame can be placed on them, they will pick someone else who can be linked to the error or mistake. These people are often not expecting the blame and are caught off guard. Backstabbers often focus on a person who is well liked or respected in the organization and will chip away at that persona. They will do it subtly at first, such as by making small statements about the individual to start placing the seeds of doubt in another person's mind. In other cases, backstabbers will focus on the people who are quiet and won't push back when something happens. The goal of the backstabber is to diminish an individual while promoting themselves or dodging accountability. Backstabbers are often incompetent and struggle with succeeding on their own merit. Because of this, they are often insecure and focus their attention on eliminating individuals who they view as a threat. They prefer to take credit and to ride on the coat-tails of others.

Davies (2013) suggests not taking the backstabber's negative behavior personally. When you witness this type of behavior, take a step back and be a spectator to what is happening. While it appears this behavior focuses on your incompetence, this behavior actually focuses on the backstabber's lack of self-awareness, insecurity or past experiences. The backstabber may have learned this behavior from others in order to get ahead in the workplace. The environment might be one that encourages this type of behavior. The best approach is to address the behavior quickly and to fix the problem. By proving the backstabber wrong, the target can quickly regain their credibility.

Master manipulators

The master manipulator is an expert in manipulation; it is their most powerful weapon. Manipulating people to get what they want is their way of controlling situations. The manipulator controls and influences the behaviors and actions of the people with whom they are associated. Think of the politician who manipulates others for their vote, never revealing their true agenda. They will say what people want to hear and do the direct opposite. Their goal is to manipulate others by gaining their followers' respect. Once earned, the manipulator then goes in for the kill, looking at how they can control the way someone feels, behaves and thinks about something. This is done through three different tactics:

Distortion of relationships: When we have healthy relationships, they are genuine. There is real concern, collaboration, empathy and honesty associated with the relationship. The exchange within the relationship is one of mutual respect and trust; even if the people have different agendas, the healthy relationship lets them work together for a positive solution to problems and continue to support one another during difficult times. The master manipulator, on the other hand, needs to wedge themselves between individuals in order to divide and conquer. The manipulator will find any means to come between people through lying, enticing, creating chaos, adding more complexity to situations than there needs to be, and typically looking to supercharge the emotion around them. Within the workplace, their interactions will be completely focused on control and negative interactions.

Lack of respect: As is the case with most of the dysfunctions in the workplace, there is a lack of respect for individuals. The master manipulator views themselves as being at a higher level than others, regardless of their status or power. In their mind they are better than others, and to prove this theory they will manipulate individuals into believing how good they are. Because the manipulator thinks they are better than others, they do not recognize their own flaws, but they can identify the insecurities and imperfections of everyone else and use this information to set themselves apart from others. Because of this lack of respect, they don't view individuals as having feelings or emotions and they don't believe that other people have choices or are able to make decisions for themselves. They force people to pick sides. If you are in with a manipulator then domination and control is at the root of the relationship. Everything you think, feel, believe and do will be controlled by the manipulator. If you go against them, they will punish you emotionally so that you fall back into their control. If you are against them, they do not really feel sorry for you and they will sabotage or undermine you, turn others against you through manipulation, or even try to get you fired. They view you as flawed since you can't or won't see how superior they are.

Honing in on your flaws: As mentioned earlier, the master manipulator will focus on your flaws and insecurities. They have a keen radar when it comes to finding these insecurities. They love the person who is kind-hearted and hardworking, the person who might have insecurities or the person who is new to the organization. The master manipulator especially enjoys the latter because they understand that the person will be nervous, insecure about their new position and may be trying too hard to make a good impression. Because of these insecurities, the new employee might even let their guard down and share all sorts of interesting tidbits with the manipulator (personal and professional). The manipulator is usually the first person to introduce themselves to the new employee, to invite them to lunch to make them feel welcome, to offer to help them, or to take them under their wing and be their new friend. They will portray themselves as someone who is well connected within the organization and can help the new person understand the complexities and politics. They will also appear to be concerned with their well-being as they try to navigate their new position. Nevertheless, the manipulator is not at all concerned about the new person. During this time, the manipulator is noticing the insecurities of the new person and starting to identify what they can control and manipulate. Before the new employee even knows what is happening, they have become entangled in the sticky web that the manipulator has created and they struggle to free themselves. Then, either they move into submission and stay in the clutches of the manipulator, or they move away and form a new social group. If they move away, the manipulator will believe that they have shown disrespect towards them. The target may do this intentionally or unintentionally, but once this occurs, the trust has been broken. The manipulator will now use the tidbits shared during that early bonding time and will now look to eliminate that person, as they no longer serve a purpose for them.

What is important to understand about the manipulator is that they have many flaws that they do not or will not recognize in themselves. They are typically very dominating in their behavior, judgmental, suspicious of people and situations, demanding, aggressive and they can come across as cold and calculating. Alongside these flaws, the manipulator has a quick temper when challenged. The manipulator lacks compassion, empathy or a desire to promote and build up a person. Their goal is rather to tear people down so they are not a threat. The only thing that the manipulator believes in is the need to preserve their ego and get ahead. At the end of the day, it is all about the manipulator. Nothing else matters and what is important to them is status, fame, being the center of attention and ensuring that everything revolves around them. They lack emotional intelligence and self-awareness of their behaviors and they believe their own lies. During their career they will have learned that in order to get ahead they need to be in control, and they will be aggressive to get what they want and what they think they deserve.

Emotionally abusive co-workers

Most employees in the workplace focus on emotional attacks versus physical altercations. There are a number of emotional tactics used by individuals in the workplace. Forms of mental or emotional abuse can include gaslighting, aggression and undermining, to name a few. We will discuss these approaches in further detail in this section.

Gaslighting

Gaslighting is one of the most dangerous forms of mental manipulation in the workplace. Most of the time victims of gaslighting don't see it happening, but they do feel the effects of the manipulation that takes place. These effects may include self-doubt, diminished self-esteem and a reduced sense of self-worth.

The term "gaslighting" was developed in 1944 from a play, which was later made into a movie. The plot focuses on a husband who works to make his wife and others believe that she is slowly going crazy. He does this by making subtle changes to her environment by slightly adjusting a gas lamp to cause the room to brighten or dim, causing her to question what is happening. When the wife first points out these changes, he tells her nothing has changed. Eventually he begins to insinuate that she is wrong and crazy. She gives in to her self-doubt, especially related to the changes to the gas lamp. Later, the term evolved from "gas lamping" to what we refer to today as "gaslighting" (Ni, 2017).

The goal of gaslighting is to alter a person's perception of reality. The perpetrator focuses on causing the target to question the reality of either themselves or their environment. Gaslighting is done to all of us on a daily basis when we are confronted with advertising that makes us feel as though we are less than. This advertising makes us feel that, if we purchase the product, we will be just like the model in the advertisement or our lives will be so much better. When we buy the product and do not see this change, we feel emotionally unfulfilled and look to something else.

Gaslighting in our work lives focuses on an individual causing their co-worker or direct reports to question their sanity, abilities and/or competence. The perpetrator wants their target to feel as though they are incompetent or inadequate. By making the target question their self-worth or abilities, the individual focuses on trying to position themselves, all the while holding their target back and limiting the target's potential. Here's an example of gaslighting in action.

Susan constantly belittles Angela. She calls Angela incompetent and tells her she lacks the basic abilities to do her job. Susan often tells Angela about meetings that are scheduled to start at a certain time, but Angela later finds out that the meeting was held at a different time. When Susan is called out on the behavior, she shrugs and says that Angela is disorganized. Angela does everything to organize her work; she begins to become compulsive with her behavior, ensuring that she is early to meetings; she is diligent in taking notes and double-checking emails. Angela has become so focused on making sure that she is not making mistakes that her work is suffering and people notice this. Then Susan hires a new person, Eliza. Eliza is the new star in the department and Susan begins to focus her time and efforts on Eliza. Angela now feels as though Eliza was hired to replace her. She begins to get paranoid around Eliza and Susan. This results in awkward conversations and Angela not feeling confident or having the ability to do what needs to be done. Susan continues to add pressure until, finally, the organization lets Angela go. However, the manipulation does not stop even after Angela has left the organization, since she still feels as though her self-worth is lacking. She questions her abilities and this comes across in interviews. The vicious cycle continues and Angela's self-worth and self-esteem continue to diminish. Her talents and skills are now wasted.

Emotional abuse

Emotional abuse does not show itself in physical signs such as scars or bruises. There are no physical signs of emotional abuse, but it can be more detrimental than physical abuse. The scars of emotional abuse remain hidden and can last a lifetime. The tactics used by emotional abusers are often very subtle and the victim may not be aware at first what is happening to them. In some cases, the person inflicting the abuse is not aware of the impact that they are having on an individual. For example, subtle comments that are meant to be a "joke" are taken in a hurtful or negative manner by the other person. A subtle comment might be something like, "Wow, that's an interesting blouse you're wearing. I would never have picked that color for you." The person receiving this message may take it as a compliment or may question whether it was meant as a negative comment. They might think, "What is wrong with this color?" or "Maybe this isn't a color I should be wearing." The person may start to doubt the blouse and in some cases may never wear that color again. A work-related statement can be something as simple as, "Your style of presenting is a little different." The person receiving this statement may not be sure what the hidden message is.

On the other side of emotional abuse is the person who knows exactly what they are doing to another person. One definition of emotional abuse is any behavior that isolates or confines an individual. This is done through intimidation, humiliation or any act that diminishes a person's self-worth or self-esteem. Some examples of emotional abuse include:

1. Embarrassing or humiliating you in front of others.
2. Ignoring your needs and wants, diminishing your viewpoint or overlooking your beliefs.
3. Making remarks that are sarcastic or biting in an attempt to shame you.

4. Trying to blame their behavior on you being overly sensitive, weak or thin-skinned.
5. Treating you as a child.
6. Punishing you for things you don't do right, no matter how large or small.
7. Making you feel as though you need the other person's permission to do something.
8. Taking charge of things or projects that you oversee.
9. Never admitting that you have done something right or that you are correct. You are always wrong and you are always at fault.
10. Using condescending non-verbal actions including eye rolls, smirks and eyebrow lifts.
11. Constantly focusing on your flaws and not your strengths.
12. Making false accusations about you.
13. Being unable to handle constructive feedback or criticism. The abuser is good at giving criticism but not at receiving it, and views feedback as an attack.
14. Constantly bringing up something that happened years ago. Not letting you forget if you did something wrong.
15. Coming up with excuses to justify their behavior and usually claiming someone else is at fault.
16. Pushing your limits and, if asked to stop, intensifying the behavior because they know that it bothers you.
17. Muttering comments under their breath so that, even if you might not hear them, you know something was said and it feels negative. When asked, "What did you say?" they will respond with, "I didn't say anything."
18. Being withdrawn, not speaking to you for days, weeks or months. You may ask them what is wrong or if you did something, but they will be passive-aggressive and say nothing is wrong and they are just fine.

Conclusion

We have scratched the surface when it comes to the topic of dysfunction in the workplace. In this section, we were able to understand what motivates each of these dysfunctional individuals in the workplace. For some, their intentions are not meant to be harmful, while for others these behaviors are focused and intentional. The ultimate goal of any of these dysfunctions is to erode personal self-esteem, confidence and to get the target to become submissive. For the dysfunctional individual, it is about positioning themselves to gain power over another. By gaining power over another, they are able to exert their dominance. Many people believe that when a dysfunctional individual targets them they are somehow at fault. It is easy to believe the tactics and approaches of a dysfunctional individual as they come across as self-confident and powerful, but that is not the case at all and they are really the direct opposite, possessing low self-esteem and feeling incompetent and unsure of themselves.

References

Adams, A. 2014. *Bullying at work: How to confront and overcome it*. London: Little, Brown Book Group.

Barrow, L. 2009. *In darkness light dawns: Exposing workplace bullying*. London: Crown Publishing.

Bond, S., Tuckey, M., & Dollard, M. 2010. Psychosocial safety climate, workplace bullying, and symptoms of posttraumatic stress. *Organization Development Journal*, 28(1), 37–56.

Davies, N. 2013. The backstabber personality. https://healthpsychologyconsultancy. wordpress.com/2013/03/15/the-backstabber-personality.

Einarsen, S. 1999. The nature and causes of bullying at work. *International Journal of Manpower*, 20(1/2), 16–20.

Einarsen, S. 2000. Harassment and bullying at work: A review of the Scandinavian approach. *Aggression and Violent Behavior*, 5(4), 379–401.

Einarsen, S., Helge, Hoel, H., & Notelaers, G. 2009. Measuring exposure to bullying and harassment at work: Validity, factor structure and psychometric properties of the Negative Acts Questionnaire—Revised. *Work and Stress*, 23(1), 22–44.

Einarsen, S., Hoel, H., Zapf, D. & Cooper, C.L. (Eds.). 2003. *Bullying and emotional abuse in the workplace: International perspectives in research and practice*. London: Taylor & Francis.

Einarsen, S. & Raknes, B. 1997. Harassment in the workplace and the victimization of men. *Violence and Victims*, 12(3), 247–263.

Einarsen, S. & Skogstad, A. 1996. Prevalence and risk groups of bullying and harassment at work. *European Journal of Work and Organizational Psychology*, 5(2), 185–202.

Ellis, H. 1927. The concept of narcissism. *The Psychoanalytic Review. A Journal Devoted to an Understanding of Human Concept*, 14(2), 129.

Felblinger, D. 2009. Bullying, incivility, and disruptive behaviors in health care setting: Identification, impact and intervention. *Frontiers of Health Services Management*, 25(4), 13–24.

Fields, T. 1999. Bully in sight. How to predict, resist, challenge and combat workplace bullying; Overcoming the silence and denial by which abuse thrives. http://bullyonline. org/old/successunlimited/books/bistress.htm.

Freud, S. 1914. *On narcissism: An introduction*. Freiburg im Breisgau: White Press.

Glad, B. 2002. Why tyrants go too far: Malignant narcissism and absolute power. *Political Psychology*, 23(1), 1–2.

Harvey, M., Heames, J., Richey, R., & Leonard, N. 2006. Bullying: From the playground to the boardroom. *Journal of Leadership and Organizational Studies*, 12(4), 1–11.

Hutchinson, M., Vickers, M., Jackson, D., & Wilkes, L. 2006. Like wolves in a pack: Predatory alliances of bullies in nursing. *Journal of Management and Organization*, 12(3), 235–251.

Keashly, L. 1998. Emotional abuse in the workplace: Conceptual and empirical issues. *Journal of Emotional Abuse*, 1, 85–117.

Keashly, L. & Jagatic, K. 2003. Conflict, conflict resolution and bullying, in S. Einarsen, H. Hoel, D. Zapf, & C.L. Cooper (Eds.), *Bullying and emotional abuse at work: International perspectives*. London: Taylor & Francis, 339–369.

Kets de Vries, M. 2001. Creating authentizotic organizations: Well-functioning individuals in vibrant companies. *Human Relations*, 54(1), 101–112.

King, G., Rosenthal, S., & Pittinsky, T. 2007. Narcissism and effective crisis management: A review of potential problems and pitfalls. *Journal of Contingencies and Crisis Management*, 15(4), 183–193.

Leymann, H. 1990. Mobbing and psychological terror at workplace. *Violence and Victims*, 5, 119–126.

Maccoby, M. 2016. *Narcissistic leaders: Who succeeds and who fails.* London: Crown Publishing.

Mikkelsen, E. & Einarsen, S. 2002. Basic assumptions and symptoms of post-traumatic stress among victims of bullying at work. *European Journal of Work and Organizational Psychology*, 11(1), 87–111.

Morin, R. 2013. *The most narcissistic US presidents.* Washington, DC: Pew Research Center.

Namie, G. & Namie, T. 2009. US workplace bullying: Some basic considerations and consultation interventions. *Consulting Psychology Journal: Practice and Research*, 61(3), 202–219.

Ni, P. 2017. 7 stages of gaslighting in a relationship. *Psychology Today.* www.psychologytoday.com/us/basics/gaslighting

Olweus, D. 1993. *Aggression in schools: Bullies and whipping boys.* Washington, DC: Hemisphere.

Paulhus, D.L. & Williams, K.M. 2002. The dark triad of personality: Narcissism, Machiavellianism and psychopathy. *Journal of Research in Personality*, 36, 556–563.

Rayner, C. and Keashly, L. 2005. Bullying at work: A perspective from Britain and North America. *American Psychological Association*, 329, 271–296.

Rosenthal, S. & Pittinsky, T. 2006. Narcissistic leadership. *The Leadership Quarterly*, 17(6), 617–633.

Roter, A., 2016. A phenomenological study: Understanding registered nurses experiences related to dysfunctional leadership in a hospital setting. *Journal of Organizational Psychology*, 16(1), 57–70.

Roter, A., 2017. *Understanding and recognizing dysfunctional leadership: The impact of dysfunctional leadership on organizations and followers.* London: Routledge, Gower Publishing.

Tepper, B., Duffy, D., Henle, C., & Lambert, L. 2006. Procedural injustice, victim precipitation, and abusive supervision. *Personnel Psychology*, 59(1), 101–124.

Thomas, D. 2010. *Narcissism: Behind the Mask.* Lewes, East Sussex: Book Guild Publishing.

Yamada, D. 2000. The phenomenon of workplace bullying and the need for status-blind hostile work environment protection. *Georgetown Law Journal*, 88, 475–536.

4

DEVIANT BEHAVIORS IN THE WORKPLACE

Throughout this book we have discussed the dynamics of individuals and how dark behaviors play out in the workplace. At the root of a majority of the issues within the workplace, we find that interpersonal dynamics are the most common cause of dark side behaviors. These dynamics are at the core of most workplace complaints and conflicts. To this point, in previous chapters we have explored two levels of dark behaviors in the workplace: incivility and dysfunction. Now we will look at the final end of the spectrum of dark behaviors: deviant behaviors. Deviant behaviors apply to all industries, businesses and for-profit and non-profit organizations. These are the most extreme of all of the behaviors that we have discussed up to this point.

There have been many different terms used to describe deviant behavior in the workplace. Storms and Spector (1987) termed these behaviors "counter-productive"; Hogan and Hogan (1989) referred to them as "anti-social"; Perlow and Latham (1993) called them "maladaptive". For the purpose of this book, we will use the definition from Robinson and Bennett (1995) of deviant workplace behaviors: "voluntary behavior that violates significant organizational norms and in so doing threatens the wellbeing of an organization, its members, or both" (Robinson & Bennett, 1995, 557). As can be clearly seen in this definition, the focus is on the voluntary violation of norms within organizations. There is an intentional threat that is imposed and the target of deviant behavior can be the organization, individuals or both. This chapter will explore deviance from both organizational and personal aspects.

Corporate deviances

Nair and Bhatnagar (2011) pointed to recent incidents of corporate greed related to corporate deviance. These incidents include: Wall Street meltdowns; risk-taking by corporate CEOs; scandals including Enron, Tyco and Wells Fargo; extraordinarily high salary levels for executives; and a lack of accountability within organizations, governments and society all contributing to deviant organizational behaviors. Corporate deviance can be identified as organizational deviance that happens on the behalf of the corporation in the course of working in it (Shichor, 1989). In the past, these behaviors have been labeled "unethical", "white-collar crimes" and "corporate greed", to name a few.

Deviant behaviors can be linked to acts such as theft, abuses of privileges such as power, and lack of physical and psychological safety. These are actions that jeopardize the well-being of followers and stakeholders along with the financial goals of the organization. Deviant behaviors contribute to 30% of all business failures (Nair & Bhatnagar, 2011). Theories related to deviance in the workplace link back to what is referred to as "amoral calculus", whereby individual decision makers weigh the costs and benefits of their actions. As these scandals occur, we tend to look at the individuals at the core of the actions versus the organizational system and culture that allow these behaviors to happen (Cullen et al., 2009). Many corporate deviant acts occur as an outcome of the often conflicting pressures from goals of profit maximization and free competition (Shichor, 1989).

Researchers have shown that deviant decision making stems from a culture that supports risky behaviors. In some cases—such as unethical behaviors related to companies such as Volkswagen and NASA, and financial sector meltdowns—industry behaviors are redefined as normal and acceptable because of autocratic and bureaucratic pressures (Vaughan, 1998; Larson & Powell, 2015). To understand corporate deviance, it is important to define what it is. One definition describes corporate deviance as "criminal acts committed by individuals or groups of individuals during the normal course of their work as employees of organizations, which they intend to contribute to the achievement of goals or other objectives thought be important for the organization as a whole, some subunit with the organization, or their own particular job duties" (Bromley, n.d.). Many individuals involved in corporate deviance rarely see themselves as doing anything wrong or participating in criminal activities. Many believe they are doing what is in the best interest of the organization to make money, as well as for them to benefit as well.

Types of corporate deviance include:

- **Anti-trust violations:** Reduction of competition in order to increase market share and increase economic power.
- **Securities fraud:** Creation of financial capital by sale of fraudulent or falsely inflated stock in order to gain increased profitability.
- **False advertising:** Increased market demand through the creation of artificial demand.
- **Labor law violations:** Reduction in labor costs through unlawful practices.

- **Environmental, safety and public health violations:** Reduction in production costs through unsafe practices (e.g. improper disposal or safety cutbacks).
- **Illegal political campaign contributions:** Increased political influence in the making and enforcement of laws (Bromley, n.d.).

Murphy (1993) reported that deviant behaviors lead to organizational costs ranging from $6 billion to $200 billion annually in the United States alone. Over 25 years later, in 2018, we can assume the costs to organizations are substantially higher. More recent estimates have placed global costs of deviance at nearly $1 trillion dollars per year, which is approximately 7% of organizational revenues (ACFE, 2008; Christian & Ellis, 2011).

Awareness related to deviant workplace behavior has been increasing. As employees are asked to do more with fewer resources, including money and talent, individuals are faced with increased stress and burnout in the workplace. We are seeing fewer support systems in workplaces following reductions related to compliance and Human Resources. With the reduction of compliance and Human Resources controls, individuals are more inclined to participate in deviant behaviors, either indirectly or directly, by cutting corners or participating in acts where they know they will not be caught. Many of the dysfunctional behaviors we have explored so far all have elements of stress, as well as psychological components, linked to dark behaviors. Stress can heighten the level and type of deviant behavior that occurs in workplaces, from minor theft of office supplies, to extreme examples such as shootings.

Behaviors associated with deviance

As discussed earlier, in order for these behaviors to happen in the workplace, there needs to be a culture that permits them to happen. In addition, there are people behind the actions. This section will explore the different deviant behaviors associated with the workplace.

Identifying deviant behaviors

Employee deviance can take many different forms and researchers have broken down these behaviors into different categories. In one instance, deviance is defined as a voluntary behavior that goes against an organization's normal way of operating, which in turn threatens the well-being of the employees and the business (Robinson & Bennett, 1995). Zoghbi-Manrique-de-Lara (2010) states that the organizational setting and environment may influence an employee's desire to participate in deviant behavior. Studies indicate that the organization's ethical climate may significantly influence employee behavior in relation to deviance (Peterson, 2002).

With ambiguous approaches to and definitions of deviant workplace behavior, it can be confusing to understand the true definition. In order to understand deviant behavior, an understanding of the categories of behavior can be helpful. Robinson and Bennett's (1995) study attempts to create an understanding of these behaviors. They break up deviant workplace behavior into a four-quadrant grid that includes: 1) production deviance, 2) property deviance, 3) political deviance and 4) personal aggression. Let us look at each of these quadrants in more detail.

- **Production deviance:** Slowing down work or calling in sick when an individual is not sick, creating delays or safety issues. Includes violating organizational norms regarding the quantity and quality of work performed.
- **Property deviance:** Stealing company property, sabotaging equipment or lying about hours worked. This can include acquiring or damaging property that belongs to one's employer, including theft.
- **Political deviance:** Blaming others and/or showing favoritism.
- **Personal aggression:** Sexual harassment, stealing from co-workers, endangering co-workers and targeting verbal or physical abuse at another individual.

What triggers employee deviance?

Robinson and Bennett (1995) identified in their typology two levels or dimensions of workplace deviance: minor versus serious deviance, and organizational versus individual deviance. Minor deviance includes minor thefts such as stealing supplies, while serious deviance includes violence or large-scale theft. Organizational deviance is targeted towards the organization and relates to damaging company property, while individual deviance targets individuals.

Some have argued that deviant behaviors are related to self-esteem issues, while other researchers point to self-regulation. Work from Christian and Ellis (2011) finds that acting in a deviant or inappropriate manner is determined by an individual's ability to control their behaviors and/or emotions.

If we examine what triggers deviant behaviors in people, the simple version would break down deviant behavior into a lack of motivation to conform to organizational expectations or the desire to violate those expectations (Robinson & Bennett, 1995). For example, in the realm of inequities in the organization, one could argue that inequity could be linked to both a lack of motivation and violated expectations. A person may act out based on personal inequities related to an organization. For example, Sally has been working for an organization for a number of years. Dale has been hired into the same position as Sally, doing the same work. One day Sally finds out that Dale has been making more money for the same job. Sally is angry at the inequity of pay and says something. The company does not respond or change the inequity. Sally starts to lash out at the organization, resulting in Sally sabotaging Dale's work in order to make him look bad; when that does not work she begins to sabotage the work efforts of the team by slowing down productivity, resulting in an impact on the customers they serve. In addition to slowing and sabotaging work efforts, Sally begins to steal from the organization: removing supplies and equipment, taking them home and in some cases selling them at a discounted rate to friends who own their own businesses. This is an example of how personal and organizational norms provide inequity in regards to workplace norms and the associated deviance.

One study ties the root cause of employees acting in a deviant manner to perpetrator power and task inter-dependency as the key to predicting employees' actions (Hershcovis et al., 2012). Zoghbi-Manrique-de-Lara (2010) suggests that the organizational setting and the perception of procedural justice and fairness are indicators in predicting deviant workplace behaviors. Lastly, job stress has a positive relationship with deviant behavior, where higher job stress leads to a more predictable indication that employees will act in a deviant manner (Farhadi et al., 2015). The following discusses some of the ways employees may act out based on perceived injustice, inequity or lack of fairness in the workplace.

Types of deviant behavior in the workplace

There are a number of types of deviant individuals in the workplace, from people involved in theft (including petty theft and embezzlement), to psychopaths (the harassers in the workplace), to evil individuals. There are a number of different types of deviant behaviors we will explore. The following provides further insights into these types of individuals.

Thieves

Theft can manifest in many different ways in the workplace. It may include taking small items such as pens or stationery, or it may involve stealing items from others, taking credit for the work of others and stealing ideas and making them one's own. Theft can escalate into falsifying reports and embezzlement. An example of theft in the workplace that seems minor to an employee but has a significant impact on the organization is falsifying time reporting—for example, coming in at 8:15 A.M. and reporting on your time card that you arrived at 8:00 A.M. Other examples of falsifying working hours include taking sick time when not sick, working fewer hours than scheduled but reporting full time worked, and extending work in order to gain overtime pay. Many believe that this type of theft is an entitlement. After all, the company is a multi-million dollar company—surely they won't mind if I add a few extra minutes to my time card or take time off? However, all of these acts have costs associated with them. In the United States alone, it is estimated that organizations lose $50 billion annually to these types of actions (Applebaum, Iaconi & Matousek, 2007).

Psychopaths

Recognizing a psychopath is a challenge for most individuals. Typically, when we think about psychopaths, our minds go to the criminal acts that we see on television, or in the movies. We recognize and associate the term "psychopath" with the serial killer or the individual participating in devious acts of crime and evil. Our minds do not enjoy entertaining thoughts of working side by side with a psychopath. However, there are different levels of psychopathy and the corporate psychopath is very real. They come across as charming, confident and friendly, all the while luring people into their webs. This type of psychopathy borders on dysfunctional and deviant behavior. Researchers argue about the number of psychopaths present in the workplace, with estimates ranging from 1% to 4% (Boddy, 2005).

Psychologists have found a type of psychopath that is not prone to the same impulsive, violent or criminal behavior as other psychopaths (i.e. the ones we are most familiar with from mainstream media). These psychopaths live normal lives and often go undetected in our societies, comfortably ensconced in professional positions (Boddy, 2005). These types of psychopaths are found leading organizations, non-profits and governments, as well as working in leadership and individual contributor roles. There are various labels for these types of psychopaths which may include "corporate psychopaths", "industrial psychopaths", "executive psychopaths" and "organizational psychopaths". For the purpose of this chapter, the popular term "corporate psychopaths" will be used.

The corporate psychopath wreaks havoc in organizations and corporate positions rather than choosing a criminal career (Boddy, 2012). Typically these individuals come from normal, often strong socio-economic backgrounds. They learn early on that it is easier to get power, prestige and money from a corporate position while leveraging their psychopathic personality (Boddy, 2012). Corporate psychopaths are simply described as psychopaths working in the corporate sector (Boddy, 2014). Considered to be snakes, con artists, thrill-seekers and daredevils, there is nothing that will inhibit the way they behave. For the purpose of this book I have chosen to include the psychopath in the category of deviant behaviors because of the psychology associated with their behavior.

To date, there is very little research or literature on the topic of the corporate psychopath and little is known about how they function or what makes them operate the way they do. However, it is agreed that the deviant influence of corporate psychopaths is worthy of further investigation and research. Limited research does exist and the emergence of this topic has laid the foundation for further research (Gudmundsson & Southey, 2011).

Corporate psychopaths are motivated by many different influences including: money, prestige, power, greed, success and admiration. The tactics that they utilize to reach these goals include lying, manipulation, egotism and callousness towards others. They have learned that their behavior can pay off in lucrative ways. They have mastered the skill of using their traits and they often go unnoticed until it is too late and damage has already been inflicted onto their targets. Examples of how their behavior may play out negatively in the corporate world include white-collar crimes like embezzlement, harassment, blackmail and falsifying numbers to report gains or altering numbers for personal gains. The corporate psychopath's behavior is often considered parasitic. They feed off the generosity, kindness and gullibility of others. These individuals take advantage of other people's trust and their kind human nature. Psychopaths are also more inclined to move from place to place and person to person in order to feed their psychopathy (Babiak & Hare, 2006, 19). If one person no longer feeds their psychopathy or suits their needs, they move on to someone else. The corporate psychopath pays little attention to the feelings of others. They are unable to feel remorse or shame for any harm they may inflict on others. They are often found to be unreliable and have little follow-through. When caught, they will charm their way out of the situation.

On the surface, they will appear to be in control, charming, sincere, highly intelligent and very approachable. They will use corporate jargon which lacks substance behind the words and they will dress to impress, thus coming across as pulled together, exuding confidence and control. Individuals will at first find them to be non-threatening, reassuring, fun and exciting to work with. For individuals who are not familiar with the corporate psychopath, they may find themselves drawn to their confidence, charm and what appears to be sincerity. This person appears too good to be true; they appear to have everything together.

Another way to define the corporate psychopath is as a chameleon, because they will take on whatever persona is needed to fit the individual they are working with or setting. They will switch directions very quickly in order to fit the mood or situation. They are masters at assessing people and situations. From the first time they meet a person, they will identify that person's strengths, needs, weaknesses and motivations. Based on their assessment they will then adjust their persona in order to meet the needs of the person they are targeting. They will use manipulation with messages that are specifically crafted to meet these needs (Roter, 2017). In addition, the corporate psychopath will assess situations through feedback, through which they will either maintain their control or adjust accordingly. When confronted or challenged on their behavior, they will maneuver themselves in order to take control, often manipulating the situation so that it becomes the fault of others. They will know who to align themselves with in order to gain formal and informal power and to manipulate circumstances to their advantage.

A bully or a psychopath?

Before exploring the tactics of corporate psychopaths, it is important to address the crossover between the behaviors of the bully and the psychopath. These behaviors are very closely related and people may become confused trying to distinguish between them. In many cases, they can be considered the same; psychopaths will use bullying behaviors to get what they want. What separates the bully from the psychopath is that the psychopath lacks any type of remorse, guilt or recognition that their behaviors are hurtful or wrong in any way. For the psychopath, they use bullying behaviors for two main reasons.

The first is predatory. They do it because they like it and they enjoy making people feel uncomfortable. They derive joy from ruining careers and destroying individuals. This type of behavior is difficult for many to understand. Why would a person find joy in hurting or harming another individual?

The second reason psychopaths use bullying is known as "instrumental bullying". They will use these behaviors to cause chaos and confusion in the workplace so that they can forward their own agenda, be it personal, political or other gain. During the chaos the psychopaths have created, individuals become emotionally distracted and do not pay attention. While everyone is focused on the emotional turmoil and stress, the corporate psychopath is the only one that is cool, calm and collected. To upper leadership, they come across as being able to work well under pressure, to effectively manage stress and to keep their act together while everyone else is falling apart. As a result, they are often promoted to leadership positions, but ultimately they are the ones that started the turmoil. The confusion and chaos are instrumental to promoting their own personal gain (Boddy, 2012).

Tactics of the corporate psychopath

The following will discuss the psychopath's pathology and provide insights into how they operate. This will include the tactics they use and how they may have a distorted view of these tactics versus how others may view them.

Lack of remorse: Many of the incivilities and dysfunctions explored so far within this book are behaviors individuals will feel a level of remorse or regret about. The average individual knows that they are doing something wrong and there is a level of remorse or regret on their part. With the psychopath, they are not aware that their behavior is wrong. They lack the ability to feel any type of emotion and believe their behavior is normal. Often when corporate psychopaths are asked if they feel any type of remorse or regret for their behavior, they respond with a bewildered "no". They believe there is nothing wrong with their tactics or behaviors. They do not have a conscience and sleep well without experiencing any guilt, remorse or fear. They are unable to experience these feelings and they view negative events as the fault of others and not associated with themselves. As a result, they will deny responsibility for their behavior and will not hesitate to pass the blame onto other people around them.

Relationships: There is a psychological abnormality in how psychopaths interact with others. They do not have the ability to connect to others on an emotional level and as a result they are unable to feel empathy, sympathy or a connection with others. The psychopath does not view people as human beings, but objects that can be manipulated and utilized to advance their personal agenda and needs. The behavior of the psychopath is often viewed as inappropriate to others. For example, normal behavior for the psychopath is the use of aggression, inappropriate thrill-seeking, and deceit. There is no sense of the norms of behavior for the psychopath. What others believe to be immoral or unethical, the psychopath views as normal and perceives these behaviors as ways of doing business or getting ahead. The long-term consequences of those behaviors are not on the mind of the psychopath as long as there are instant gains and gratification. They do not believe in or recognize the moral implications of their behaviors, providing them the rationale they need in order to continue using the patterns of behavior that work best for them (Shouten & Silver, 2012). In addition to not feeling remorse or regret, the psychopath does not experience fear. For the majority of individuals, they know right from wrong, and when they do something wrong there is an element of fear. For the psychopath, fear is an adrenaline rush and they will push the envelope further and further to see how far they can go. In some cases, this pushing of the envelope results in dangerous activities that can endanger the safety of others and themselves. Each psychopath will deal with situations differently. Some will use violence and aggression, while others will use power, greed and money to achieve their goals. The thrill-seeking psychopath is fueled by pressured situations. The corporate psychopath's motto is, "Whatever needs to get done."

Arrogance: Psychopaths possess an extreme level of arrogance inflated by their own sense of self-importance. They believe they are the best at everything they do within the workplace. There is no one like them and they believe they possess traits and characteristics others do not. As a result, they believe they are above everything including rules, regulations, standards and norms. In some cases, they believe they are above the law. Because of their ability to maneuver themselves, they usually get away with their actions because of their charm and their ability to navigate sticky situations. When this happens it just reaffirms their beliefs that they are untouchable.

Manipulation: We have discussed the topic of manipulation in previous sections of this book. Manipulation is the key tactic used by a psychopath. For the psychopath, manipulation is not just a tactic, but a key and essential part of the game they play. Manipulation is used to see how far they can push others. Based on the situation, they will tell half-truths or lies in order to manipulate the person in front of them. With their charm and manipulation, they will make promises the target will believe, but which the psychopath has no intention to carry out.

Charm: When first meeting a psychopath in the workplace, they will be extremely charming and engaging. One is drawn to the magnetic charm and charisma the psychopath exhibits. They will use flattery, false compliments and a vivid personality so people feel attracted to them. While being drawn into their magnetic pull, the target of the psychopath will slowly let their guard down. What is there not to like about this person? But while the target is looking to build a relationship with the psychopath, the psychopath is unable to maintain the relationship. They have no interest in doing so, since they are using the target as an object to get what they want. Once that person is no longer of value, they will be discarded, left confused, frustrated and aggravated, and the psychopath will move on to charm others.

Looking down: The psychopath will maneuver people like pawns in a chess game across the game board they are playing on: their lives. They look down on others and view them as nothing more than a means to an end and not having any value. They view the person they are targeting as insignificant; the only one who is significant in this game is the psychopath. All others are just a way for them to move forward. Psychopaths also tear down the people they are dealing with. At the end of an interaction with a psychopath, the target will feel as though they have done something wrong and need to apologize for things that have nothing to do with them. They will apologize even if the fault is that of the psychopath. Through the psychopath's charm, manipulation and inability to feel remorse, the target will walk off feeling worse than when they started.

Chameleons: The psychopath is a chameleon; they are masters at changing who they are. When walking into a room or meeting a person for the first time, they size up the crowd or person in front of them. Based on their assessment, they will become the person they believe the target needs. For example, when a male psychopath meets a female, he will assess her to determine if she needs a boost to her confidence. Is she strong-willed? If so, does she need someone who is also strong-willed to match up with? Is she someone who needs companionship? Based on his assessment he will adjust his personality. He will be the man who will boost that woman's confidence to build her up, only to later tear her down. He will match up to a strong-willed woman only to later shatter her strength. He will become a companion to the woman who is lonely and she will feel as though she is the most important person in the world, only to be left off worse and lonelier in the long run. The chameleon will take on the moods and personality that will best fit the situation. The chameleon will effortlessly change for each person they meet and is able to compartmentalize the disguises they use in order to fit the situation, remembering what is best for each interaction.

Thrill-seeking: The corporate psychopath lives for thrills and for winning. Winning for them might mean moving up in the organization or gaining prestige, an increased salary and bonuses. These are easy wins for the psychopath and eventually they will move on to thrills that surge their adrenaline. Because they feel they are above the law, they will move on to other thrill-seeking activities in the belief that they won't get caught. These may include gambling and risk-taking in the workplace, skimming money off the top and pushing the envelope to see how far they can take it, taking risks that jeopardize the safety of themselves and others, stealing from the organization or pushing the boundaries. The psychopath is looking to see how far they can go and they will escalate their behavior until they are finally caught. When caught, they will show they don't understand what they have done wrong. Since they can't recognize what they have done, they will be confused as to why they were caught.

Example of a corporate psychopath

Through current media reports we can see many examples of corporate psychopaths. The first one we can identify is Bernie Madoff (Winarick, 2010; Quow, 2013). When meeting Bernie Madoff, he came across as a kind, gentle man with a slight stutter that caused people to have sympathy for him. His victims all say he was unassuming and disarming. Yet he was able to pull off the biggest Ponzi scheme to date. Madoff was a stockbroker and investment advisor. His father, Ralph, was not a successful financer, and while his father was failing at financing, Bernie was working odd jobs and saving to start up his own business. During this time, he was focused on his future wife, Ruth. After they married, Bernie took out a $50,000 loan from this father-in-law and partnered with him to build his business. His client list included the Hollywood elite. Madoff was able to provide reliable returns that were modest but steady. Through word of mouth and a steady return on investment, people came to Madoff's investment firm. Madoff was successful in his business endeavors. He was adaptable and embraced new technology for trading. As this technology took off, the National Association of Securities Dealers Automated Quotations (better known as NASDAQ) was formed. Later, Madoff would serve three one-year terms as chairman of NASDAQ. He was ahead of the trends and able to adapt quickly to changes that came his way (Lee, 2013).

As his business grew, it became a family affair with the addition of his younger brother, Peter, who joined the firm to oversee compliance. Later, Madoff's sons Andrew and Mark joined the firm, as well as his son Roger, who worked for his father until he passed in 2006. Later, Madoff's niece, daughter of Peter, joined the firm as well.

While Madoff ran the investment firm, he also secretly led the Ponzi scheme. After his arrest in December, 2008, he admitted to losing approximately $50 billion of his investors' money. However, his investors knew nothing about these losses as they had received statements showing steady returns on their investments. After all was said and done, the loss was in the range of $80 billion. To date, Madoff's victims have received restitution of approximately $1.2 billion, a mere fraction of what was lost. Madoff did plead guilty to 11 accounts of fraud and other charges and was sentenced to 150 years in prison. Approximately six years after pleading guilty, he shared in emails that his crimes were not as bad as what had been reported by the media or the court-appointed trustee (Cohn, 2015). He claimed that he warned his clients to pull their investments, close their accounts or at a minimum withdraw the profits that had been earned on the accounts. In an email to a CNBC reporter (Cohn, 2015), Madoff responded that most of his clients did profit. The following is a quote from Cohn's article about the email sent by Madoff:

> "Unfortunately, human nature being as it is, the people that are the most vocal are those that either did lose money, and certainly there were some," he wrote. "The facts were that a majority of my individual clients were net winners."

Madoff claims the amount lost was not nearly close to the $50 billion he pled guilty to or the $80 billion that others have reported. He explained that the actual net loss was closer to $2 billion. In many cases, Madoff points to his investors as individuals who were adept at hiding and not reporting their profits, funneling profits through trusts, foundations and various charities from the investor to only report write-offs.

Madoff has repeatedly said that he has some level of remorse: "Please understand I truly regret being responsible for any loss. I also am fully aware that no clients should expect to be betrayed as I clearly have done" (Cohn, 2015). While he shows some level of remorse, others argue that Madoff is just saying what he believes people want him to say. Reporter Sital Patel (2013) from the *Wall Street Journal* sat down with Madoff for an interview at the Butner, a North Carolina prison. Madoff shared that the prison was more like a camp than a prison and that it was a laid-back place and as good as it gets. He went on to place the blame on investors, saying that they should have known better and they were at fault because they didn't ask good questions. He went on to fondly remember the days when he was considered a financial power player. Madoff showed no emotion for his acts during this interview, but despaired as at the time of the interview his son Andrew and his wife were refusing to speak to him (Andrew later passed away from cancer). During the interview he did mention his son Mark, who had committed suicide, saying he regretted the suicide, but he did not show any level of emotion over the loss.

In this example, Madoff has shown signs of shifting blame back onto his targets, denying wrongdoing to a certain extent and having the ability to play the victim. In interviews he shows little to no remorse or emotion and does not take full ownership of the events that happened. He denies the extent of his participation in the activities. During his crimes, he thought he was above the law and blames his targets because they didn't ask the right questions. In this example, Madoff's targets trusted him and were pulled in by his charm, his "knowledge" of the services and the scale of the con.

When the psychopath is in a leadership role

Many corporate psychopaths have an uncanny ability to move into positions of power and influence. In executive leadership we can be exposed to the non-criminal psychopath, though less than 1% of the population falls into the definition of the corporate psychopath (Boddy, 2015). These people will display behaviors similar to the narcissist, including high levels of self-confidence, charm and manipulation. Because of their high levels of self-confidence, they are able to maneuver effectively up the corporate ladder and become comfortably ensconced in the C-Suite. As a result of their ability to use persuasion, confidence, charm and their willingness to take risks, they are viewed as capable leaders. In addition, they have mastered the political landscape and maneuver through landmines in the corporate setting. They are well connected to the right people and have stepped on many toes to get to the top. People don't challenge these leaders because they recognize the behavior too late and by then it is not helpful, or they believe that corporate leadership should be able to spot deviant and outright dark behaviors in the workplace.

The corporate psychopath will be recognized for their ability to make "tough decisions" that others do not want to make. Because the corporate psychopath does not experience emotions, it is easy for them to make these "tough decisions" because there is not an emotional attachment to the people or situations involved in the decision-making process. They thrive under pressure and will be calm, cool and collected. The psychopath is actually driven by the thrill of the situation and is fueled by the discomfort of others. They enjoy the events that others stress over. They like change and the challenge that change offers. In some cases, they are known to purposely seek out organizations going through change in order to stir up havoc and turmoil. By doing so, they are able to keep people focused on the ever-shifting landscape and not on their actions.

Keeping people busy with turmoil provides little opportunity for followers to observe the corporate psychopath in action. The corporate psychopath thrives on drama, and as they move into positions of power they will create further drama. They will either be drawn to the drama and chaos and add fuel to the fire, or if drama and turmoil does not exist they will be the ones to start it. The corporate psychopath leader will state to team members that they do not like drama and will not tolerate it, but in reality they love the thrill and chaos caused by the drama. When people come forward to discuss issues, the leader will not want to hear about them and will blame the follower for causing the problem or spreading rumors. This will cause the follower and others to believe they are the ones at the center of the drama, not the psychopath. The leader will not help to find a solution for the drama and will often work behind the scenes to escalate it instead. Again, for the corporate psychopath, conflict, chaos and drama are a thrill and they find it exciting. Eventually, as people begin to question the behavior of the psychopath leader, the psychopath will move on to another position and wreak havoc in a new environment.

In the shifting landscape that is caused by the corporate psychopath, individuals will feel on edge and will begin to experience paranoia about the events happening around them. The psychopath leader likes to cause followers to question their feelings and sanity in order to throw them off and make them start believing that the leader is not the problem, they are. The follower walks away from meetings questioning their own abilities, competence, skills and intuition. When a problem comes about and the follower questions it, the psychopath leader will often state that the follower has misunderstood. A tactic the corporate psychopath likes to use is gaslighting (discussed in Chapter 3). They will use phrases such as "You over-think everything" or "You're reading too much into this" or "You're just crazy and should seek help." Another tactic the corporate psychopath leader is very familiar with is denial. They will deny that an interaction or conversation ever occurred. This is a tactic used to throw the follower off and again make them question their own sanity. This type of behavior will continue to occur, causing the follower to question their role and what truly happened.

Recognizing the psychopath's behavior

It takes a while to recognize the actions of the corporate psychopath. They will be cloaked in charisma, charm and a sense of competence like no other. We are thrown into the hypnotic trance they utilize and we become blinded by their actions, until we learn the hard way that they are not at all who we thought them to be. People who have been burned by a corporate psychopath in the past usually catch on to the behavior right away when they experience it again, but because this is not a constant occurrence, people don't always identify or recognize these deviant behaviors for what they are. For some it can take a week to recognize the behavior and for others it may take years, or they may never see it. However, once we get to know the person and their dysfunctional behavior we can start to notice signs of this pathology.

I have had the opportunity to work with a corporate psychopath. I will call him Charlie (not his real name). The first time I met Charlie I had to escort him upstairs to his office on his first day. I went downstairs to meet him and while shaking his hand I was struck by the feeling that something was not right. He was well dressed with perfect hair, but his smile did not reach his eyes. I thought maybe he was nervous. I walked him upstairs and introduced him to people in the office. As he was meeting with individuals his demeanor would change based on the person to whom he was speaking. I watched as Charlie would pick up on the body language and expressions of the people he was meeting. Charlie walked into offices with a smile and just as quickly mirrored and mimicked the expression of the person he was talking to. If the person was serious, Charlie quickly turned serious; if the person was smiling, Charlie was happy and cracking jokes. It was uncanny how he shifted his actions so quickly based on who he was talking to. As we got to know and work with each other, I knew that my instincts about Charlie were correct. Here were the signs that I noticed right away. The following provides insights into the corporate psychopath.

Conscience: You will start to notice that they don't have a conscience. While working with Charlie, this was the first thing that I picked up from him. We were having layoffs and he volunteered to do the layoff meetings. Charlie was the last person we thought would want to be involved in the layoffs. This was not going to be easy and we figured he would want to take the easy way out. But Charlie volunteered for the meetings, saying, "But someone has to do it." My boss was beside himself because he did not have to do the uncomfortable and difficult task of laying people off. What we learned was that Charlie loved being the person to do layoffs. I remember watching people leave the office crying or upset and he would come out displaying concern on his face, but as soon as the person was out of sight he would start laughing, smiling and clapping his hands, ready for the next one. I remember him saying, "We should have a number system like a deli. Now servicing number—." The rest of the office was emotionally drained watching people go in and out, receive their severance package and then leave. However, Charlie was more and more invigorated as the day went on. He didn't miss a beat and his energy just seemed to increase with each meeting. When the last person came out of his office, Charlie came out with the severance spreadsheet highlighted with amounts. His only concern was that several of the people had received too much in severance, in his opinion, and they did not deserve the amounts they were getting.

He was disappointed that the day was over and asked if there would be more the next day. He enjoyed the feeling of power he had during those meetings. I asked him if he realized that he was changing the course of their lives and his only reply was, "As long as it isn't me." He never saw his reaction or the consequences of his behaviors as negative, and at the time we didn't know how to label his behavior. We just thought he was a cold-hearted jerk.

Emotional switch: The corporate psychopath knows the right emotional switch to flip on a person and will flip it depending on the circumstances and the events that are happening. While they don't experience emotion, they are able to mirror whatever emotion is in front of them or to portray the emotion needed for the situation. They can flip the switch to a different emotion. Watching this is quite interesting. One moment they are showing despair that matches the conversation and then they will walk off and mirror another group that is demonstrating happiness and joy.

Charlie was good at this and it was interesting to watch. He knew each person's emotional triggers. For example, he knew his assistant was getting divorced and he played to her moods each day. However, depending on what he needed, he would either empathize with her situation or he would use the emotional terms her husband used on her; she often said it was like working with her ex-husband. She reported that she often felt as though she was in the same emotionally abusive relationship with Charlie as the one she had just left.

Drama: If there is an innate amount of drama following this person, or they seem somehow to be in the center of the storm, this is a signal that there is an issue. Whenever there was drama in my workplace, I just had to sit down, listen to the situation and eventually all roads would lead back to Charlie. Every drama or turmoil in the office, we found him in the middle of it. He was the puppet master of the drama happening in the office.

What Charlie did not bank on was that the administrative assistant was close to the vice president of the office. Charlie was not able to read this situation well because the vice president worked remotely and could not see the interactions in the office; he could only hear what his administrative assistant told him. It was not until the vice president got word of Charlie's abusive behavior towards the administrative assistant that Charlie was let go. Charlie found work right away through his well-connected network and was able to land on his feet, creating the same turmoil within his new organization.

Harassment

The next level of deviant behaviors we will examine is harassment. We will look at both emotional harassment and sexual harassment, which is the most common form of harassment in the workplace. Harassment can take many different forms and approaches. In the deviance area of dysfunction, we will look at harassment as causing both emotional and physical harm to an individual or individuals.

According to York and Brookhouse (1988), harassment is defined as any kind of annoying, alarming or abusive act from one person to another.

Emotional harassment

Emotional harassment is linked to bullying behaviors in the workplace (addressed in Chapter 3). Bullying behaviors can become deviant as they become more consistent and increasingly threatening to an individual (Namie & Namie, 2003). In this section, we will explore another level of emotional abuse that can become deviant: emotional harassment. In the case of emotional harassment, the behavior is deliberate and psychologically damaging. The repeated behavior can paralyze an individual to the extent that they can no longer work. In other cases, the abuse can drive individuals to contemplate and/or commit suicide. Another form of emotional abuse is an individual threatening another with potential physical abuse, so they live in fear of this physical abuse being played out. Emotional abuse can be extremely damaging and it chips away at the psyche of the individual.

Emotional abuse is grossly disrespectful towards an individual and their rights. This abuse can be harmful and injurious to the individual. Types of abusive behavior may include aggression, deceit, maltreatment and suppression. The broad definition of emotional abuse is maltreatment or neglect inflicted by one individual onto another who is perceived to be weaker, resulting in a form of psychological trauma (Keashly & Harvey, 2005). This trauma may include depression, anxiety and fear which may evolve into physical trauma.

Characteristics of emotional harassment

Emotional harassment can be found in all of the spectrums discussed so far. We can find mild levels of emotional harassment in the uncivil behaviors of harassing body language and in dysfunctional bullying behaviors. I have chosen to discuss the topic of emotional harassment in further detail as it relates to deviant behavior. In this chapter, we examine how emotional harassment can evolve into deviant types of behavior that escalate. By exploring emotional harassment at this level, we can get a full understanding of the behavior and the tactics used. As emotional harassment escalates, the blatant violation of human rights that occurs through this type of behavior is clear to see. The following highlights and provides context for these behaviors.

Non-physical behaviors: Behaviors associated with emotional harassment are not physical but are attacks on the person's emotional well-being. Non-physical behaviors may include verbal threats, open humiliation, insults and intimidation. In other cases, there may not be any type of verbal interaction whatsoever and the abuse could take the form of intimidation, whereby the person does not lay their hands on another but enacts behaviors such as stalking, neglect and isolation.

Isolation can come in the form of physical or social isolation; another form of isolation is the silent treatment, which is usually coupled with strong body language such as glares, eye rolling, heavy sighing and other looks of hostility. When this form of abuse takes place, the target often wonders what is happening and is confused by the behavior they are experiencing.

Use of power: Emotional harassment is used when there is an imbalance of power, when one person has higher levels of power or authority than another. They will use this power to manipulate or control another. Public humiliation is a form of harassment the abuser will use to deliver attacks. If the abuser sees the target as a threat, they will use public humiliation to cause others to wonder about the target and to demonstrate their control.

Intentional behavior: The acts of emotional harassment are intentional and calculating. There are times when the behavior is random—e.g. lashing out at others who happen to be around—but the goal of this type of behavior is to intentionally hurt and cause emotional distress to another person. In this case, the behavior is something the abuser is not shy about. They will use intimidation, for example, to demonstrate power and to assert the upper hand over another. The attacker may yell, ridicule and humiliate their target, especially when they have an audience. They might say they are using tough love and it might come across to others that the behavior is acceptable, but to the target this will not be the case.

Steady and recurring behavior: The abuse is not a one-time event, but happens over a prolonged period of time. The behavior comes at a steady rate and increases in frequency, duration or both. As time goes on, the aggression and abuse escalate, causing more psychological harm to the target. The behavior continues over long periods and gets harder and harder for the target to endure, causing them to either leave or become submissive to the harassment.

Verbal aggression: Words are used as a tactic or weapon against another person. The abuser will intentionally use words to cause the other person to become upset, annoyed and/or offended. These comments may range from mild to outright verbal attacks, and they may be used in public or private. The tactic used will be determined on what the aggressor believes will be the best way to control another individual. Abusers will more than likely enjoy delivering insults either directly to their target or behind their backs. In some cases, the target knows they are being targeted when the abuse is outright, but when it comes about in a roundabout way the target is left wondering what is happening and whether they are being attacked. Often the target is caught off guard and is unable to properly defend themselves.

In other cases, the verbal aggression will come in the form of name-calling or shaming. The language used can be offensive or insulting, but it is used to gain power in a conversation. Sometimes, if the power is equal, the abuser will shame the individual in order to attack their self-esteem and to assert dominance. Their comments may be directed towards body shaming, gender bashing or making discriminatory or derogatory comments. Once the abuser finds the right button to push, they will continue to escalate the attacks on the individual they are focused on.

Dominating behaviors: Through verbal attacks, the abuser asserts their dominance over their target, to control them. They want to make sure the target understands who is in charge. Dominant behaviors include exclusion, verbal threats and humiliation. The abuser will use whatever tactics are needed in order to let the target know they have no control over the situation.

Jealousy: This form of attack is used to cause the target to become suspicious. Creating jealousy and suspicion is a form of control the abuser will use to make the individual insecure about friendships, relationships or workplace dynamics. Once a person begins to feel insecure, the abuser will use this against them, causing them to make errors or become paranoid.

Sexual harassment

The most common form of harassment in the workplace is sexual harassment. With sexual harassment, the abuser may use forms of emotional harassment, bullying and other forms of dysfunctional behavior. In the case of sexual harassment, it is not about the sexual act or about sex itself but about power and the abuse of power. Sexual harassment is the one form of uncivil, dysfunctional and deviant behavior in the workplace that we have discussed thus far that is addressed in our legal system. It is the only behavior that in the United States is covered under formal policies in the workplace, education and training. Yet, it is still under-reported in the workplace.

Sexual harassment can take several different forms in the workplace, including inappropriate texting, crude or uncomfortable looks, comments, words and tone of voice, non-verbal gestures, sexual advances, inappropriate touching and sexual assault. These behaviors are all used to make a target uncomfortable and to exert power over that person. A misconception of sexual harassment is that the behavior just focuses on the man as the aggressor and the woman as the target. In a majority of the cases that are reported, that is the case, but we also see sexual harassment in the forms of male to male, female to male and female to female, and in some cases mobbing, or groups of individuals targeting one or several individuals (Yildirim & Yildirim, 2007). These cases are not openly shared and often ignored or not addressed in the workplace because of shame or doubt.

Since late 2017, we have witnessed an increase in sexual harassment claims ranging from Hollywood to the political arena. Awareness of the topic has increased exponentially because of these events. It seems that each week a new report is shared related to sexual harassment claims from all areas of the public and private sector. With recent social events including the #MeToo and #TimesUp movements, we have watched several individuals called out regarding inappropriate behaviors related to sexual harassment. In addition to these movements, we have seen more women come forward to state that at some point in their careers they were sexually harassed. These movements have further come to light following comments made by Donald Trump while a US presidential candidate about inappropriately touching women; after Trump was inaugurated more women came forward to share inappropriate comments, attacks and affairs with the now president. Other political figures have been disgraced for sending inappropriate photographs to women; news anchors have been terminated because of accusations of sexual harassment; and Hollywood moguls have been called out for inappropriate behavior and sexual attacks.

These behaviors are vile and offensive and they have attracted extensive media coverage. However, the topic of sexual harassment is not new and it has always been in the workplace. The earliest public claims regarding sexual harassment came to light with public hearings in 1991 discussing inappropriate comments made by Clarence Thomas to his assistant at the Equal Employment Opportunities Commission, Anita Hill. During his confirmation hearings for a position on the Supreme Court, Anita Hill testified to the nature of these comments. At the time it was a defining moment with regard to how the United States viewed the topic of sexual harassment in the workplace. It is important to note that, regardless of conformational hearings and testimony on behalf of Anita Hill, Clarence Thomas was confirmed to the US Supreme Court, but this event helped to raise awareness of sexual harassment in the workplace. Prior discussion regarding sexual harassment was often ignored; these behaviors were often swept under the rug and, as we later discovered, not reported for fear of how the target would be perceived. However, after Anita Hill testified, the number of sexual harassment cases reported in the US and Canada increased by 58% and continued to climb (Black & Allen, 2001).

History of sexual harassment

Anita Hill's testimony and Clarence Thomas' hearings helped to shed light on the topic of sexual harassment. The term "sexual harassment" developed in the 1970's, helped to raise awareness of this issue. Attorney Lin Farley suggested that harassment is a form of discrimination. Harassment claims were rooted in the efforts of the 1960s, which were embedded in the civil rights movement. Many of the claims of discrimination were considered "open secrets", whereby people were aware of incidents of harassment or discrimination but were encouraged to avoid discussing these topics in public. Cases of secretaries being harassed by their male bosses, or the "casting couch" of Hollywood being used for gender and sexual harassment, were well known and considered an open secret. Sexual harassment in Hollywood was something that was being dealt with during the time of Judy Garland filming *The Wizard of Oz*, and it was experienced by Shirley Temple. During these types of incidents, the men who perpetrated them were labeled "fresh" or "womanizers". As a result, their behavior was excused; people knew what was happening but didn't talk about it or address it head on. It was not until recently that the subject began to unfold as brave women came forward to report incidents of harassment and sexual assaults they had endured in the workplace. These claims were just the tip of the iceberg, and the issues that were under the surface quickly started to emerge as we saw more and more powerful executives in Hollywood, politics and the media were exposed for their unacceptable behavior.

Starting in the 1970s and coming to further light in the 1980s, sexual harassment has moved from being an open secret to a full-blown topic, with organizations providing policies and training to address the behavior in the workplace. Yet fast-forward more than 30 years and it is still known as an "open secret". Recent social movements have begun to surface as more and more people come forward to discuss the harassment that has happened to them during the course of their careers. While public media has provided a platform for individuals to speak up in high-profile cases, there continue to be women and men who endure sexual harassment in the workplace and are not willing to report it.

The first large organization to face and address issues regarding sexual harassment was the Massachusetts Institute of Technology (MIT). Mary Rowe, a Professor at MIT, authored a report entitled "Saturn's Wings" (1990). This report was the first to include females as targets of aggression including discrimination and harassment (Paludi, 2010). The report was presented to the president and chancellor of MIT. During this time the term sexual harassment emerged. Mary Rowe argued that she did not believe that she was the first to use the term "sexual harassment" since it was a topic that was being discussed in women's groups in Massachusetts. Regardless of how the term came to be, because of Mary Rowe's report MIT was the first large-scale organization to openly discuss the topic and to develop policies and procedures to address issues such as racial harassment and harassment against women of color, which included both racial and sexual harassment. The then president of MIT took a stand, stating that these behaviors were not acceptable and were intolerable for individuals. There have been debates about who was the first person to coin the term "sexual harassment". Cornell University activists claim that they came up with the term in 1975 while discussing sexual coercion and sexual exploitation in the workplace. However, none of the terms they were discussing linked back to the subtle and not-so-subtle behaviors related to this conduct. It was then that the term "sexual harassment" was mentioned and it was quickly agreed upon as the nomenclature for the behavior. This group of activists went on to form the Working Women's Institute. It was the work of this group—as well as the Alliance Against Sexual Coercion, founded in 1976—that brought the topic of sexual harassment to the public in the late 1970s.

In 2018 women and men continue to be targets of sexual harassment in the workplace and that it has taken so many years for these secrets to emerge into the public eye. Despite mandatory sexual harassment training in organizations, this behavior still occurs in the workplace. It still remains an "open secret".

Definition of sexual harassment

The Equal Employment Opportunity Commission (EEOC) in the United States addresses harassment, including sexual harassment, as follows: "It is unlawful to harass a person (an applicant or employee) because of that person's sex". Harassment can include "sexual harassment", which comes in the form of unwelcome sexual advances, requests for sexual favors, and other verbal or physical harassment of a sexual nature. While laws exist, they do not prohibit behavior such as simple teasing, off-hand comments and isolated incidents, nor do they impose a general civility code. In the workplace, harassment may be considered illegal when it is frequent or severe and creates a hostile and/or offensive work environment, or when it results in an adverse employment decision including demotion, firing or quitting.

Sexual harassment can range from mild transgressions to sexual abuse or sexual assault. In many countries outside of the United States, sexual harassment is a form of illegal employment discrimination and includes sexual, psychological abuse, and in most countries it is viewed as a form of bullying. Depending on the anti-bullying laws of that country, it can be treated as a civil crime, punishable with fines and/ or jail time.

Types of sexual harassment

Sexual harassment can be found in any realm of our society, including workplaces, places of education (e.g. K-12 or higher education) and other industries. Most of the time, the perpetrator is in a position of power or is trying to exert power over another individual. However, it is important to note this is not always the case, but the majority of cases do link power to the abuse. This power may be linked to differences in age, social status, politics, education or employment power. The following are key facts about harassment.

- Perpetrators of sexual harassment may include a client, co-worker, customer, relative, legal guardian, teacher, professor, student, friend or stranger.
- Harassment can take place in schools, universities, workplaces and outside of workplaces during work hours.
- There may or may not be witnesses.
- The perpetrator may or may not be completely aware that their behavior is offensive or is even considered sexual harassment, or they may be unaware that their behavior is unlawful.
- The target may not be aware of or understand what is happening at the time.
- The incident may be a one-time act or it can be repetitive.
- Adverse impacts may include stress, social withdrawal, sleep, eating difficulties and overall health impairment, etc.
- The victim and perpetrator can be any gender and do not have to be of the opposite sex. Male-to-female, female-to-male, male-to-male, and female-to-female harassment occur on a day-to-day basis.
- The harassment may result from a situation in which the perpetrator thinks they are making themselves clear, but is actually not being understood the way they intended. The misunderstanding can either be reasonable or unreasonable. An example of an unreasonable misunderstanding is when a woman holds a certain stereotypical view of a man such that she does not understand the man's explicit message to stop and thinks he may be enjoying the conversation.

With the increase of technology, there has been an increase in social interactions through technology related to sexual harassment, including cyberstalking, sexting and sending inappropriate pictures (Giumetti et al., 2012). In a 2014 study conducted by PEW Research it was found that online harassment was an issue: of those surveyed 25% of females and 13% of males between the ages of 18 and 24 stated they had experienced some form of sexual harassment while online (Duggan, 2014).

The EEOC defines workplace sexual harassment as "unwelcome sexual advances, requests for sexual favors and other verbal or physical conduct of a sexual nature". These behaviors constitute sexual harassment when this conduct explicitly or implicitly affects an individual's employment, interferes with an individual's work performance or creates an intimidating, hostile or offensive work environment (EEOC). Sexual harassment is also considered a form of sexual discrimination which violates Title VII of the Civil Rights Act of 1964, which is a federal law that prohibits employers from discriminating against employees on the basis of sex, race, color, national origin and religion. It generally applies to employers with 15 or more employees, including federal, state and local governments. Title VII also applies to both private and public colleges and universities, employment agencies and labor organizations.

Challenges linked to sexual harassment

One of the challenges related to sexual harassment is understanding that it involves a wide range of behaviors. In most cases, though not all, it is difficult for the target to describe what has happened or what they have experienced. This could be related to the stress of the event, humiliation or fear of retaliation if they speak up. For example, there are cases of males being sexually harassed by females, but males are less inclined to come forward to report that they have been sexually harassed by a woman because of possible humiliation and stereotyping from their male peers. In addition, each case of sexual harassment is not cut and dried and each incident may differ greatly.

Let us take a look at the different types of harassers. Dziech and Weiner (1990) explain that there are two very broad types:

- **Public harassers** are straightforward and blatant in their seductive and sexist attitudes towards colleagues, students, subordinates, etc. They do not hide their actions or comments. In many cases, these harassers' behavior is considered a part of their personality. They may have been reprimanded in the past, but they continue their behavior. For example, the construction worker on a job site who whistles at or catcalls a woman as she walks past, or makes an inappropriate comment.
- **Private harassers** carefully cultivate a restrained and respectable image on the surface, but when alone with their target, their demeanor changes. In many cases, this is what we have witnessed with the recent charges against

Hollywood and media personalities. Their public personas are respectable, but behind closed doors their behavior is completely different, and as a result, many individuals are shocked when this behavior is reported to the public, as this is not the persona they have portrayed of themselves.

Another challenge related to sexual harassers is understanding the different categories their behavior may fall under. By understanding the different types of harassers and sexual harassment, one can identify the behavior that is being experienced. Langelan (1993) describes four different classes of harassers:

- **Predatory harassers:** Individuals who get sexual thrills from humiliating others. This type of harasser may become involved in sexual extortion and may frequently harass just to see how the target responds. Those who don't resist may become targets for rape as the predatory harasser takes this as permission or consent, but that is not the case on the part of the target.
- **Dominance harassers:** This is the most common type of harasser, someone who engages in harassing behavior in order to boost their own ego and dominate their target. They are able to gain and maintain power and control over their target.
- **Strategic or territorial harassers:** Harassers who seek to maintain their privilege in jobs or physical locations. For example, a man's harassment of a female in a predominately male occupation. They exert their level of power over a particular gender not welcomed into their gender-dominated world. We can find this in the nursing profession, which is predominately female, and male nurses are harassed in order to be put into their place. Sexual comments or statements are made to make the male nurse uncomfortable and for the female to dominate the male. Another example is the female who works in a male-dominated industry such as construction, and who is subjected to comments by the males who wish to see how far they can take these behaviors with the female present. In many cases, this type of harassment is a way for the harasser to push out their target to maintain the gender majority in that field.
- **Street harassers:** Another type of sexual harassment is performed in public places by strangers. Street harassment includes verbal and non-verbal behavior, and remarks that are frequently sexual in nature and usually consist of comments on physical appearance or presence in public. Examples include catcalls, whistling or making comments in public about a person's appearance.

Impact

The impact of sexual harassment is just like any other type of dysfunctional or deviant behavior we have discussed and may vary depending on the event and the individual. The EU Fundamental Rights Agency conducted research on over 17,335 female targets of sexual harassment who were asked to name the feelings that resulted from the harassment they experienced. The following outlines these feelings:

- 45% anger.
- 41% annoyance.
- 36% embarrassment.
- 29% fear.
- 20% shame.

Prolonged exposure to harassment can manifest itself into temporary or prolonged episodes of stress and depression, depending on the target's abilities to cope with the situation and the type of support system the person has in place. It is also noted that targets that do not submit to harassment may also experience forms of retaliation, isolation and continued bullying. In many cases, they are left out of promotional opportunities. These individuals will not speak up for fear of retaliation and will often give in to sexual advances or leave the organization. One of the most significant stigmas associated with harassment in the workplace is the abuse received when coming forward to report the act; targets are often victimized again by having to endure an investigation to determine how their behavior was associated with the act. In a sense, targets are forced to relive these acts, and at times they are wrongfully blamed for the inappropriate behavior. As a result, targets have learned not to speak up. For example, men who are being harassed by women will not speak up because of the idea that men could stop the behavior of women. It may be unwelcome, but they may be blamed for encouraging the behavior and not stepping up to the female harasser. However, once again, if the female is in a position of power, the male may not be able to step up or speak out for fear of losing their job and/or having to withstand public humiliation.

Evil in the workplace

There are times when deviant behaviors in the workplace does get out of control and results in violence. There are people who will take their behaviors to another level and there is no better word to use for that person than "evil". In the workplace, evil behaviors are an extreme form of deviant behavior. Evil individuals are often focused on destroying, having complete control over and submission from another individual. In some cases, evil may not surface until it is too late. Like a pressure cooker that slowly simmers, eventually the pressure will cause the individual to explode. The following provides further insights into evil in the workplace.

Counter-productive workplace behaviors

People with an extreme level of psychopathy often demonstrate one or several types of behavior which are very similar to the behaviors of the corporate psychopath. However, at this point the behaviors can become extreme and the individuals may need mental health interventions. It is impossible for organizations to step in to address these behaviors alone, and it is important to have a professional assess them. Some of these behaviors include:

1. **Denying reality:** The evil individual has their own story which is their reality and their truth. Their reality shows their true motives. This reality is often distorted to demonstrate what they believe to be accurate and there is no changing this perception. They will deny the reality others see and will focus on their own reality of the situation.

2. **Twisting and turning:** The evil individual will twist and turn the facts. They will twist truths and link these truths back into their reality and perceptions. They will take things out of context and provide alternative facts instead of speaking the truth.

3. **Information is power:** Withholding information is a key aspect of the evil person's motive. Leaving others in the dark and not giving them information gives the evil person power over them. Keeping information from individuals on purpose is a common power play used to alter facts, lie about the information and even cause individuals to feel guilty for not trusting or believing them. In addition, the evil person will use information to gain power over another individual. This can come in the form of stalking and learning about what the other person does and how they act. With the use of the internet as a whole, and in particular social platforms such as Facebook, Instagram and LinkedIn, the evil individual has access to a wealth of information they can learn about their target and use against them. They will use this information as a way to get into the lives of others.

4. **Misleading others:** The evil person will use lies and cons to mislead others, and twist the truth in order to leave them feeling scared, attacked, uncertain, confused and vulnerable. They have mastered the way they use their words in order to cause individuals to question their own beliefs or even sanity. Individuals may start to believe what they are being told and the other person's agenda. The evil person can cause them to question other people's motives and intentions. We see this type of behavior in corporations and political offices all the time.

5. **Lying:** Evil individuals lie so much that they don't even recognize the truth. The lies become their reality and their truth. The truth is never as colorful to them as the lie. When they hear something, they have to add more to it in order to add that little extra spice to the situation. They even start to believe the lie and believe it to be the truth. When caught in a lie, they will tell you even more lies to throw you off or make you believe something else instead. They will let you know why they lied: it might be to protect you, and it might be that they were protecting themselves or others from the truth. They will let you think that their lies were noble, to protect others or the situation. In reality it is just another lie. In other cases, they may deny the lie because in their minds the lie does not exist, since it has become their truth and their reality.

6. **No remorse:** Just like the psychopath, these individuals are never sorry for their actions or for ruining the lives of other people. It is all part of their master plan and the reality they have created for themselves. They view others as indispensable, and as pawns to get them to where they are going. Destroying others and focusing on other people's lives is part of their master plan and what they need to do in order to get themselves ahead. When meeting individuals, the evil person will find their weaknesses and use these weaknesses to their benefit and personal gain.

7. **Avoiding responsibility:** Responsibility and accountability are just not something the evil person wants any part of. They take no responsibility for their actions, and if their actions cause harm or pain to others then that is not their problem. They take no blame for their actions and if they feel blame is headed towards them, they will redirect it to others. "I'm sorry" is not in their vocabulary and they don't know what it means. When others apologize, they view this as a weakness and a sign that the other person is vulnerable and gullible.

8. **Friendship:** The evil individual is not a friend. Even if others feel that they are, in fact they are constantly calculating the best way to position themselves and may be focusing on fake friendship. If they come to assist you, know that they are there to position themselves and that their intentions are not positive. Instead, they are focused on ensuring they can best position themselves for their own advantage. This is not to say everyone in the workplace is evil and not your friend. However, the evil person uses friendship as a means to gain information, control and to gain insights.

9. **Monopolizing your time:** The evil person typically doesn't have respect for your time. If they know you have a deadline or an important project coming up, they will do everything they can to cause you to be late. They will distract you and waste your time so you can't focus on your project. They do this in order to prevent you from completing the work and to cause you to fail on your project. They will act as though they are concerned with your timeline, while monopolizing your time to draw you away from the work you are trying to finish.

10. **Living a double life:** Just like the corporate psychopath, the evil individual tends to live in a fantasy world that is a façade not based in reality. You never get to know these individuals on a real or personal level. In many cases, *they* don't know who they are as they have come to believe in the fantasy life they have concocted. They never want anyone to know who they really are and as a result they create a whole new life and persona. In other cases, they won't lie but will conjure up what they think their façade is based on, or what they think will appeal to the person in front of them. In other cases, they will live life to the extreme: driving cars and buying homes they cannot afford, or buying designer clothes and jewelry to impress others and to inflate their own ego. In many cases, they will live beyond their means. They will begin to falsify records, lie and embezzle in order to maintain the life they have created. With each individual, the evil person will show themselves in a different way based on what they need from that person. They are never authentic and constantly live a lie about who they really are.

11. **Control freaks:** In order to keep things moving and to organize the lies they tell, the evil person is constantly focused on control. They will control the situation, the person and the environment. They will become possessive of others and control individuals. By doing this, they are able to feed off others, which gives them the feeling of power. When they begin to lose control of a situation, they begin to unravel.

Evil behaviors in the workplace may lead to aggression against the organization. This type of evil may come in the form of theft from the organization, embezzlement or falsification of records. An individual looking to fuel their reality of a life they lead may find themselves getting in over their heads. They may be found skimming money from the organization or diverting funds to maintain the lives they lead. In other cases, if bonuses are linked to their salary, they may falsify records such as sales numbers to reflect higher revenue than actually earned in order to obtain larger bonuses.

Another form of evil comes in the form of sabotaging operations to deliberately harm the organization or individuals. Evil individuals may feel as though they have suffered some level of injustice in the workplace. For example, the person may have experienced some form of mistreatment that the organization has not addressed, or they might experience a form of injustice such as being treated unfairly by the organization, being overlooked for promotions or not receiving pay increases. As a result, they may act out towards the organization, by sabotaging operations, sales, production, customer relationships or other organizational elements.

Workplace violence

The final deviant behavior that we will discuss is workplace violence. We have discussed several uncivil, dysfunctional and deviant behaviors. One could argue that individuals who engage in verbal abuse, pranks, arguments, property damage, rumor spreading and swearing are associated with workplace violence. As we have discussed, these behaviors can be classified as a form of incivility or dysfunctional behavior. However, this chapter explores workplace violence as deviant behaviors that involve physical harm to individuals, such as anger-related incidents, rape, arson, and murder.

Violence can happen inside and outside the workplace. It can take the form of emotional threats, verbal abuse and physical/sexual abuse. The National Institute of Occupational Safety and Health (NIOSH) defines workplace violence as any physical assault, threatening behavior or verbal abuse occurring in the work environment (Kennedy et al., 2011). Another definition of violence relates to incidents that abuse employees through threats or assaults in circumstances involving an explicit or implicit challenge to their safety, well-being or health. Violence affects not only the target, but also the people connected to the target. Incidences of workplace violence drain employees both physically and emotionally.

Categories of workplace violence

Type 1: Criminal intent. This is focused on workplace violence where the perpetrator has no relationship with the targeted establishment and the primary motive is usually theft or a random act of violence. This is when the act starts off as theft, for example, and then turns violent. We often see this type of violence in the workplace associated with people who deal with large sums of money or work late at night—for example, at banks, gas stations or thrift stores—where the violence is targeted towards an employee for the sole purpose of personal material gain.

Type 2: Customer/client. During this type of workplace violence, the perpetrator may be a customer or client of the organization and the violence occurs in relation to the employee's normal work. We often see this type of violence in healthcare settings, where a patient acts out against a healthcare employee or social service worker, and in some rare cases there are reports of sexual assault by a client towards a sales employee in order to close a deal.

Type 3: Employee to employee. This type of violence happens between current or former employees. The individuals who are most often targeted are supervisors and/or managers who the perpetrator believes have incited an injustice against them.

Type 4: Domestic violence. The workplace is experiencing more and more domestic assault complaints from people who are not employees or former employees, but who are married to, separated and/or divorced from an employee. This type of violence will usually be perpetrated by the spouse, who knows exactly where their target will be during certain hours. Typically these events happen when the target is alone, for example walking to their car in the parking lot (Scalora et al., 2003).

Type 5: Ideological violence. This is violence that is targeted towards a particular organization, their employees or property due to ideological thinking related to religious and/or political reasons, and includes terrorist shooters or active shooters with specific targets. They justify their acts as a way to protect the ideology they believe in.

For the sake of this chapter we will explore employee-to-employee violence in the workplace, recognizing that this type of behavior is not limited to one act.

Employee-to-employee violence

Employee violence in the workplace has been most commonly referred to by the term "going postal", which relates to employees who become extremely angry towards individuals or an organization, often resulting in violence in the workplace. This expression was linked to several incidents, starting in 1986, where postal workers shot and killed managers, co-workers and members of the public. Between the years of 1970 and 1997 more than 40 employees were killed by current or former employees in 20 separate incidents of workplace violence. However, since 1994, homicides in the workplace have been declining. In 2014, homicide accounted for almost 10% of fatal workplace injuries, which is a decrease of 62% compared to 1994. In 2014, 68 women and 341 men were victims of homicide in the workplace. Of the women, 32% were killed by a relative or domestic partner, compared to 2% of men. 16% of women were killed by a co-worker or work associate, compared to 15% of men. It is important to note that while the numbers appear to be declining, evidence shows that violence in the workplace is often under-reported (Seungmug & McCrie, 2012). In 2015 the Occupational Safety and Health Administration (OSHA) reported: "Nearly 2 million American workers report having been victims of workplace violence each year" (www.osha.gov/SLTC/workplaceviolence).

Violence in the workplace may include threats of physical harm or acts of violence against another person or property. These threats are sufficiently severe, offensive and/or intimidating and should result in immediate action from the organization. These offenses create an environment that is hostile or intimidating to an employee or employees. While incidents of violence are not commonly reported, we continue to see examples of this type of deviant behavior within the workplace. The following reports on acts of violence in the workplace come from the Bureau of Labor Statistics (2014):

- One out of every six fatal work injuries is related to violence in the workplace.
- Shootings are the most frequent manner of death in the workplace.
- Homicides account for 52% of fatal work injuries; suicides account for 35%.

Examples of workplace violence include but are not limited to the following:

- Causing physical injury to another person; this is intentional injury through unsafe practices, sabotaging of equipment or acts of violence against another.
- Making threatening remarks of physical harm to another person and creating an environment of fear.
- Engaging in aggressive or hostile behavior that causes another to experience emotional distress or fear of injury because of a person's actions or words.
- Intentional sabotage or damaging of property of the employer or an employee.
- Making harassing or threatening phone calls to another person.
- Sending harassing or threatening messages, or posting harassing or threatening messages on social media.
- Committing acts that are motivated by or related to sexual harassment or domestic violence.
- Willful, malicious and repeated following of another person, which is also referred to as stalking. In addition, cyberstalking through theft of another person's identity or stalking on social media platforms.
- Unauthorized possession of a weapon while on the job site or in the place of employment with the intent to threaten or cause harm to another.

What can organizations do to prevent deviant behavior?

There are many suggestions for preventing and addressing deviant behavior depending on the severity as well as the culture of the organization. One of the more noted suggestions involves having an organizational climate with a strong ethical emphasis that shows a concern for employees and their well-being (Peterson, 2002). Peterson suggests that an organization's mission statement and strategy should focus on a genuine concern for the employees, along with developing an acceptable model for leaders to follow in the organization. Addressing aggression immediately, creating less formal reporting systems for employees to report an incident, and educating higher-powered employees on task inter-dependency consequences with lower-powered employees are all suggestions for creating a healthy culture (Hershcovis et al., 2012). Zoghbi-Manrique-de-Lara (2010) points out that creating an environment of task satisfaction and promoting procedural justice are ways to create an effective strategy for limiting deviant workplace behavior. The final suggestion revolves around developing policies to address deviance by focusing on reducing employee stress and understanding the personalities of employees (Farhadi et al., 2015). Also helpful is having expectations throughout the organization that focus on ethics and employee well-being, having task orientation that aligns with the culture and mission statement, and encouraging the positive actions of leaders to contribute to an environment that is proactive in its approach to stopping deviant behavior.

In addition to having strong mechanisms such as culture, values and norms in place that address behaviors in the workplace, other mechanisms are also needed. Risk factors should be identified and addressed quickly. Zero-tolerance protocols should be implemented that are not just limited to the employee, but apply to all workers, clients, patients, contractors and anyone else that comes into contact with employees (OSHA, 2015). In addition, programs that provide elements to address prevention are also called for. These elements include addressing the work environment, fostering an environment that is both physically and psychologically safe for employees, and providing security measures or employees that have the proper resources (training and equipment) to address violence in the workplace. Education and training should be provided for all employees. These programs should focus on expectations, responsibilities, awareness, conflict training and ways to deescalate situations. Finally, there should be a focus on awareness, the observation of potential warning signs and advice about how to report these issues to the appropriate people. Typically there are signs prior to a person losing control and lashing out. The following can be used as indicators of concern and signs for managers to address.

- Excessive attendance issues, such as coming in late or calling in sick from work.
- Decreased productivity, lack of engagement, seeming to withdraw from work obligations, self-imposed isolation.
- Work patterns that are not consistent.
- Difficulty with concentration.

- Reckless safety issues.
- Decline in health or hygiene.
- Evidence of drug or alcohol use.
- Increase in work and/or personal stress factors.
- Sudden outbursts, uncontrolled or explosive temper flare-ups, frequent arguments or conflicts with co-workers, excessive swearing and derogatory comments.
- Verbal threats of harm to another.
- Domestic disputes.
- Dramatic behavioral changes.

Many of these indicators demonstrate issues with stress, depression and other psychological issues. It is key for managers to identify issues and to seek assistance for the employee. It is important to note that it is not up to the manager or supervisor to assess or diagnose behavioral or psychological issues, as they are not equipped to assess these issues. Their responsibility is to identify issues and seek to identify the proper resources through which the employee can be properly diagnosed and their issues addressed.

Conclusion

Deviant behaviors in an organization can spiral out of control rather quickly if the business is not taking steps to prevent or address them. Whether the deviant behavior is stealing time, taking office supplies, harassing individuals emotionally or physically, or endangering another employee's life, the consequences can be astonishing and costly in both monetary value and the reputation of the organization, not to mention the costs of physical harm, not limited to death. Organizations need to focus on proactively addressing deviant behavior and nurturing a culture that does not condone this type of conduct. Keeping a focus on employees in a caring fashion and instilling expectations across the entire organization are ways to help prevent deviant behavior from growing. In the following chapters, we will discuss in further detail the impact of these behaviors and the ways in which organizations can properly address them.

References

ACFE, 2008. Report to the nation on occupational fraud and abuse. www.acfe.com/uploadedfiles/acfe_website/content/documents/2008-rttn.pdf.

Applebaum, S., Iaconi, G., & Matousek, A. 2007. Positive and negative deviant workplace behaviors; causes, impacts and solutions. *Corporate Governance: The International Journal of Business in Society*, 7(5), 586–598.

Babiak, P. & Hare, R. 2006. *Snakes in suits: When psychopaths go to work*. New York: HarperCollins.

Black, A.E. & Allen, J.L. 2001. Tracing the legacy of Anita Hill: The Thomas/Hill hearings and media coverage of sexual harassment. *Gender Issues*, 19(1), 33–52.

Boddy, C. 2005. The implications of corporate psychopaths for business and society: An initial examination and a call to arms. *Australian Journal of Business and Behavioral Sciences* 1(2), 30–40.

Boddy, C. 2012. The impact of corporate psychopaths on corporate reputation and marketing. *The Marketing Review*, 12(1), 79–89.

Boddy, C. 2014. Corporate psychopaths, conflict, employee affective wellbeing and counterproductive work behavior. *Journal of Business Ethics*, 121(1), 107–121.

Boddy, C. 2015. Organisational psychopaths: A ten year update. *Management Decision*, 53(10), 2407–2432.

Bromley, D. n.d. Corporate deviance. www.people.vcu.edu/~dbromley/corporate.htm.

Bureau of Labor and Statistics. 2014. Injuries, Illnesses, and Fatalities. www.bls.gov/iif/

Christian, M. & Ellis, A. 2011. Examining the effects of sleep deprivation on workplace deviance: A self-regulatory perspective. *Academy of Management*, 54(5) 913–934.

Cohn, S. 2015. In new emails, Madoff says fraud wasn't so bad. CNBC Report.

Cullen, F., Hartman, J., & Jonson, C. 2009. Bad guys: why the public supports punishing white-collar offenders. *Crime, Law and Social Change*, 51, 31–44.

Duggan, M. 2014. Online harassment report: Summary and findings. Washington, DC: Pew Research Center.

Dziech, B. & Weiner, L. 1990. *The lecherous professor: Sexual harassment on campus.* Chicago, IL: University of Illinois Press.

Farhadi, H., Nasir, R., Omar, F., & Nouri, A. 2015. Understanding employees' deviant behaviour: The role of agreeableness and stress related to work. *E-BANGI Journal*, 10, 102–107.

Giumetti, G.W., McKibben, E.S., Hatfield, A.L., Schroeder, A.N., & Kowalski, R.M. 2012. Cyber incivility @ work: The new age of interpersonal deviance. *Cyberpsychology, Behavior, and Social Networking*, 15(3), 148–154.

Gudmundsson, A. & Southey, G. 2011. Leadership and the rise of the corporate psychopath: What can business schools do about the "snakes inside"? *Journal of Social and Behavioral Research in Business*, 2(2), 18–27.

Hershcovis, M. S., Reich, T. C., Parker, S. K., & Bozeman, J. 2012. The relationship between workplace aggression and target deviant behaviour: The moderating roles of power and task interdependence. *Work & Stress*, 26(1), 1–20.

Hogan, J., & Hogan, R. 1989. How to measure employee reliability. *Journal of Applied Psychology*, 74, 273–279.

Keashly, L., & Harvey, S. 2005. Emotional abuse in the workplace. In S. Fox, & P. E. Spector (Eds.), *Counterproductive work behavior: Investigations of actors and targets* (pp. 201–235). Washington, DC: American Psychological Association.

Kennedy R., Burks, E., Calhoun, S., Essory, M., Herring, S., & Kerner, L. 2011. Workplace violence: A discussion and ongoing study. *International Journal of the Academic Business World*, 5(1), 35–40.

Langelan, M. 1993. *Back off! How to confront and stop sexual harassment and harassers.* New York: Simon and Schuster.

Larson, R. & Powell, A. 2015. Corporate Deviance. Society Pages. https://thesocietypages.org/trot/2015/10/06/corporate-deviance.

Lee, A. 2013. No remorse: Bernie Madoff still doesn't care what you think of him. *Business Insider*, 91(1–2), 114–121.

Murphy, K. R. 1993. *Honesty in the workplace.* Belmont, CA: Brooks/Cole.

Namie, G. & Namie, T. 2003. *The bully at work: What can you do to stop the hurt and reclaim your dignity on the job?* Naperville, IL: Sourcebooks, Inc.

Nair, N. & Bhatnagar, D. 2011. Understanding workplace deviant behavior in nonprofit organizations. *Nonprofit Management and Leadership*, 21(3), 289–309.

OSHA. 2015. United States Department of Labor. Occupational Safety and Health Administration. Workplace Violence Report. www.osha.gov/SLTC/workplaceviolence.

Paludi, M. 2010. *Victims of sexual assault and abuse: Resources and responses for individuals and families (Women's Psychology)*. Westport, CT: Praeger.

Patel, S. 2013. My interview with Madoff. *Wall Street Journal*. www.wsj.com/articles/my-sitdown-with-madoff-1386429356.

Perlow, R. & Latham, L.L. 1993. Relationship of Client Abuse with Locus of Control and Gender: A Longitudinal Study in Mental Retardation Facilities. *Journal of Applied Psychology*, 78, 831–834.

Peterson, D.K. 2002. Deviant workplace behavior and the organization's ethical climate. *Journal of Business and Psychology*, 17(1), 47–61.

Quow, K.L. 2013. An introspective analysis of the etiological relationships of psychopathy in serial killers and successful business men. *Modern Psychological Studies*, 19(1), 9.

Robinson, S.L. & Bennett, R.J. 1995. A typology of deviant workplace behaviors: A multidimensional scaling study. *Academy of Management Journal*, 38(2), 555–572.

Roter, A. 2017. *Understanding and recognizing dysfunctional leadership: The impact of dysfunctional leadership on organizations and followers*. London: Routledge, Gower Publishing.

Rowe, M.P. 1990. People who feel harassed need a complaint system with both formal and informal options. *Negotiation Journal*, 6(2), 161–172.

Scalora, M.J., Washington, D.O.N., Casady, T., & Newell, S.P. 2003. Nonfatal workplace violence risk factors: Data from a police contact sample. *Journal of Interpersonal Violence*, 18(3), 310–327.

Seungmug, L. & McCrie, R. 2012. *Mass homicides by employees in the American workplace. CRISP Report*. ASIS Foundation.

Shichor, D. 1989. Corporate deviance and corporate victimization: A review and some elaborations. *International Review of Victimology*, 1(1), 67–88.

Shouten, R. & Silver, J. 2012. *Almost a psychopath: Do I (or does someone I know) have a problem with manipulation and lack of empathy?* Cambridge, MA: Harvard University Press.

Storms, P.L. & Spector, P.E. 1987. Relationships of organizational frustration with reported behavioral reactions: The moderating effect of locus of control. *Journal of Occupational Psychology*, 1987, 60, 227–234.

Vaughan, D. 1998. Rational choice, situated action, and the social control of organizations. *Law and Society Review*, 32(1): 23–61.

Winarick, K. 2010. Thoughts on greed and envy. *The American Journal of Psychoanalysis*, 70(4), 317–327.

Yildirim, A. & Yildirim, D. 2007. Mobbing in the workplace by peers and managers: Mobbing experienced by nurses working in healthcare facilities in Turkey and its effect on nurses. *Journal of Clinical Nursing*, 16(8), 1444–1453.

York, K.M. & Brookhouse, K.J. 1988. The legal history of work-related sexual harassment and implications for employers. *Employee Responsibilities and Rights Journal*, 1(3), 227–237.

Zoghbi-Manrique-de-Lara, P. 2010. Employee deviance as a response to injustice and task-related discontent. *The Psychologist-Manager Journal*, 13(3), 131–146.

5

IMPACT OF DARK SIDE BEHAVIORS ON THE WORKPLACE

Introduction

Incivility, dysfunctional and deviant behaviors exist in some form in most organizations, whether they are for-profit or non-profit organizations. These behaviors have a cost, whether direct or indirect, for the organization, the target or the employees, and customers served by the organization. While these behaviors may start out as unintentional, they will still have a cost and impact for others. As the behaviors escalate, we find the impact and costs escalating significantly. In regards to impact, the targets and employees who are bystanders may experience psychological pain, emotional abuse, physical symptoms and financial impacts. The organization is also impacted by the direct and indirect costs incurred.

The ramifications of these behaviors affect both the individual and the organization. Table 5.1 provides a high-level overview of some examples of impact that can be experienced by individuals and the organization. This chapter will review these in further detail.

TABLE 5.1 Individual and organizational impact (Roter, 2017)

Individual Impact	Organizational Impact
Physical illness	Increased staff turnover
Psychological symptoms	Absenteeism
Social and professional isolation	Decreased commitment to the organization
Anxiety	Decreased productivity
Insomnia/sleep disturbances	Impact on civil rights in the workplace/lawsuits
PTSD	Reputation of the workplace

Impact on individuals

This section will explore the impact on individuals. These individuals may include the target of the behavior as well as the bystanders. Many infer that the abuse is focused on the target only, but the abuse can be far-reaching, impacting many individuals indirectly as bystanders and witnesses to the abuse. They also suffer from these behaviors. This section will explore the impact and costs to both targets and bystanders.

The impact on individuals who are the targets of incivility, dysfunction or deviant behaviors include psychological, physical and financial concerns. Individual impact affects the target as well as bystanders, which will ultimately impact the organization as a whole as well. The following sections will discuss both the emotional and physical impact of darkside behaviors in the workplace.

Psychological distress

All of the behaviors discussed so far in the book will elicit some form of reaction from the target. The reaction may be psychological manifestations which can surface in the form of fear, anxiety, anger, sadness and depression (Roter, 2017), to name a few. The stress that is caused by these negative interactions will eventually present themselves in some form. The following discusses the psychological manifestations.

Work and family conflict: Targets exposed to dysfunctional leadership experience an increase in work, relational and family conflicts. As a target is exposed to negative behaviors, relationships with peers, family members, friends and associates begin to suffer, as targets are either isolated by the perpetrator or begin to socially withdraw from the situation in order to protect themselves. In other cases, the target may seek to speak to others and may repeatedly share the situation, become obsessive about the problem and over-analyze the topic; as a result, other individuals may begin to resent these conversations. Friends or family may begin to pull away from the target for fear of being consumed in conversations about the situation. Family members or friends may struggle with trying to understand the situation or how to help. They may become resentful as the target obsesses over what is happening so much that they forget to ask others how they are doing. Nothing matters to the target but their situation. In other cases, the target may leave work and take their frustrations out on family members or friends through depression, anger, withdrawal or abusive behaviors. Conversations are focused on what is happening to them, and the needs of others are not addressed as the target is consumed by nothing else. As the target suffers from emotional distress, they may begin to withdraw from social and family obligations. They will begin to feel friends distancing themselves from them or tuning them out. As a result, distance forms between friends and family, all the while perpetuating the negative feelings experienced by the target, who feels as though they are suffering in silence or alone.

Depression: Targets of dark behaviors in the workplace often experience feelings of helplessness or depression. They often feel alone, stuck in a situation they can't escape, and they believe that no one can understand what it is they are going through. They used to love their work or career and now they dread going into work and feel stuck. They look for ways to remove themselves from an abusive situation, first by taking time off, then by looking for ways to transfer out of the department or unit, and if that is not an option, by beginning to look for employment outside of the organization. However, in some cases the depression can be so severe that they experience feelings of worthlessness, hopelessness and feel unable to leave the abusive situation. As a result, they stay and endure the negative situation. As their work lives become dark, so too does their personal and family life. If left untreated, the target may find negative coping techniques to deal with the depression. These negative coping mechanisms include self-medication, over- or under-eating, abuse of drugs and/or alcohol, self-harm and, in some situations, contemplation of suicide. For some, death is believed to be the only option for escape and a form of relief from a difficult situation. Through my research, I have spoken to several people who shared stories of contemplating suicide as they believed this was the only way that they could escape the situation. For some, suicide feels like the only option that will release them from the physical and emotional pain they are experiencing. They did not think they can find another job and believe the emotional abuse used is warranted by their attackers.

One person I spoke to fantasized about their death during their commute home on a busy expressway. They thought of what it would be like to drive their car into a concrete barrier at a high speed. He would often find his mind wandering into this escape and find himself speeding along the expressway. One day he was upset after being verbally humiliated at work; the attacks were relentless. While driving home, his mind wandered to what life would be like without this pain he felt. He started with thoughts of killing himself and found himself driving recklessly at high speeds. After a near miss that involved another driver, he stopped his car and realized that he was not just endangering himself, but innocent people as well. He went home and spoke to his wife about his thoughts. She encouraged him to get help and to quit his job. He admits that his thoughts were an escape when he did not want to focus on the humiliation and the pain; focusing on death was a relief for him.

Anxiety: Another form of emotional distress experienced by targets is anxiety. Anxiety is associated with focusing on things that have happened in the past or focusing on the future. The target is not present in the moment and becomes fearful of future interactions with the other person. They live in constant fear of what will happen and when the next attack will take place. They become anxious in their work environment and question their own competence and decision making. Some explain the anxiety as waiting for a bomb to explode: "You know it is going to explode. It is not a matter of if, it is a matter of when, and wondering if today will be the day." Others say they feel as though they are walking on eggshells in the workplace, fearing when they might do something that will set the other person off. At times when nothing happens, the target may let their guard down, only to be caught in the crosshairs of the next attack. The target becomes anxious when they see the person causing harm, or when they anticipate or think about the next time they will have to meet with that person. This anxiety permeates all levels of the target's life, interrupting sleep, entering into waking thoughts and creating worries about what the next day holds for them. They prepare for what they will say in the future and visualize standing up to that person.

In terms of focusing on the past, the target will fixate on events that have happened. They will replay the events in their heads over and over again, thinking about what they should have said or done, dissecting the interaction to determine what they did to deserve this attack. They will be confused and frustrated, thinking of ways to react if it happens again. They will think that they should have said something, or beat themselves up for not being more assertive or standing up to the dysfunctional person.

Humiliation: Targets often experience humiliation because of attacks related to dark behaviors in the workplace. Forms of humiliation include feeling diminished or belittled, being the subject of gossip or repeated unfair criticisms. Personal attacks in the form of accusations of incompetence, finger-pointing or purposefully not being given time to prepare for last-minute meetings can also occur. As individuals experience humiliation, they feel the need to go back and do damage control to prove the attacker wrong. As the humiliation continues, the target gets tired of doing damage control and just gives up.

Isolation or avoidance: Targets will experience some form of isolation or avoidance when dealing with negative behaviors in the workplace. Isolation may be self-imposed, where the target intentionally distances themselves from the person causing harm, or from people overall, as they withdraw into a protective mode. The target may become paranoid and start to question who they can trust and they may sever ties with people they work with. As a form of self-preservation, the target will often attempt to avoid or isolate themselves from the person causing the harm. They may also avoid associates of the dysfunctional person to protect themselves from any negative attacks or sharing of information. Targets often feel humiliated, embarrassed by the attacks and choose to keep to themselves as much as possible. They begin to build emotional barriers as they stop trusting the people they work or interact with. The target begins to shut down, and will stop contributing in meetings; creativity diminishes and the person does not speak up for fear their ideas will be attacked. When the culture is dysfunctional, individuals will often say they keep to themselves, keep a low profile and stay out of the way of the dysfunction. When dysfunction within an organization exists, individuals will isolate themselves and the culture will change from one of trust to one of mistrust and suspicion.

Loss of control: When subjecting a target to dark side behaviors in the workplace, the goal of the person is to control their target. Slowly the target begins to feel as though every aspect of their life is out of control. In a sense, they do begin to lose control. First, they lose control over their work life. Emotionally and/or physically, they begin to lose control over their health. They feel as though they are unable to control any aspect of their work life and eventually their personal life. The target begins to feel as though they are spinning out of control. The dysfunctional individual begins to control the target's work through overload of work, sabotage, blocking, hoarding resources, etc. Eventually, the target is unable to effectively perform their job. As their work life begins to spiral, they feel that, overall, their professional life is out of control. They start to question their professional career choice. Individuals who experience dysfunction might say, "Maybe I should have chosen a different profession?" or "This is not what I signed up for." Within healthcare, there are approximately 500,000 licensed registered nurses who have left the profession because of issues of lateral violence or bullying in the workplace. As the target's work and professional life begins to spiral, their personal life may also become out of control. Personal relationships are eroded and, because of increased depression, anxiety and isolation, the target begins to distance themselves from social events and relationships. Because of the constant strain, targets begin to doubt themselves, their abilities, their relationships and their lives. Targets may choose to gain control by standing up to the dysfunction, addressing the behavior with those higher-up or eventually just removing themselves from the situation.

Post-traumatic stress disorder: Post-traumatic stress disorder (PTSD) is common in targets of dark behaviors. After the situation has been eliminated or alleviated, targets often suffer for months, if not years, from the after-effects of recalling the incident. Targets continue to suffer from anxiety, nightmares and fears as they may relive the trauma. They will question what happened, why it happened, what role they played in the events and how they could have prevented or stopped it. Emotional issues, if left unresolved, can morph into anger, resentment and bitterness. For years after the events, targets often refer back to the incident, discussing the injustice, unfair treatment and feeling of being singled out. Feelings of humiliation, shame and depression bubble up to the surface as well. Leymann (1990) explained that PTSD associated with dysfunctional behaviors in the workplace was actually more traumatic than the suffering of train engineers who had witnessed people jumping in front of trains.

Self-harming behaviors: Targets of dysfunctional behaviors may turn to negative coping mechanisms, including self-harming behaviors. Individuals report increased use of alcohol, recreational and prescription drugs, abuse of food, cutting and hair pulling. Other destructive coping mechanisms include overspending, gambling and physical abuse to others, along with sexual promiscuity.

Table 5.2 shows additional psychological issues related to targets of dysfunctional behavior in the workplace.

TABLE 5.2 Psychological distress (Roter, 2017)

Forgetfulness/confusion and inability to concentrate	Disturbance in sleep patterns: loss of sleep, nightmares and physical and emotional fatigue	Agitation, irritableness
Indecisiveness and inability to solve problems	Mood swings, including uncontrollable crying spells, outbursts of anger, resentment	Panic attacks
Obsessive thinking or worrying about the future	Feelings of worthlessness	Shame, guilt, embarrassment
Feelings of incompetence	Feelings of fear/anger/grief/sadness/shock/rage	Inability to function properly
Feeling diminished		

Physical distress

There is a correlation between stress and the manifestation of physical symptoms. Targets of dark behaviors in the workplace often suffer from some level of physical distress. The frequency and severity of this will depend on the individual and how they deal with stress. Some individuals will report minor physical distress such as headaches, nausea and mild flu-like symptoms. Others may experience more debilitating effects. Based on my research, one person experienced paralysis; they woke up one morning unable to move. There was no physical reason why the individual suffered paralysis and doctors explained that it was stress. Once the individual applied for short-term disability leave from her dysfunctional work situation, she became healthy again. When she returned to work and was confronted by the stress of the negative behaviors, the symptoms returned. Another individual reported smelling phantom smells such as burning. In the stressful work situation she would experience smells of burning leaves and often thought there was a fire in the vicinity. At first she became so panicked that she thought there was a fire in her home and called the fire department. She shared that she drove her family "crazy" and the next time this happened they told her nothing was burning. When she went to the doctor, she went through a series of tests to rule out health issues. Eventually she was asked to see a neurologist, who performed a CT scan. Since the smell of burning is often an indicator of a severe physical issue, she was hospitalized, fearing seizures or a potential stroke. While in the hospital she did not experience these symptoms, until the discussion turned to the work she did; she then started to smell smoke. On the final day of being hospitalized, the patient's physician told her that it might be in her best interest to quit her job, since they could not find any neurological reason for the phantom smells. The patient did leave the organization, and approximately three months later the smells disappeared. However, to this day, when the target visits or talks to someone about what happened within that organization, the burning smells will manifest.

The most common physical distress reported by targets is gastrointestinal issues: many suffer from weight loss or gain from the experience. Frequent complaints include headaches, which range from tension headaches to migraines and cluster headaches. Cardiovascular symptoms may also arise when exposed to darkside behaviors for long periods of time, including hypertension, heart attacks, irregular heart rates and other cardiovascular symptoms. In addition, because of the stress caused by these events, targets may experience a compromised immune system, leading to increased frequency in colds and flu, and susceptibility to autoimmune symptoms.

Table 5.3 shows other physical symptoms that may manifest during dysfunctional experiences in the workplace. This list is not exhaustive, but it does give further insights into physical symptoms.

Financial and economic impact

In addition to physical and emotional impact, targets can begin to struggle with financial issues. As the target experiences increased issues related to emotional or physical distress, they will increase their time off. At first the employee will exhaust their sick days, then their vacation days and when their allotted days are depleted they will begin to take time off without pay. In other cases, employees may begin to use short-term disability once all their vacation and sick days are depleted. Eventually, they will use long-term disability at a decreased percentage of their pay. As employees take time off, they run the risk of neglecting work and decreasing productivity. Because of increased absenteeism, employees may be put on disciplinary actions that can affect salary increases or bonus payouts. As employees run out of options for time off and experience a decrease in pay, they may leave their organization without having another job in place, or they may accept another job with lower pay just to escape the situation. In some cases, targets have reported that they have left their organizations without another job and used their retirement or children's educational savings to supplement their loss in income. In addition to loss

TABLE 5.3 Physical distress (Roter, 2017)

Shakes/tremors	Sweating and chills: Flu-like symptoms	Dizziness/lightheadedness
Rapid heartbeat, palpitations, chest pains	Rapid breathing/ shortness of breath	Increased blood pressure
Body and muscle aches	Paralysis or numbness in body parts	Insomnia
Self-inflicting harm including drug use, abuse of alcohol, overspending, cutting, self-mutilation	Neurological issues	Autoimmune symptoms
Increased allergies/asthma	Hair loss	Weight loss or weight gain
Increase in hormone fluctuations	Issues with fertility	Rashes/hives

of wages, employees may face loss of health insurance coverage and/or increased medical bills, and they will have no way to pay these bills off. In the case of illness, and depending on the extent of the illness they suffer from, employees may never be able to return to work due to PTSD, extenuating physical ailments or emotional issues. When employees are terminated, they may face issues whereby the employer disputes claims for unemployment insurance and they may suffer further financial loss (Roter, 2017).

Ruined careers

Ultimately, for some individuals, the mistreatment they receive prompts them to leave their professions entirely. One physician I spoke to, who had endured a dysfunctional environment and incivility on a daily basis, said that many times he had dreamed of being a long-haul truck driver. He said he was tired of dealing and interacting with people who were dysfunctional, backstabbing and uncivil. He just wanted to get behind the wheel of a truck and drive. I asked him why he would give up his talent and years of training to be a physician. He said it was not what he signed up for. Early on, as a resident, he endured hazing, long working hours and bullying from other physicians and nurses. He accepted this behavior as a rite of passage and thought that one day he would be out of the hazing process. But he came to realize that no matter how good he was, no matter how many patients he saw or lives he saved, the behavior would continue. Ultimately, this physician retired at the age of 55 and did not become a truck driver, but he sold all his belongings and he and his wife bought a recreational vehicle as their new home and traveled around the country. He now picks up odd jobs for additional spending money. He and his wife live out of their RV and he has given up the career he loved.

Clive Boddy (2012) shared that, through dark workplaces, individuals become stalled in their careers; their lives become disrupted through job switching and unemployment. In other cases, individuals have no choice but to leave their careers because they find that they have been ruined by rumors and gossip they cannot overcome. These individuals are forced to find work in another industry because they have been wrongly accused or blocked. Many people have contacted me over the years to let me know that they have left their chosen profession because they have been wrongly labeled by their dysfunctional co-worker or leader. They are unable to find employment in their chosen careers. Boddy (2012) goes on to explain that, because of dysfunction in the workplace, the resourceful now become hesitant, the confident become doubtful, and the effective become ineffective. As a result, it can be a challenge for employees to come back when exposed to dark work behaviors.

Bystanders

We have discussed so far the target of the incivility, dysfunction and deviant behaviors. However, there is another group that suffers from this behavior: the bystanders, or the people who are witnessing the dysfunction. While perhaps not in the direct line of fire, these individuals witness what is happening and may have mixed feelings. In some cases, they may be asked to participate in the dysfunction. Bystanders may participate, not seeing the harm in the behaviors or perhaps out of peer pressure. They may participate in the dysfunction for fear that if they do not they may be the next target. Many bystanders report witnessing dysfunction in the workplace and feeling guilt or shame. When pulled into the dysfunction, many bystanders have stated that they were ashamed of their behavior, yet they did not know what else to do. Others report feeling helpless as they want to provide assistance but are afraid or do not understand what is happening.

Organizational impact

Incivility, dysfunctional behaviors and deviant behaviors have negative impacts on the organization. These dark behaviors can work against the organizational culture, norms and values. Abuse and dysfunction in the organization can leave organizations damaged and struggling to recoup for many years.

Moore and Lynch (2007) found that organizations exposed to darkside behaviors experienced work cultures that were autocratic, bureaucratic and hands off. Of course, organizations that were not exposed to darkside behaviors found work environments to be friendly, supportive, creative, innovative and productive. Darkside behaviors may influence many different levels within the organization. From the frontline staff to the executive office, darkside behaviors are embedded into the organization and can be difficult to remove from the culture. These behaviors impact several areas of the organization including staff turnover, lost time, creativity, production, etc. Table 5.4 demonstrates some of the behaviors experienced within organizations as a result of uncivil and dysfunctional behaviors in the workplace.

Organizational costs

Healthy organizations demonstrate signs of well-being and focus improvement towards their employees, which allows the employees to feel valued and respected. Healthy organizations have a culture that embraces, respects their employees and focuses on developing and promoting civility, respect and mutual trust. Within unhealthy organizations, employees experience cultures that impede creativity, trust and respectful interactions. Instead of focusing on the needs of the organization and the customers they serve, the focus is on the needs of individuals and their own personal agendas.

While most costs of incivility remain hidden and present psychological damage to the targets, they can affect organizations in extreme ways. A *Harvard Business Review* study found that 48% of targets of incivility decreased their work effort, 78% reported a decline in their commitment to the organization, 12% left their job and 25% took their frustration out on customers (Porath, 2013). Another recent study shows that 75% of the sample of American employees

TABLE 5.4 Impact of dark behaviors (Roter, 2017)

Avoidance	Ostracism	Increase in gossip or rumors
Withholding important information to complete work	Elimination of proactive behaviors	Lost time/lost productivity
	Behaviors become more reactive	
Employees become less committed to the organization and/or work	Decreased time in the workplace and increase in absenteeism	Reduced psychological safety and willingness to share ideas
Lack of trust	Higher staff turnover rates	Reduced creativity

had experienced some type of incivility in the last five years. This same study goes on to point out that incivility cultivates decreased psychological and physical health, lower job satisfaction, work withdrawal and increased absenteeism, intentions to quit and staff turnover (Giumetti et al., 2016). To build on this point, incivility targets perceive a social rejection that stems from not understanding the intentions of the uncivil treatment that threatens their need for self-esteem, control and meaningful existence. Another interesting point is that top-down incivility has a greater effect on victims than peer-perceived uncivil behavior (Caza & Cortina, 2007). One of my own experiences concerns a manager called Rick, who had his favorites but would not admit it. Whenever there was a team meeting Rick would spend most of his time recognizing his favorites and providing kudos to these people. When someone who was not in Rick's inner circle had something positive to share, they were either ignored or downplayed. The team began to realize that Rick was not even aware of what he was doing. When he spoke to Pat, his favorite, he always pointed out the amazing things he did, even the trivial things that were part of his job. When Ann, another direct report of Rick's, shared that she had received recognition for a project she was working on, Rick just shrugged and said, "That's part of your job, it's expected." Eventually, the team realized that Rick liked certain people and if you were in that group then things were good. They started to believe that if Rick did not care about his team members, why should they care? When budget numbers were down, Rick tried to rally the troops, telling them how great they were as a team and how they would be just fine in a downturn. The team did not believe him and knew that when the time came to make cuts, his favorites would be just fine—the rest, not so much. Rick did not know what the rest of the team was doing and did not really even care. For them, it seemed as though he only cared about what Pat did. That was how the team perceived Rick as a leader, and some on the team stopped caring. Others were angry, frustrated and got to a point where they did not say anything. Why would they, when it was not recognized? Some left the organization or transferred to other areas within the organization.

Regardless of the intentions of negative behaviors, individuals may perceive these acts in a negative light. This perception will ultimately alter their views of the organization as well. The following provides further insights into the organizational costs of incivility and dysfunctional behavior.

Business impact

Decreased financial results: A measureable and tangible result of darkside behaviors is the impact on financial performance, and lack of achievement related to organizational goals and strategic performance. These factors all contribute negatively to the bottom line. Employees experiencing and/or witnessing negative behaviors in the workplace are less inclined to perform at their best, are less productive, experience lost time and opportunity costs, and have an increase in waste and inefficiency (Roter, 2017).

Lack of team synergy: Whether the negative behaviors are coming from organizational leadership or employees, these behaviors can affect team synergy. When the leader is at the root of the negativity, they will often cause chaos and turmoil within the team in order to motivate their agenda. When this happens, the team is at a loss for direction and is disrupted by these behaviors. Organizational disorder within a team causes division and individuals being pitted against one another. The team can become stalled and team members can lose focus on the team's goals and agenda. The synergy needed to move the team forward is also disrupted, as well as its creativity, healthy decision making and open dialogue, causing the team to become stagnant and stale.

Positive and negative conflict: Organizations should encourage healthy conflict. It is through healthy conflict that decisions are made, creativity and innovation flourish and outside-the-box thinking is encouraged. Individuals rightfully tend to want to avoid unhealthy conflict. Because of the negative behavior, employees will want to go with the flow rather than be at the center of the storm. When unhealthy conflict is present, creativity, innovation, productivity and creative thinking stagnate and the organization does not move forward. In addition, concepts of change are extremely difficult to implement with increased resistance. Healthy conflict is replaced with unhealthy conflict, turmoil and chaos.

Low morale: When there is abuse in the workplace or employees feel mistreated in any way, they begin to question the organization. If the organization does not address these behaviors and allows them to continue, employees will question the values and norms of the organization. As a result, morale drops and employees become less engaged and satisfied with their work. In addition, employees begin to disengage from the mission and vision of the organization for allowing these behaviors to continue.

Lost time: The amount of time that is spent discussing incivility and dysfunction is high. In addition, there is the time spent addressing the situations with personnel, fixing problems of sabotage and, in many cases, the actual time spent on the incivility and dysfunction—for example, the time spent gossiping about or sabotaging another person. All of this is time away from work. The following provides further examples of lost time that occur through darkside behaviors:

1. Increased absenteeism as employees who are caught up in the negative behavior experience either physical or emotional distress.
2. Time spent by employees gossiping, spreading rumors or discussing the situation and not focusing on the work that needs to be done.
3. Lost time for leadership or the organization in addressing or investigating the situation.
4. Lost opportunity costs because of sabotage, or not focusing on the work but on the negative situation.

Staff turnover costs: With negative behavior comes the cost of turnover as employees begin to give up, and look for work elsewhere. The turnover may be to another department, which means the employees are retained in the organization. However, there are still the costs of filling the position the employee has transferred to and the back costs to fill their previous position. In other cases, the employee leaves the organization completely. In that case, there are the costs associated with filling the position, overtime costs for employees who have to fill in for the lost employee and other lost opportunity costs. Other hidden costs include recruitment costs, orientation of new employees, training costs and decreased morale, to name a few.

Impact on organizational culture: Darkside behaviors play a role in changing the organizational culture. When examining organizational culture, we can focus on the values, norms and behaviors of the organization. Incivility and dysfunctional behavior can permeate many different levels within the organization. As the behavior seeps into these levels, the culture starts to morph and can quickly shift from a healthy culture to an unhealthy one.

When organizations are faced with darkside behaviors in the workplace, most organizations struggle with understanding how to address or change the behaviors of the individual(s) involved. Organizations often struggle with how to address the culture of the organization and whether the culture is conducive to providing an environment that allows these dysfunctional behaviors to thrive. Research indicates that dysfunctional workplace cultures provide a breeding ground for employees to openly display their negative behavior. Ways in which organizations contribute to this type of negativity include stressful environments, uncertain or ambiguous roles and a sense of inequity in treatment or injustice. Typically, organizations will use cultural surveys to gauge the environment and culture of the organization. If used properly, these surveys can provide a wealth of data. However, if the organization or certain departments within it are dysfunctional, these types of cultural surveys can be ineffective. For example, managers may "suggest" that employees rate the department high so they are not pointed out as having problems. If employees rate the manager or department low and indicate that there are issues, then the manager focuses their efforts on trying to figure out who has made these comments and will have conversations with employees that are less than comfortable. At times, individuals are sought out who may have rated the manager or department low, or the whole department may be looked at. As a result, in most cases, the next time the culture surveys come around, employees will rate the department as highly functioning, as they do not want to be singled out by the organization. This type of behavior only increases the disconnect between the employees, the manager and the organization, since the full picture of what is happening is not being discussed. Van Fleet and Griffin (2006, 669) defined a dysfunctional workplace culture as one that "constrains or limits individuals—and group level performance often resulting in dysfunctional behaviors". Some indicators of a dysfunctional culture include:

- Increased staff turnover.
- High levels of stress and burnout.
- Lack of trust and safety.
- Apprehension towards change, innovation or new initiatives that can further the department or organization.
- New ideas being discouraged and people ceasing to bring ideas forward for fear of what will happen.
- Groupthink.
- Low participation in company events.
- Increased health issues and increased absenteeism.

Managers typically take a hands-off approach when it comes to low levels of workplace aggression or conflict. Typically, leadership relies on Human Resources to address the conflicts. As a result, uncivil workplace acts are considered difficult to address, especially a sarcastic word or an eye roll, which can be hard to call a person out on. Employees who are the targets of these types of acts may have a difficult time expressing what they are feeling or dealing with. However, the feelings associated with these acts can leave the target feeling abused, psychologically stressed, experiencing a decline in physical health and overall job satisfaction. On the other side, leadership and the organization are left wondering how and whether to address these behaviors.

Financial impact

In many cases, organizations do not know what to do with these types of behaviors. As a result, the organization will pay targets not to discuss these issues and ask them to leave. Meanwhile, the dysfunctional individual stays with the organization; they will be promoted because the organization sees them as a high performer because they are achieving the goals of the organization. While the organization believes that sweeping these behaviors under the rug and paying employees off will solve the problem, we find the moral and ethical fiber of the organization begins to slowly diminish as bystanders watch the dysfunctional individual rewarded, the target dismissed, and the bystanders are left questioning the ethics of the organization. Slowly they move into their own self-preservation mode by cutting back hours, becoming less engaged in the organization and often acting out towards others, resulting in a dark culture that is difficult to repair. Employees start to question the values of the organization, wondering, if this type of behavior is acceptable, then what other behavior is accepted in the workplace?

Costs that cannot be quantified

It is often challenging to quantify the costs associated with incivility, dysfunction or deviant behaviors in the workplace. Since it is such a challenge, one needs to take a step back and not look at the dollars and cents but instead at the emotional and physical toll this behavior takes on others. With each negative interaction that takes place, there is an increase in the stress level of the target, resulting in a decline in their ability to perform at full focus and thus impacting organizational performance. While incivility such as an eye roll might seem harmless at the time, there is still an emotional trigger for the target. Time is spent wondering:

- What did I say or do to trigger that response?
- Why does that person not like me?
- Am I incompetent or inadequate?
- What did I do or say to offend them?
- Should I apologize? Approach them? Ignore them? How do I handle the situation?
- If I ignore the behavior, will it stop?
- Do I need to set boundaries, and if I do, what will happen?

This type of behavior leaves self-doubt in the target's mind, along with feelings of inadequacy. As the behavior continues, the employee spends more time thinking about the relationship and less time focused on work. They may talk to others in the organization about what is happening and more people will now be focused on the behavior rather than the tasks that need to be done. Eventually, the person feels demoralized and disengaged and may eventually lash out at others or quit the organization. In some cases, they might not physically quit the organization, but mentally check out and become less engaged in helping the organization reach its strategic goals and objectives. It is difficult to measure the toll that these behaviors may take on individuals and the organization.

The costs associated with the health and psychological impact can be measured through absenteeism and increased health costs. However, the physical and emotional toll can be difficult to quantify. The impact these behaviors have on family members and relationships can also be a challenge to quantify. Finally, the personal costs to a person's life can never be measured.

Conclusion

Incivility, dysfunction and deviance cost both the organization and the target. For the organization, there are consequences to these types of behaviors that affect the bottom line negatively. Pearson and Porath (2009) have stated that the monetary costs to employers are in the millions of dollars. In addition, organizations face issues such as loss of productivity, creativity, innovation, employee loyalty and energy. While the organization suffers, the target suffers as well through emotional, physical and financial distress. It is important for organizations to address these issues and to identify how to properly address these behaviors.

References

Boddy, C. 2012. *Bullying and corporate psychopaths at work: Clive Boddy at TEDxHanzeUniversity*. TED Talk.

Caza, B.B. & Cortina, L.M. 2007. From insult to injury: Explaining the impact of incivility. *Basic and Applied Social Psychology*, 29(4), 335–350.

Giumetti, G.W., Saunders, L.A., Brunette, J.P., DiFrancesco, F.M., & Graham, P.G. 2016. Linking cyber incivility with job performance through job satisfaction: The buffering role of positive affect. *Psi Chi Journal of Psychological Research*, 21(4) 230–240.

Leymann, H. 1990. Mobbing and psychological terror at workplaces. *Violence and Victims*, 5, 119–126.

Moore, M. & Lynch, J. 2007. Leadership, working environment and workplace bullying. *International Journal of Organization Theory and Behavior*, 10(1), 95–118.

Pearson, C. & Porath, C. 2009. *The cost of bad behavior: How incivility is damaging your business and what to do about*. New York: Portfolio.

Porath, C. 2013. *The price of incivility*. Harvard Business Review, 91(1–2), 114–121.

Roter, A. 2017. *Understanding and recognizing dysfunctional leadership. The impact of dysfunctional leadership on organizations and followers*. London: Routledge, Gower Publishing.

Van Fleet, D. & Griffin, R. 2006. Dysfunctional organization culture: The role of leadership in motivating dysfunctional work behaviors. *Journal of Managerial Psychology*, 21(8), 698–708.

6

WAYS TO ADDRESS THE DARK SIDE

We have explored the different types of uncivil, dysfunctional and deviant behaviors that we can run across in the workplace. In addition, we have explored the impact of this type of behavior on the organization as well as the individual, which can be costly in relation to health, profits, organizational systems, etc. Even with an understanding of the costs of these types of behaviors, organizations and individuals struggle with finding effective ways to address this type of behavior in the workplace. In this chapter, we will explore ways that individuals and organizations can address these behaviors; however, it is important to mention that, while these ideas make sense in theory, applying these concepts can be challenging and difficult for even the most expert individual.

Organizations need to take a proactive approach to combating workplace incivility; this begins even before employees are hired. It is important to address these behaviors from both an organizational and individual standpoint. There are challenges related to identifying and properly addressing these types of behaviors. Once identified, it is often easier for organizations to ignore these behaviors and hope the problem will go away or resolve itself on its own. This is especially true when the behavior begins as a minor incivility such as idle gossip or rude behavior. Most of the time, the goal of organizations is that employees will resolve these behaviors on their own, but in many cases these behaviors will continue, fester, and often escalate into further dysfunction and/or possible deviant behavior.

Addressing dark behaviors in the organization

Early screening

Ideally, organizations want to identify these problem behaviors before the employee enters the ranks of the organization. When screening and interviewing potential employees, organizations look at the tactical qualifications of candidates. Identifying the behaviors of a candidate can be difficult. Having the ability to identify key characteristics, traits and behaviors early on, prior to interviewing candidates for the position, is the first step. Porath (2016) suggests using structured, behavior-based interview questions and completing in-depth reference checks to help prevent incivility or dysfunction from entering the workplace.

The challenge with in-depth reference checking is multi-fold. When listing references, individuals will list the best people they can think of who will give glowing recommendations. These individuals will be friends or co-workers and the relationship will be a positive one. Nobody is going to put down a person who could potentially provide a negative reference. In some instances, people have made up references using cell phone numbers for friends who have not even worked with the candidate and who will provide a positive reference. Actual references more than likely will not share negative information about the employee because of potential liability issues. In some cases, references provide only short answers that verify the employee's work history, including the dates of the start and end of employment. Information is limited.

It is the job of the person doing the reference checking to spend time with the reference. Many times this task is assigned to a recruiter who has to complete several different calls and is focused on completing the task and getting someone hired. When checking references, listen for cues that something is not right, including tone of voice, hesitation, quick or short responses and non-committal comments. While this is not a sure-fire way to recognize if there is an issue, these are subtle cues that something could be wrong. Some organizations will conduct checks into a person's background that might provide clues as well. Off-record reference checking is often used, where people are contacted outside of the listed references. It is important to inform the candidate that this is being done, but it can provide insights, especially if there is an informal network of individuals to turn to. Through the use of social media and websites such as LinkedIn, we are able to identify individuals who are connected with the candidate, with whom we may also be connected. This person may or may not be able to provide further insights into the candidate.

While reference checking is one way to gain insights into a person's background and behaviors, it is not foolproof. Resume checking is another point of data that can provide information regarding a candidate. If a candidate seems too good to be true, more than likely this is a red flag. Explore any questions you might find on the resume with the candidate and their references to get answers. Listen to the wording that is used. Narcissists and psychopaths will embellish their resume and will highlight themselves as being the superstar or the person who has saved the organization. Look for wording that might be concerning. Establish a pattern in their work history and movement. If the candidate is someone who should be brought in for an interview, follow up with them in regards to the questions about their resume and work history.

When bringing a candidate in for an interview, be sure to ask questions that focus on their skills and abilities as well as their behaviors. Ask behavior-based questions that help to establish behaviors and trends. When asking behavior-based questions, it is okay to ask for negative examples. For example, "Tell me about a time when you had a conflict with another person on the team that did not go well. What happened and how did you address it?" This type of question can help to establish how the candidate deals with conflict. Follow up later with probing questions on conflict to see how the person addresses this. This approach may help to establish or define a pattern of behavior. Ask for specifics and further details. If the details or specifics are vague, continue to probe for further details and information. It is important to note that psychopaths and narcissists will be adept at interviewing and will sell themselves effectively. Again, if the candidate seems too good to be true, don't be afraid to investigate further. If they are good at what they do, then you will be happy you landed this strong candidate. However, if they are too good to be true, then you will also be happy not to have brought them into your organization. The challenge is educating others on the interview committee on red flags that might come up. Many individuals will look at the resume and be sold right away. Education about the need to do one's due diligence when hiring is important to the success of landing a strong employee.

While these approaches are helpful for identifying potential problems, they are not foolproof. Someone who is quite good at selling themselves will also be good at masking their dysfunctional behaviors. These people will slip through the process and find their way into organizations. It is inevitable, but it is important to try to stop them from even entering the organization. The key is to be able to address these behaviors early on in the process.

Onboarding new employees

It is important to educate an employee during the first three months of them starting with the organization, about the organizational values, norms and goals. Use these components in interview questions when interviewing a candidate. During the onboarding process, it is critical to address the values and behaviors of the organization. Focus on the vision, mission and values of the organization. Organizations should have clearly defined norms, behaviors and codes of conduct in place. During the onboarding process is the time to reiterate these behaviors to new employees. For example, some organizations have established a zero-tolerance rule against bullying and/or harassment in the workplace. In healthcare, the Joint Commission (2008) mandated that healthcare organizations have policies in place that address disruptive behaviors. By reiterating this information to candidates, employers are able to identify and address what are acceptable and unacceptable behaviors. Having employees sign a code of conduct is another way that organizations can address dark behaviors. This code can be used to hold employees accountable for negative behaviors in the workplace.

Once employees have been onboarded, provide them with the necessary tools to be successful in dealing with dark behaviors, including training them on how to work with difficult co-workers (Porath, 2016). Research supports the idea that it is important to take action before a formal complaint has been filed (Sidle, 2009). Training courses and clear codes of conduct can lead to a reduction in uncivil behavior (Sidle, 2009). Carefully designed orientation programs introducing and defining the "organization's structures, systems and cultures" can help newcomers experience autonomy and identity within the organization (Reio & Ghosh, 2009).

Once uncivil, dysfunctional or deviant behavior has been detected, employers tend to follow a progression of disciplinary actions, starting with minor conversations about the occurrence and intensifying the severity as the discipline progresses (Irani Williams, et al., 2013). The problem with many workplaces and institutions is that they do not have policies in place that address or hold individuals accountable for negative behaviors (Marchiondo et al., 2010). Irani Williams et al. (2013) suggested the organizations may attempt to implement solutions to address dark behavior ranging from supervisors finding different assignments for the person, enlisting allies, transferring individuals to other areas in the organization, ignoring the problem or even suggesting that employees seek alternative employment elsewhere. The researchers determined that the outcomes of these solutions were often inconsistent and there is not one strategy that can work for all situations.

Some employers who choose to confront uncivil behaviors head on often feel as if their efforts can further fuel the dysfunction, and only 15% report being satisfied with the outcome (Porath, 2016). Porath also suggests that employers use a holistic approach, focusing on improving behaviors the can be changed rather than changing the wrong doer's behaviors. She also advocates that creating positive relationships and helping employees find value and purpose in the work will help to offset the feelings of dark behaviors in the workplace.

Educating organizations

Now that we understand the impact of the dark side of the workplace, it is critical to understand how organizations can educate themselves to address these behaviors. Organizations need to pay attention to small acts of rudeness, derision and ostracism (Caza & Cortina, 2007). When an organizational environment becomes dysfunctional, leaders need to be able to make difficult decisions and have tough discussions with the individuals displaying these types of behaviors. At the end of the day, the conflict needs to be addressed quickly and effectively. This requires organizations to create a culture of respect and one where people feel safe to speak up about conflict, incivility, dysfunction and deviance. If employees are unable to speak up or address these behaviors, the organization will face increased issues related to dark behaviors, including lack of mutual trust, decreased psychological safety and issues related to lost productivity and creativity, all while experiencing an increase in the dark behaviors. Leadership needs to be open to listening to and addressing these issues. When the leader is the one causing the conflict, employees need to know there are resources available to them, such as Human Resources and policies and procedures in place to address these issues.

Confronting the dark side

The following section explores further suggestions for how organizations can work to address these behaviors in the workplace. All of these components can build upon each other to help to provide a healthy work culture.

1. **Make sure that the executive team is cohesive:** Ensuring that the executive team is working together and not against each other is important. If individuals within the organization feel or notice that the executive team is not working together, there will be a sense of suspicion as well as lack of trust in the strength of the leadership. Having an executive team that works together, focuses on the goals of the organization and moves in one direction allows for a culture that thrives.

2. **Ensure that the organizational core values are clear:** Ensure that the core values are at the center of what the organization does. Employees who are aware of the core values and are aligned with the behavior will have a sense of buy-in with the organization.

3. **Identify the culture that best aligns with the organization:** The culture of the organization is fluid and it needs to be harnessed. Understanding what the current state of the culture is, along with where the culture wants to go in the future, is key to a healthy organization. Cultures also need to embrace accountability when actions do not align with the desired culture. When hiring employees, focus on developing and managing performance according to the culture and values of the organization.

4. **Have a strong leadership development plan:** Leaders play a role in modeling correct behaviors when dealing with their followers. Teaching leaders to use positive reinforcement and recognition is important for encouraging positive behaviors in employees. Utilization of forms of recognition, appreciation and acknowledgement of acceptable behavior is key to shifting from an uncivil environment to one of civility. Simple things such as a handwritten note thanking an employee for living the values and treating people with respect can go a long way. The leadership development plan that is employed by the organization should align with the strategic vision and culture of the organization. Developing leaders that have the skills to develop a healthy culture is important for providing a culture that is not dysfunctional. In addition, training and education of leadership and employees in how to identify and address incivility is important. It is key to discuss ways to cope with and minimize the impact of dark behaviors (Beattie & Griffin, 2014).

5. **Communication:** Having a strategy that allows for strong communication is important for reducing incivility and other dark behaviors. The organization should define the channels of communication and share information, as well as be transparent in their communication methods. Organizations that hinder their communication and are less than transparent run the risk of the communication channels being driven by rumors and gossip. Ensure that messages and

communications are consistent. This links back to having a cohesive leadership team that shares consistent and clear messages. Communication is not just limited to the distribution of information; it is also focused on actively listening and engaging with the recipients of the messages. What are the reactions from employees? How are they engaged in the process? What are their insights? Providing an avenue through which employees can share their insights and feel as though they are listened to creates trust and strength within the culture.

6. **Educational opportunities:** Leadership development has already been identified, but education regarding employee incivility is another area of exploration for organizations. It seems that, early on in our lives, we are taught to treat people with respect and dignity, but this is not always the case. Some organizations have taken on the task of educating employees about civility and respect in the workplace. In addition, they provide training regarding the etiquette of online communication. Online technology norms and etiquette are not clearly defined to within most organizations. Most online communication may take on the vibe of incivility through the tone of the message. Abrupt, poorly written emails or text messages can signal perceived rudeness or incivility. Online communication training or interventions to educate people on the effects of online incivility are often ignored and as a result are needed in order to build civilized organizations (Giumetti et al., 2016).

7. **Set expectations:** Set expectations within the organization, teams and units that have clearly identified norms and expectations pertaining to behavior. It should be recognized that people will disagree on problems at work, but mutual respect needs to exist in order for the organization to be successful (Porath & Pearson, 2013). Dark behaviors do not just happen by themselves. People come from many different backgrounds and cultures, which can provide a platform for conflict. It is easy to perceive actions in the wrong way and to recognize these behaviors as disrespectful. Setting expectations for all levels of the organization, along with continuous education on the subject of incivility, can bring the awareness that organizations and employees need.

8. **Managing conduct:** Organizations need to assess the climate and culture pertaining to dark behaviors. Appraising, addressing and discussing negative behaviors when they happen, regardless of the hierarchical level, will help to contain the costs and incidents of incivility (Porath & Pearson, 2012).

9. **Promote and reward healthy behaviors:** Saying that an organization does not promote or tolerate negative behaviors is not enough to create a healthy environment. Focusing on positive behaviors, such as effective problem solving and healthy conflict resolution, is key to addressing negativity in the workplace. Encourage healthy behaviors by rewarding and recognizing positive behaviors within the organization and by demonstrating them within top leadership.

10. **Consistently monitor and check behaviors:** Validate positive behavior and address negative behavior quickly. Organizations complete yearly training on

civility, sexual harassment and diversity, yet these programs are only good until a new employee enters the workplace. When a new employee enters the organization, the dynamics within the organization shift. The shift can occur on a team level and then permeate into the organization. As the saying goes, "One bad apple can spoil the bunch." If an employee comes in from an environment where the values and norms were toxic and negative, the new employee can bring these behaviors into their new environment. This may or may not be intentional. Many times, these employees believe this type of behavior is acceptable at other organizations and they might not know anything different. In other cases, they might be the person who caused the dysfunction in the workplace. They may come into the organization and try to test the boundaries and limits. Regardless of the situation, organizations must confront how they will address unhealthy behavior when it happens. If it is noticed that there has been a shift towards a negative dynamic, leadership and employees should address the behavior immediately. Explain to the new employee the values of the organization, what acceptable behavior looks like and the expectations of the organization. Coach the new employee and be sure that other employees recognize that the behaviors are being addressed. Keep in mind that negative behavior may not surface right away and may slowly creep into the organization. Frequent monitoring and checking of the behavior is key to addressing issues as they come up and morph into something substantial.

Interventions

Identifying interventions that can help address dysfunction in the workplace is important for the organization and the individuals working within it. The following provides some recommendations for interventions that can be used by the organization.

Private informal meetings: These types of meetings help leaders/managers gauge how an employee is doing. In cases where the manager knows the people they are working with, they can see signs of distress or changes in personality. By having informal meetings to see how employees are doing, the leader is able to find out if things are bothering an employee either professionally or personally. If a problem related to negative conflict or incivility is brought to the discussion, the leader is able to help coach employees and provide insights into how to address the problem before it escalates. These types of meetings should happen often and should be a platform that can help to address these issues quickly and with minimal interruptions. The leader can also intervene for the employee and help to address the behavior quickly, before it gets out of control.

Be proactive: As leaders, it is important to know your employees and their emotions. Understand when they are energized or de-energized. Relying on the fact that employees are adults and should handle the situation is not enough. In addition, relying on Human Resources to address these issues is not effective either. In cases of incivility, the aggression can be mild and may never get to the full-blown level of needing to call in HR. Regardless, conflict causes negative impacts on an employee and the team. As a leader, you must be proactive in finding out what is happening, so ask questions and listen to the underlying messages to find out what the problem is.

What managers can do to address these behaviors

Previously we have discussed what an organization can do in order to address dark behaviors in the workplace. In addition, we have explored some interventions that can be used by leadership and management. The following section goes into further detail about what can be done to address these behaviors in the workplace, along with addressing these behaviors in managers.

Incivility

For a manager or leader it is important to constantly monitor the environment and the culture of the organization. There are ways to address uncivil behaviors in the workplace before they fester and escalate to higher levels of dysfunctional and deviant behavior.

1. **Self-awareness:** As a leader, be aware of how you are handling your emotions. It is natural to experience stress. However, as a leader or a manager it is important to understand how you handle yourself when you are stressed, busy or preoccupied, as this will set the tone for how your employees address stress as well. Your employees can read these emotions and they will pick up on how you are acting. As a leader, employees are looking to you all the time to see how you address the situations you are experiencing. Focus on your behaviors and reactions to situations.

2. **Model acceptable behavior:** Model the behavior that should be demonstrated in the organization. Many times managers will model the behavior of past or current managers. If their manager was dysfunctional of uncivil to them, they may tend to do the same to their direct reports. Research from Porath and Pearson (2013) found that 25% of managers admitted to behaving poorly because the leaders who were their role models were being uncivil. If employees see rude and disrespectful individuals move up in the organization, they tend to think that this type of behavior is rewarded. When meeting with employees, think about how you want to be treated and look at your own behavior. It is so tempting to check your phone for messages or to be distracted and prepare in your mind for your next meeting, but try to stay present in the conversation and focus on what is being discussed. In addition, appreciate your employees. Recognize them for the work that they do. Be equitable in your recognition: if you recognize one, then also recognize others when they do something. Too often a manager will focus their recognition on one star employee. While

praising that employee is great, after a while the other staff will pick up on the favoritism and start to resent you and that employee.

3. **Ask for feedback from others:** Don't be afraid of feedback. Ask your employees for feedback on what they like and don't like about your leadership style (Porath & Pearson, 2013). Take the comments that they provide you and apply any necessary changes to help you grow as a leader. Ask for feedback from your peers as well and ask what they have observed about your behavior and the way you treat them.

4. **Pay attention to your actions:** Pay attention to how you react to certain circumstances or individuals. What is causing you to react the way you are and what can you do differently to address these reactions? For example, if there is co-worker or direct report you don't like but have to interact with, check how you are feeling before meeting with them. If you are not in a positive place, how can you get yourself there? Remember that this is business and it is not personal. Whatever those negative personal reactions are, hold off on them and focus on what needs to be done for the organization. If you feel as though you are starting to become uncivil, walk away or excuse yourself and come back when you are in a better frame of mind.

5. **Hire people for civility:** This is challenging. When people interview they tend to be on their best behavior. Earlier in the chapter we discussed ways to interview individuals. You can only control your own actions, so look for subtle clues of negativity and ensure that employees can demonstrate the behaviors and norms that the organization embraces. Include others in the hiring process, including team members, peers and others, to get as many perspectives about the employee as you can. If employees come back and say that the potential employee is not a good fit for the team, listen to them. Even if you like that candidate, listen to what employees are saying or what they have observed. The candidate could be putting on a mask when they are talking to you, but with their potential peers they might have let their guard down or asserted themselves in a different way. Consider the role of civility in the hiring process. Many organizations focus on the candidate that looks good on paper and has the skills they need, but look to make sure that the person fits the organization, the culture of the team and the behaviors that the organization is expecting. Just because a person has the skills and looks good on paper does not mean they will have the ability to work with others. Remember that you can train and develop individuals to do the job, but it is challenging to change negative behaviors.

6. **Provide education and coaching:** Provide education on civility to the employees. When you see behaviors that are uncivil, pull the employee aside and address these behaviors in the moment. These can include body cues or tone of voice. Be sure to address the behavior quickly, provide coaching and feedback. Remember, a majority of individuals are not being uncivil intentionally. Many times they are acting this way without even being aware of these behaviors. Give them feedback so they can address the behaviors and make changes. If the behavior continues, address it again.

7. **Create ground rules:** Develop ground rules that the team can refer to in order to hold others accountable for the behavior they are looking to address. By focusing on behaviors and norms, employees will have a level of accountability. Allow team members to refer back to the norms and ground rules so they can address these behaviors early on and create a level of accountability within the team. There is something to be said about the power of peer relationships.

8. **Reward positive behavior:** When you see an employee doing something positive or acting in a positive way, address the behavior. Focus on the positives and focus on what good behavior looks like so that others can demonstrate these behaviors in the workplace as well. Others will be able to refer to that positive behavior as a model for their interactions. Also, initiate a program whereby employees can recognize other employees. As a leader, you can't be everywhere and you may miss good actions. Allowing peers to recognize behavior helps to promote positive interactions. There is one bit of caution to be advised when implementing reward programs: when leadership implements and rewards behaviors, this can be a good thing, but it can also be viewed negatively. Be sure to be equitable in rewarding behavior as focusing on just one person can quickly backfire.

9. **Don't shift people around:** If an employee is hired who is not a good fit, address the situation quickly. Don't opt to move them to another location in the company. In many cases, leaders and managers think the best way to get rid of the problem is to shift them to another area within the organization, but this won't change their behavior, and more than likely, will only make another unit or team negative. Try to coach the employee, but if that does not work, don't be afraid to let them go. At the end of the day, the costs and impact on the organization are too great to keep negative behavior in the workplace.

10. **Exit interviews:** When an employee leaves the organization, be sure to take the time to conduct an exit interview. Find out the real reason that a person is leaving. During exit interviews, employees tend to be more open about the reason they are leaving. If they share that they have experienced a leader or individual who has been uncivil, dysfunctional, unethical or deviant, use this information and address the situation. More than likely you won't get that employee to stay, but you can prevent more employees from leaving the organization if you address the behavior.

Addressing team-level dysfunction

Organizations are based on team environments which should be able to embrace diverse thoughts and concepts. When conflict or dysfunction occurs within a team, the team faces obstacles such as groupthink, a reduction in creativity, lack of cohesive team interactions and a shutdown of positive interactions between team members. Other team impacts may include theft, team sabotage, undermining and anti-social behaviors against other members of the team. The following provides some insights into addressing dysfunction in a team.

1. **Establish team ground rules:** Conflict is inevitable in teams. Positive conflict should be encouraged in order to foster healthy interactions, creativity and a mechanism to move teams forward. Negative conflict, on the other hand, can cause teams to stagnate, promote groupthink, halt productivity and damage relationships within and outside the team. Teams need to establish ground rules early on, in regards to how they will address conflict. In addition, acceptable and unacceptable behavior need to be identified by the team, and the team then needs to discuss how these behaviors will be addressed.

2. **Team accountability:** At the heart of incivility, dysfunction and deviant behaviors lies a lack of accountability. Negative norms of behavior include blame and finger pointing. When accountability measures are in place, there tend to be fewer issues related to blame. To address accountability, it is important to understand the protocols for addressing negative behaviors within the team, the organization, etc. Ask team members to hold themselves and others accountable for behaviors such as bullying, intimidation, rudeness, gossiping and other negative behaviors. By addressing these behaviors early on and linking them back to their established ground rules, the team has a platform through which to hold team members accountable for this type of behavior. The critical component of this is that leadership must support the team in holding others accountable.

In conclusion, educating staff, quickly addressing dark behaviors and carrying it throughout the culture of the organization is critical to the success of dealing with dark behaviors. Depending on the organization's background, implementing these suggestions will help bring a more civilized organization forward and prevent new uncivil behaviors from entering.

Culture of the organization

The culture of the organization plays a critical role in determining how and whether incivility and dysfunctional behavior will be tolerated. Leadership has the power to influence and motivate employees by demonstrating appropriate and inappropriate behavior in the workplace. Scholars have demonstrated a link between aggressive behavior and poor working conditions (Lawrence & Leather, 1999; Roter, 2017). These feelings of negativity and aggression lead to unhealthy and unresolved levels of conflict, which provide a culture that is ripe for dysfunction. Organizational cultures built on strong standards and protocols are needed to address negative behaviors. We have addressed the damaging impact that these behaviors can have on the organization and the individual. By building an organizational culture that promotes a healthy environment while ensuring that the organization provides support to its employees is key to helping to diminish these behaviors (Roter, 2017).

How leadership addresses these behaviors, as well as how they act, sends clear messages to employees. If the leadership team is rude, gossiping and acting in uncivil ways, these behaviors send a very clear message to employees that this is acceptable behavior, and identifies that these behaviors are tolerated in the organization. If the employees see that leadership does not tolerate or participate in these behaviors, then employees are less likely to engage in them too. While not always true, employees will test the boundaries. When they do, it is important to address these behaviors quickly and to provide coaching and/or some form of approach to address the behavior. Building a strong culture is key to minimizing these types of negative behaviors. As discussed previously, having open communication helps to eliminate the need for employees to fill in the gaps of communication with false information and rumors. While one could hope that open communication will completely eliminate negativity in the workplace, the reality of the situation is that these behaviors will still exist. However, being proactive in communications about the organization and what is happening is key to helping to minimize these behaviors. Continue to establish expectations of behaviors that are acceptable in the organization.

Finally, develop a culture that promotes psychological safety. Organizational cultures should strive to build work environments in which employees feel safe to express ideas, learn and speak up when there are issues. Kahn (1990, 705) defined psychological safety as the employee's "sense of being able to show and express one's self without fear of negative consequences to self-image, status or career". Research related to psychological safety indicates that there is a positive correlation between employee work engagement and psychological safety. Research conducted by Edmondson (1999) highlighted psychological safety as a way for employees to express their ideas and take risks without fear of retaliation.

Organizational investigations

Once there has been a report of harassment, abuse or other dark behaviors, it should be immediately investigated. Inaction should not be an option. When sharing information with upper leadership or Human Resources, employees should know that materials (e.g. documentation) related to the report will be kept confidential to an extent that is reasonable. Human Resources should try their best to handle the investigation discreetly, but at some point the complaint will be shared with the person being accused of the negative behavior. This person does have the right to defend themselves and due process should be allowed. While the investigation happens, all parties should be treated with respect. All sides should be heard and facts should be reviewed objectively. If the investigation confirms that misconduct has occurred, then leadership should ideally take appropriate corrective action, which may include discipline, coaching, referrals, and in some cases, termination of employment. Likewise, discipline may also be issued when an employee knowingly makes a false accusation of harassment or lies about someone's standing in the organization.

Removing retaliation in the workplace

Policies in the organization should address uncivil and dysfunctional behavior. In addition, policies should be created that strictly prohibit retaliation of any kind against an employee for making a good-faith report or for participating in the investigation of a complaint. When an investigation occurs, the person making the complaint, the complainant and any witnesses may be asked to share information. It is important that the organization ensure that employees are free from any form of retaliation. Retaliation is defined as a negative action or inaction against a person who has made a complaint in the workplace in good faith. Many people believe retaliation is about someone "getting even" with another person, but it is so much more and it is usually used as a form of intimidation by causing fear and preventing employees from feeling free to speak up. Examples of retaliation include negative behavior such as threatening, intimidation and derailment. Examples of inaction include shunning an employee, not sharing information with another person or isolating them. When a claim is made and then investigated, any adverse action should be reported and addressed as well. Employees should feel empowered to speak up, whether as a target or a bystander witnessing the action. Any issues of retaliation should be addressed and stopped in order to ensure that employees feel safe to speak up.

Individuals dealing with dysfunction and incivility

Introduction

Dealing with dysfunctional behavior in the workplace is a challenge for individuals. When an uncivil or dysfunctional event first takes place, individuals tend to be shocked, confused or may dismiss the behavior as a one-time event. It is human nature to want to find the positive in others and to believe that people come to work with good intentions, which is usually true. Therefore, when these behaviors are first experienced it is easy to write them off as the person just having a bad day; we may give them the benefit of the doubt. The natural inclination is to stay quiet and not say anything, believing this is a rare incident. Often these behaviors are ignored in the hopes that the situation will be resolved as a simple conflict or that, over time, the problem will go away by itself. In other cases, individuals hope their assessment of the negative situation was not accurate and was blown out of proportion.

When a person is first exposed to negative behavior in the workplace, it can happen very subtly, usually through body language such as sighing in frustration, eye rolling or smirking. This type of behavior does not always show itself right away. Employees might catch a glimpse of the behavior and write it off. When left unaddressed, the problem can continue and begin to escalate. At this point, the person noticing the behavior is trapped in a web of dysfunction and it is a challenge to escape.

How to recognize if you are a target

Targets of incivility and dysfunction will often question whether they are truly being attacked. They will first question the behavior and try to make sense of it. Meanwhile, the perpetrator will focus on ensuring their target questions themselves and their competence at all times. Many times, the target will think they are going crazy, but that is a tactic of the dysfunctional or uncivil person. As the events progress, eventually the target will become submissive and start to believe the insults and attacks that are hurled at them, yet they may still struggle to identify if they are truly a target. The following information can be helpful in determining whether or not a person is a target.

1. **Something does not feel right:** At the end of a weekend or extended time off, a feeling of dread starts to creep in. The individual starts to feel depressed and/or physically ill. There is a sense of relief on Friday, Saturday feels good, but Sunday arrives and the feelings of dread begin to creep in. Identify what is not feeling right and determine what is causing these feelings of dread.
2. **Relationships are impacted:** Loved ones and friends complain that the target is obsessing over work or the person attacking them. Conversations are monopolized by the actions or the negative experience of the workplace. No other conversation matters. As a result, the person's relationships begin to suffer and individuals begin to pull away from them.
3. **Escaping:** Vacation and sick days are used as a way to escape the dysfunctional person. They are referred to as "mental health days". If you wake up in the morning dreading the day ahead, that can be normal, but if this is constant and you find yourself using your time off as an escape from people, then there might be an issue.
4. **Emotional pain:** Feelings of depression, isolation and hopelessness take the place of joy and career contentment. The person may have once enjoyed their job or career, only now to hate work, the environment and to think they are trapped.
5. **Feeling at fault:** The target starts to believe they deserve this treatment. They begin to believe that they have done something to aggravate this person, they are incompetent or there is something wrong with them.
6. **Isolation:** The target is socially isolated or ostracized from the workplace, social events or work interactions. Other people avoid the person and work feels lonely.
7. **Exclusion from work decisions:** Decisions about the target's work are made without consulting the target. The target is removed from all decision making related to their work, or they are not given the resources to properly complete their job.
8. **Surprises:** Surprise or last-minute meetings are called to throw the target off and used to humiliate them in front of others.

9. **Criticism:** The target's work is openly criticized. Nothing positive is ever said. The target is constantly told to redo their work and yet it will never be right, no matter how much work is done on the project.
10. **Fear:** The target lives in constant fear, waiting for the next attack.
11. **Blacklisting:** The target is blacklisted and unable to move to other positions within the organization. They are derailed and unable to make a move to get away from the perpetrator.

All of these examples relate to dark behaviors. If you are experiencing any of these feelings, it is important to seek professional assistance to help address the situation.

Why me?

Individuals who have been identified as a target often ask the questions, "Why me?", "Why is this person focusing on me?" or "What am I doing wrong?" There are so many reasons why a perpetrator chooses their target. First, they identify their targets quickly. They have an uncanny knack for scanning a room to identify who they will focus on, and then they make their move. If at any point they feel resistance, they will back off and move on to another target. This resistance may come in the form of a strong personality that the dysfunctional person realizes is too much for even them to handle. In other cases, they may run across a person who is just like them, or the person will not have what they need. The goal is to find someone they feel they can manipulate or control to get their way.

What is crucial during these interactions is for the target to realize that they are not to blame. Power is handed over to the dysfunctional person when their target believes they are incompetent or weak. It is important for the target to realize quickly that it is the perpetrator who is weak and incompetent. Typically when someone hones in on a target, it is someone they are threatened by. It is a person who is competent, respected, successful, well liked by senior leadership or someone the perpetrator feels is going to indirectly threaten their security and stability. The perpetrator is compelled to take over, gain power and quickly take control over the situation.

The worst thing to show a dysfunctional attacker is weakness. Like a shark in the water, they will smell out the weakness or fear of an individual and then go in for the attack. The perpetrator is able to identify signals and behaviors that they will use against the target. The following provides examples of behaviors that the target will focus in on and identify as cues that the person is someone they can go after.

Non-verbals: The easiest cue for a dysfunctional person to assess is body language. Body language may indicate insecurity, lack of confidence or uncertainty. The way a target carries themselves, lack of eye contact, overly expressive body language and nervous laughter can all be signs to the perpetrator that the person is nervous or not feeling confident. The way an individual carries themselves also projects their self-esteem to others. If the target projects confidence in their posture, walk and tone of voice, they will appear off-limits to the perpetrator. If this is the case, dysfunctional individuals will usually steer clear of that person and focus on someone else. Other signs the perpetrator can pick up on include appearing nervous, flushed skin, rapid or shallow breathing, nervous laughter, sweating or tears in the eyes.

Verbals: Voices that appear hesitant or seem uncertain will be viewed as a weakness by the perpetrator. For example, a quiet voice or a rapid or hesitant tone may be an indicator that the target is insecure or lacks confidence. Self-effacing comments like "I can't believe I keep making these stupid mistakes" or "Sometimes, I wonder why they keep me here" are another signal. People who demonstrate a tolerance for being interrupted may indicate a willingness to be controlled. Other signs include appearing flustered in speech, signs of nervousness, stuttering or an inability to effectively communicate thoughts through speech. These types of verbal cues happen to all of us and it can be difficult for individuals to control these behaviors, but once they happen radars can be piqued and the perpetrator will keep an eye on that person to see if a pattern emerges to indicate that they can utilize that person for promoting their agenda.

Secrets and personal information: Don't share secrets or personal information that can be used against you. This is, of course, especially true with the gossiper, but it also applies to each of the dysfunctions we have discussed so far. Individuals in the workplace tend to want to share their personal lives with the people they work with. On an average day, we spend approximately eight hours or more in the workplace and it is easy to want to integrate our personal lives into our work. In addition, human nature tends to focus on the good in people, whether in society or the workplace. We want to believe that people are good and kind, so why not share our lives with the people in the workplace? However, there are people who want the information you share, in order to position themselves and to gain power and control over you. While you might think you are sharing something in confidence, know that there is always the risk that this information could be shared with others, either intentionally or unintentionally.

Boundaries: Dysfunctional individuals want to see how far they can push the limits, and they will push hard. The more they push, tear individuals down, instigate drama, gain control and manipulate, the happier and more confident they become. They feed off the negative reactions they get and these help to build their power base. It is important to set boundaries or limits in regards to these types of individuals. These boundaries need to be set immediately at the first sign of a negative interaction. While it might be easy to want to give them the benefit of the doubt and assume that what happened was a one-time event, this is usually not the case. When the focus is on them, it is all about them. They find having an audience assemble around them to be powerful. Once their platform no longer exists, they will move on. When confronted by a dysfunctional person, turn the attention away from them. Set very clear boundaries and learn techniques to stop the behavior before it starts. For example, if they constantly complain, shift the ownership back to them. Ask them, "What role do you play in this situation?" or "What are your plans to address the situation?" By switching the attention from the negative complaining back to the ownership of the person complaining, they will have to stop and refocus. More than likely they won't do this, but keep up with the questions to divert them back to their ownership of the situation. Finally, if they are not taking ownership, remove yourself from the discussion by excusing yourself from the room or situation. When they start to realize you are not playing along and are no longer entrenched in the situation, they will stop or move on to someone else (Roter, 2017). The best way not to get wrapped up in these situations is simply not to participate. This is easier said than done—we are all human and can get wrapped up in drama from time to time—but the key is to recognize the situation and remove yourself from it as quickly as possible.

The best ways to address the situation

The following provides tips and tricks for addressing a negative situation. They are not always easy and it does take time for some people to fine-tune these skills, but it is important to identify the best ways to address the negative situation in which you find yourself.

- **Know what your values are:** We all have a set of values we live by. Ask yourself what your values are and what is important to you. For example, treating people with respect may be a value. Understanding what you value and what is important to you can help you develop mechanisms to handle these types of situations, as well as to remove yourself from them. Don't compromise your values for the sake of the dysfunction. For example, if a person is a gossiper and this type of interaction makes you uncomfortable, don't compromise your values for the sake of pleasing the other person. Tell the other person you are not comfortable with this behavior and remove yourself from the situation.
- **Communicate clearly:** As mentioned earlier, you should establish your boundaries very clearly. When someone starts to gossip, stop the discussion in its tracks and bring it to the attention of the gossiper. As soon as they start a conversation about someone, stop them. Let them know that you don't want to talk about another person when they are not there to defend themselves. For people who are acting rudely, let them know you are bothered by their behavior and it is not acceptable to you. Communicate these expectations early on and as close to the time of the situation as possible.
- **Don't engage:** I had a co-worker who just did not play nice. We both clashed and we didn't like each other. That is okay, we are not all going to get along in the workplace, but we need to be civil in order to get the work done. She loved to play new-age music loudly in the office. There were times I thought about playing hard-rock channels to drown out her music. Instead, I asked her if she could turn down the music as I was trying to concentrate. She apologized and turned down the music. While I would like to say that worked,

it didn't. The next day the music was louder. Again, I asked her to turn down the music and she did. This continued for the next week. Finally, I closed my door and brought in headphones to cancel out the noise. I knew she had no intention of changing her behavior and, while tempting, I didn't engage. Once she realized it was not bothering me and she couldn't get under my skin, she stopped playing the music. She moved on to other things to irritate me, but I learned to find ways to work around them and eventually she stopped. While still uncivil, she knew she could not get under my skin.

- **Surround yourself with like-minded people:** We attract like-minded people in our lives—for example, positive people seem to gravitate towards other positive people, and negative people towards other negative people. In the world of dysfunction, the dysfunctional person gravitates towards the person who will give them the attention they need and who they perceive to be an easy target. As you work in an organization, you will be able to identify the people you can genuinely trust and the people who hold the same values as you do. Your network will be instrumental to your success. Align yourself with people who want to build you up. You want to network with these people. Some will argue that it is important to be looped into the office grapevine to know what is going on. While being informed is important, recognizing where this information is coming from and what the truth is, is just as important. Negative people tend to gravitate towards each other and feed off one another. They get their energy from other negative individuals and will do what they can to build up their own energy while depleting the energy of others. These people are draining and not worth the time and effort.
- **Don't internalize it:** When people lash out at us, it is natural for us to internalize it or take it personally. It is natural to think of it as a personal attack, a negative action against you or something that is personally connected to you. However, everything the dysfunctional person does is related to their insecurities, and is a reflection of their own faults. They are just projecting their insecurities onto you. It is important to focus on being strong, confident and not giving this person the power over you. Though their actions are directed towards you, they are using them as a weapon to build themselves up. Don't give them the power to build upon this power and continue their attacks. By not handing control over to them, you can keep your own power in order to fight back.
- **Hold others accountable:** For every dysfunction listed in this book, we have identified that these perpetrators don't have accountability or responsibility for their actions. Everything bad that happens to these individuals is never their responsibility, but always someone else's fault. They take little to no responsibility for what happens. It is easy to get pulled into the negativity and to feel sorry for them, but that is part of the game. They want to draw individuals into their drama and negative situations through sympathy and get others to drop their guard. Once pulled in, it is difficult to detach yourself from the situation and you will find yourself sucked in deeper. Remember, everyone has

some level off accountability for every situation. When you are pulled into the drama, ask the person what they own in regards to the drama. What is their role in the situation? Have them focus on their actions. Inevitably, we know they will not take ownership and they will point fingers; if that is the case, be sure to bring it back to them. Eventually they will back off and find someone else who will play along and build them up.

- **Focus and get to the point:** Dysfunctional individuals are very talented at skirting around the issue. They will never get to the point. They will maneuver around the conversation and focus on what is best for their own agenda. To get the person to focus on the point takes time and patience on your part. Be persistent, redirect them back to the point. They will redirect you in another direction, but gently guide them back to the point. Eventually they will get frustrated and soon realize that they will not be able to use their die-hard tactics. They will also pick up that you are on to their tactics. What has worked for them in the past is not going to work now and they will move on to someone else.

- **Stay in control of your emotions:** Dysfunctional people will use many different tactics to see if they can hit you in an emotional way. They will use any tactic to throw you off. It is natural to feel negative emotions and this will happen from time to time. Try your best to control your emotions and not show them how you feel. The best thing to do is walk away from the situation when you feel your emotions surfacing. Focus on your strengths and pull from your confidence, your values and your support network. When emotions are high and you are shaken, this is when you will draw on your strong network to remind you of your strengths and the reality of the situation. If you are on solid footing, it makes it difficult for the dysfunctional individual to throw you off. When your emotions are high, this is not the time to try to establish boundaries. The dysfunctional person will pick up on the emotionally charged situation and will continue to attack to elicit some sort of response, whether it is anger, frustration or tears. The best thing is to walk away, cool down and come back when emotions have calmed.

- **Forgive but don't forget:** When we forgive a dysfunctional individual, it is not about justifying their behavior. Instead, it is about releasing the hold they have on you. It is not healthy to hold on to resentment or negative emotions. To forgive is to release yourself from these negative emotions and to set yourself free from the situation. However, while it is important to forgive, it is also important not to forget, in order to protect yourself from their negative behaviors in the future. Distance yourself from the negativity that surrounds this person and remember what happened. Focus on eliminating yourself from future negative events with this person.

- **Address the behavior quickly:** When a problem occurs, don't just ignore it. Often when we are violated in some way, we ignore it and hope it will go away. In other cases, we let our frustration simmer under the surface, trying to ignore what happened, until it happens again and those pent-up negative emotions come to the surface in anger and rage. That is what the other person wants. Don't wait too long to address the problem or issue. Instead, when something happens that goes against your values or beliefs, address it quickly. Too often we don't say anything until something forces us to address it, which might happen days, weeks or months later. Ask for clarity on the agenda of these attacks: "What are your intentions?" or "What are your expectations?" They will be confused, as they do not believe the target realizes there is an agenda, and they will respond by saying that they don't know what you mean. Keep asking and asking for clarification. Why are they acting this way? It is also important to recognize that the perpetrator will more than likely deny having an agenda. That is okay: the key is to let the dysfunctional person know that you are aware there is an agenda and will not tolerate it. Keep emotion out of the situation. If you feel emotions rising, walk away and readdress the behavior when calm. Don't get into a fight or argument with them. If something goes against your values and beliefs, speak up. If a person is forceful or argumentative with you, set your boundaries on what behaviors are acceptable and what behaviors are not acceptable; this aligns with what you value.

Dealing with an uncivil or dysfunctional leader

As we have discussed, addressing dysfunction or uncivil behavior is never easy; this is especially true if the person is a leader within the organization. Uncivil and dysfunctional leaders are focused on ensuring that the target is left questioning their abilities and feeling insecure. Just like any other dysfunctional person, the dysfunctional leader is often threatened by their target. This cannot be stressed enough: it is important to recognize that in reality the one who is insecure is the dysfunctional or uncivil leader. This is not about you, it is about the fact that you have something that they either want or feel threatened by. That may be talent, intelligence, a strong work ethic or popularity among others in the organization; the target is usually more competent than the dysfunctional leader and frankly they are afraid of the target. Recognizing that the leader is the problem is the first step in regaining power (Roter, 2017).

Next, it is important for the target to find individuals they can confide in. Talking to trusted colleagues or friends is the first step. Finding individuals who are supportive and believe in you is also important. Having a strong network can help to bring sanity into the situation. If there isn't a strong network to turn to in the workplace, seek professional help in order to bring the situation into perspective. Sometimes, talking to an outsider who is not involved in the situation can bring a new perspective and insights to the situation. When asking for insights, it is important to take this information and learn from the situation. Ask individuals to provide you with honest feedback and not to sugarcoat it. Maybe there is something wrong and the leader just doesn't deliver constructive feedback properly. Don't rely on the feedback from the dysfunctional leader alone, and don't over-analyze the information. Instead, go directly to others for support and feedback. They may provide feedback that is positive and they may provide feedback on areas for development. In some cases, you might find the feedback aligns with the feedback of the leader. Don't get angry with the person giving you constructive feedback. Understand that they are coming from a place of positive intent. If the feedback they provide contradicts the feedback the leader has given you, listen to what is being said and listen to the positive message that is being given. Reground yourself into that data point.

When starting a discussion with another person, the target will inevitably start the conversation with the question, "Am I really incompetent?" Then they will go on to say, "I feel like I am going crazy." These are all normal reactions for a target, especially when dealing with a dysfunctional leader. When leaders attack or criticize the work of others, we tend to believe them. We are taught early in our careers to have a certain level of respect for and expectations of our leaders. However, our expectations aren't always met, we learn that not all leaders are perfect, and there are many who bring dysfunction to the table.

How individuals can address dark behaviors

There are times when the target feels the need to address the dysfunctional individual. As we discussed earlier regarding approaching peers who are uncivil and dysfunctional, the same rules apply with a leader. In this section, we will frame ways in which to address a leader who is uncivil or dysfunctional. These tactics can also be used with a co-worker. Confrontation should be done early on, before the leader has gained complete power and control over the individual. The following highlights tactics to utilize when addressing or dealing with a leader.

Wait to talk to them: After a dysfunctional leader lashes out, this is not the time to address the behavior. Emotions are running high. More than likely, any response will be emotional. Walk away from the confrontation and wait to talk to them. Address them at a time when the leader is not expecting it and does not have an audience to grandstand in front of.

Frame statements: When speaking with the leader, open the discussion by outlining what needs to be discussed before beginning the conversation. By framing statements, the speaker is able to set the "scene" and provide context for the goal of the conversation, and prevent the speaker from jumping into the conversation through emotions. The leader may come with emotions, but for the target it is important to stay grounded and out of this. Focus on the conversation and on facts and data. If the discussion gets derailed, refocus it. Framing the statement will help to clarify the situation and the purpose of the conversation, and provide a framework to redirect the conversation back to the point.

Stay focused and rational: When addressing the person, stay rational and focused on the problem, not the person. If the other person feels as though they are being attacked, they will fight back. The perpetrator is protecting their fragile self-esteem and will do whatever is needed to protect themselves. Focus on the problem and what the behavior is doing to the team, organization, etc. If they are shown that their behaviors are negatively impacting the performance and outcomes of the department, this may reflect negatively on them.

Document the conversation: Document what was said during the conversation. Note the time, date, location and whether anyone witnessed the conversation. Sometimes it is key to bring in a second party, whether that is another leader, Human Resources or a peer to help with the conversation and to witness what happened. Document any actions that were identified in the discussion and everything that was discussed. This information may become important if there is a need for follow-up.

Individual action as a bystander

There are times when we might not be the target of the attack but a witness to someone acting in an uncivil or dysfunctional manner towards someone else. Every day, we witness people in society being rude to a server, gossiping about a co-worker or making derogatory comments about another. All too often we witness these behaviors, we are shocked and we don't say anything. However, there are actions that can be taken.

Take a stand

Taking a stand is about not ignoring the situation, but speaking up. Not taking a stand and watching quietly is collusion, cooperation or tacit approval, which is a form of silence. While it is not at all easy to speak up, it is important to take a stand against negative behaviors. Here are some examples of how people might not take a stand:

- **Sitting quietly when a demeaning joke is told that is focused on race, gender or sexuality:** Individuals listening to the joke may be silently offended, but may never speak up or say anything. The other person may not realize that what they have said has offended others. Speaking up and saying something informs the other person that there was something offensive and that this behavior is not acceptable. Give the person the benefit of the doubt and figure that they may not realize their behavior was offensive. If the behavior continues then remind them or speak up again. Don't be afraid to say something to others about the behavior if it continues.
- **Ignoring a co-worker who is constantly putting down a particular gender or population:** Again, this may be because the person is not aware they are being offensive. Speak up and educate. If it continues, do something about it.
- **Overlooking someone who is constantly yelling at team members or demeaning others:** This can be a challenge because often we are afraid that

if we do speak up in this circumstance, we might end up being the target of this person's wrath. It can seem easier not to say anything at all than to be the target of this person.

- **Watching as someone bullies team members in the workplace:** Again, take a stand and speak up. If you do not feel as though you can do that, provide support to the target. Sometimes, when others see someone supporting the target, they will join in and this may help to address the problem; there is power in numbers.
- **Tolerating inappropriate or sexual comments, touching or other exploits in the workplace:** With the recent #MeToo movement, more people are speaking up about harassment. Actual physical harassment or harassing comments should be reported to Human Resources immediately. Even if you are not sure about the behavior, it is better to have it investigated by HR.

An obstacle to addressing these behaviors in the workplace is not reporting harassment, discrimination or dysfunctional behaviors that are witnessed or experienced. Ideally, the workplace will have mechanisms that will allow people to come forward to speak up and address these situations. However, there are other outlets if the organization does not provide these mechanisms. The EEOC is a US government agency designed to enforce federal employment discrimination laws such as those against sexual harassment and discrimination. In 2013, it was reported that they received 93,727 discrimination charges and recovered approximately $372.1 million in monetary benefits for claimants (EEOC, 2013). The following statistics, from Roter (2017), indicates the most common complaints to the EEOC:

- Retaliation complaints: 41.1%.
- Racial discrimination: 35.3%.
- Sexual harassment: 29.5%.

Individual ways to address dysfunctional behavior

In conclusion, individuals should address the issues of dysfunction and negativity in the workplace. The following provides steps that can be taken by either the target or a bystander who witnesses these behaviors taking place.

Speak up: Immediately inform the person that their behavior is inappropriate and they need to stop. Be sure to document when this discussion occurs and whether there are any witnesses.

Report it: If you are afraid to discuss the issue with the person who is offending you, or they do not respect your request to stop the behavior, report the incident and share any documentation with your supervisor or manager.

Escalate it: If you are not comfortable discussing the issue with your direct supervisor, then discuss the issue with Human Resources or a manager who will be responsive. In most organizations, executives, senior management and Human Resources are the primary points of contact for addressing harassment issues in the workplace. Find someone with whom you are comfortable escalating the matter. Note that once a report is made, it does need to be investigated and it may not be held in confidence. Regarding discrimination or harassment issues, employees can contact the EEOC or use their own country's proper reporting protocols. It is encouraged to discuss these situations with the organization to allow them the opportunity to address these situations properly. However, if they are not addressing the complaints, there are outside avenues.

References

Beattie, L. & Griffin, B. 2014. Day-level fluctuations in stress and engagement in response to workplace incivility: A diary study. *Work & Stress*, 28(2), 124–142.

Caza, B. & Cortina, L. 2007. From insult to injury: Explaining the impact of incivility. *Basic and Applied Social Psychology*, 29(4), 335–350.

Edmondson, A. 1999. Psychological safety and learning behavior in work teams. *Administrative Science Quarterly*, 44(2), 350–383.

Giumetti, G., Saunders, L., Brunette, J., DiFrancesco, F., & Graham, P. 2016. Linking cyber incivility with job performance through job satisfaction: The buffering role of positive affect. *Psi Chi Journal of Psychological Research*, 21(4), 230–240.

Joint Commission. 2008. Behaviors that undermine a culture of safety. *Sentinel Event Alert*. www.jointcommission.org/assets/1/18/SEA_40.PDF.

Kahn, W. 1990. Psychological conditions of personal engagement and disengagement at work. *The Academy of Management Journal*, 33(4), 692–724.

Lawrence, C., & Leather, P. 1999. The social psychology of violence and aggression. *Work-related violence: Assessment and interventions*, 34–51.

Marchiondo, K., Marchiondo, L. A. & Lasiter, S. 2010. Faculty incivility: Effects on program satisfaction of BSN students. *Journal of Nursing Education*, 49(11), pp. 608–614.

Porath, C. 2016. An antidote to incivility. *Harvard Business Review*, 94(4), 22.

Porath, C. & Pearson, C. 2012. Emotional and behavioral responses to workplace incivility and the impact of hierarchical status. *Journal of Applied Social Psychology*, 42, E326–E357.

Porath, C. & Pearson, C. 2013. The price of incivility. *Harvard Business Review*, 91(1–2), 114–121.

Reio, T. & Ghosh, R. 2009. The toxic continuum from incivility to violence: What can HRD do? *Advances in Developing Human Resources*, 13(1), 3–9.

Roter, A. 2017. *Understanding and recognizing dysfunctional leadership. The impact of dysfunctional leadership on organizations and followers*. London: Routledge, Gower Publishing.

Sliter, M. 2013. *What is workplace incivility? Why should we care and what should we do?* Bristol: HRZON.

Sidle, S. 2009. Workplace incivility: How should employees and managers respond? *Academy of Management Perspectives*, 23(4), 88–89.

Irani Williams, F., Campbell, C., & Denton, L. 2013. Incivility in academe: What if the instigator is a high performer? *Journal of Management and Policy Practice,* 14(1), 35.

7

THE PHENOMENON COMES TO LIFE

For the past ten years, I have devoted my research to the topic of the dark side of the workplace. During this time I have been able to collect numerous interactions, experiences and discussions about the different types of dark side behaviors. This chapter is devoted to bringing the phenomenon to life for the reader. These stories are all based on actual events from various individuals who have experienced incidents related to the dark side. For the purpose of this section, the names of organizations have been withheld and the names of individuals have been changed in order to protect them from being identified. The stories have been written to stay as true as possible to the actual events, while providing further details to bring the story to life. For the purpose of this chapter, the reader will be able to place themselves into the position of each of the participants to better understand the phenomenon.

The crossover between incivilities in society and in the workplace

It was a Friday and Amita was driving just under the speed limit because of the driver in front of her. She was in the left lane and there were two cars to her right. The driver of the first car was about 17 years old and looked like he was new to driving by himself. The car behind him started flashing its lights at him, indicating that he should speed up. It was clear to Amita that the young driver was nervous; he began to weave back and forth, not sure what he should do. The car in front of Amita, witnessing what was happening, started to slow down, concerned that the young driver might weave into the left lane. The driver who was flashing his lights came up behind Amita and noticed she had slowed down even more as the car in front of her slowed down to let the young driver pass. He continued to flash his lights and she saw him gesturing at her and mouthing words. She could see he was angry.

At the next turn Amita decided to remove herself from the situation by getting off the road. She signaled to turn left and thought that would be the end of it. Then she thought that maybe something was wrong: instead of going on, the angry driver had also turned left. Amita pulled over to the side of the road to allow him to pass, but instead he pulled over as well and stopped. Amita was not sure what was going on and began to drive off. Again, the driver flashed his lights at her and started to flip her off. Amita began to wonder if her brake light might be out and he was gesturing to her that something was wrong. Again, she pulled over to let him pass or to tell her that something was wrong. Again, he stopped his car, but did not get out; he started slamming his hand on the steering wheel. Amita decided to find a public place to check her tail lights. She took off again and sped up to get away from the driver. He sped up and started driving very close to her car. She turned again into another side street and he followed. At this point she realized that this was not a coincidence and she looked for another place to stop. Amita could see that he was still agitated and driving close to the bumper of her car, screaming. Amita continued to speed up and the enraged driver matched her speed.

Finally, Amita decided to pull her car into a public parking space to get away from the driver. The enraged driver followed Amita into the parking lot and then got out of the car and started using derogatory terms. Amita, frustrated, got out of the car and asked what was wrong. He walked close to her and started to threaten her personal space. Amita was frightened for her safety and walked to a coffee shop; he followed her and ordered a coffee. She called the police and told the man that the police were coming and they could help to figure out what is going on. The enraged driver took his coffee order, jumped in the car, screamed further obscenities and threatened her. Amita used her phone to take a picture of the car and the license plate as he drove off.

The police arrived and a police report was filed promising that "they will talk to the individual". Finally, Amita left feeling shaken, afraid and unhappy about the way the day had started. Amita began to think about the threats the man had made and to wonder what the repercussions would personally be for her, and for her family. Had the individual recognized where she worked from the hang tag on her license plate holder? Amita was left wondering, if this person was capable of this type of rage, what else was he capable of? After all, if a person acts this way because of someone not driving fast enough, how will they react after being talked to by the police?

Amita eventually made it to her workplace and was visibly shaken. During the course of the day Amita was unable to focus on the work she needed to get done. She was focused on what had happened and she started to talk to co-workers about it, and an hour later they shared similar stories of their episodes related to road rage. The day of productivity was lost because of discussions about what had happened, other people's experiences and what Amita should do. Customer needs were not addressed that day, focus on work was lost due to wondering about what had happened, and personal phone calls were made to determine who the individual was. When the identity of the individual was discovered, time was spent on social media trying to find out more about this person and to assess his threat level. An event that had happened in one person's personal life had now entered the workplace.

A simple morning drive can demonstrate how incivility linked to a personal, societal issue can enter the workplace. This part of the story looks at what happened to Amita the research participant. This event happened quite some time ago and Amita followed up with the police report and found out that a citation was issued after some traffic cameras were reviewed to investigate the incident. After the event, Amita ran into the man at the gym, two different restaurants and the grocery store. Each time she has experienced a run-in with him there has been a verbal altercation. Amita continues to call the police but there is not much that can be done to address the behavior. The times that she has run into this man, she has been frightened and worried about how he will react.

Now let's look at the impact on work from the side of the person perpetrating the rage. This is an assumed scenario designed to demonstrate the impact that this uncivil action may have from another person's perspective.

After the altercation with the woman in the parking lot, Cody got to work, where it was obvious that he was not in a good mood. He was angry about what had happened. He was frustrated that the situation had evolved to a point where the police were called. After all, it was not his fault—it was the fault of the woman who clearly did not know how to drive. Why was she driving so slowly? He thought that, frankly, no one ever drives under the speed limit, and everyone speeds, especially if they are late for work. He had been running late to a meeting with an important client and the time it took for him to pull over and confront the driver had caused him to miss the meeting. Angry and shaking with rage, Cody got to his office, where his assistant greeted him and told him the customer was not happy that the appointment had been canceled. He screamed at the assistant and told her to get out of his office. He slammed the door behind the assistant and the phone rang, but he didn't answer it because he was too angry.

Suddenly, there was a knock at his door and his assistant said, "There is someone here to see you." The man screamed at her, "I told you to get out of my office, which means I don't want to talk to you or anyone else. Can you really be that stupid?" She cringed and wanted to lash out, but instead she said, "I think you want to talk to this person." Behind her was a police officer. Cody shook off his anger and went out to introduce himself to the officer and to shake his hand. All around Cody, his co-workers stopped what they were doing, hung up phones and listened in. Why were the police here? What had happened? Cody and the officer went into his office and closed the door. The administrative assistant was asked by several people what was going on. The assistant replied that she didn't know and all she knew was that Cody was in a horrible mood.

In the office, the police officer and Cody talked about what had happened that morning. The officer heard his side of the story and of course it was different than

Amita's. The officer stated that they had been able to view the traffic camera in that location and that Cody had been driving erratically. Cody was issued a citation. The police officer warned him to stay away from Amita and not to get pulled over for speeding or any other issues, or there may be further ramifications. The officer left and Cody closed the door to his office, fuming. He decided he had better call his wife to tell her what had happened. Cody knew she was not going to be happy, but she needed to know before she found out another way. He called his wife and, as he predicted, she was angry. This was not the first time it had happened and it wouldn't be the last. She knew his temper well. She told him she was at work and would talk about it when they got home. He slammed down the phone and she worried about what would happen when they did discuss it at home. Her mind now shifted from the project that was due on Monday to what his mood would be like this weekend. She was not focused on her work, but on what was going to happen at home and during the weekend ahead. Cody, on the other hand, sat in his office focused not on his work but on the woman who called the police. His hatred for her continued to bubble up to the surface.

Looking at the two people who were originally involved in the incident, we find that both of them took a societal component of incivility into the workplace. Anger, rude comments or distress from their personal lives now entered into several different workplaces. Not much work was done during the course of the day for either side, including co-workers who provided advice and wondered about what happened, and the spouse who was now too upset to focus on her own work project. Work time was spent gossiping about what happened, speculating, worrying and being in fear. Information was shared and feelings were hurt. Amita still has fear when she sees Cody, and Cody experiences anger every time he sees Amita.

The passive-aggressive

Ellery was the picture of kindness. She came across as a loving grandmother type. She was the sort of person who would knit baby blankets for co-workers who were having babies. When someone was sick, she would share her grandmother's recipe for chicken soup and she swore by it as a cure-all. Everyone loved Ellery. She was the person they could all go to for advice.

However, there were individuals who did not like the smothering love that Ellery would sometimes offer. They wanted to focus on their work and not get wrapped up in sharing personal details. When they did not want to share personal things, she would take it personally. Ellery never let on that she was hurt. Instead she would act it out in other ways. Within her department she was the support person for several individuals. If someone hurt her in any way, she would never tell them that she was upset. Instead, she would go to others in the department and look sad or look as though she was about to cry. People would stop what they were doing and ask her what was wrong and why she was upset.

Sheldon, a new engineer, did not know that Ellery's mother had passed away. He did not sign the card and, since he was new, no one said anything to him. Ellery noticed that he had not said anything about her mother passing. One morning Sheldon came to Ellery and asked her to run copies for a meeting he had that week. She smiled and said she was happy to make the copies.

"When do you need them?" she asked.

"I need them by Tuesday afternoon," he said, and explained what he needed—over 100 copies, collated, three-hole punched and ready for binders—and stressed the importance of the copies.

Ellery responded, "No problem, I will get them to you earlier than that."

On the day of the big meeting, Sheldon looked for the copies and for Ellery. She was nowhere to be found. He began to panic. This was his first really big meeting and he wanted to make a good impression. He went around looking for Ellery, only to find out that she had sent a memo to everyone but Sheldon, letting them know she was sick and could not make it in. Sheldon asked why he was not included in the email. Everyone just shrugged and said it was an oversight and that Ellery had a lot on her mind. He asked if he could call Ellery to see if she had the copies in her office. They reached out to Ellery and she said that she had been so distraught over her mother's passing that the copies had slipped her mind. Sheldon was upset as the meeting was two hours away and he had to scramble to get the copies made. With the help of others, he was able make the copies in time, but he was clearly rattled at the meeting and it showed in his presentation.

The next day Ellery did not call to let anyone know that she was not coming in. People were concerned that something had happened to her; she was elderly and lived alone. She always contacted someone when she was not coming in. They started to call and one person volunteered to check on her. She was fine and said that she had not heard the phone ring and had not checked her email. Everyone was relieved that she was okay.

The following day, Ellery came into the office, saying that she was still not 100% but she would stick it out as long as she could. She made her rounds and everyone told her how worried that they had been about her and what a scare she had given them. When she got to Sheldon's office she said hello. Sheldon was still upset from the other day and asked her about what had happened with the copies. She said it had slipped her mind. He then asked her why she hadn't let him know that she was going to be out sick, as that would have given him time to make the copies and to pull himself together for the meeting. She replied that she thought she included Sheldon on the email and that it must have slipped her mind. Ellery explained that she was very sorry for the miscommunication. Sheldon said that he appreciated the apology, but that it didn't help the matter and that in the future, if she could let him know when she was not going to be able to make it, it would be appreciated.

At this point Ellery held on to the door and said she was feeling dizzy. Sheldon offered her a chair and had her sit down. She started to tear up, explaining that she was not feeling well and that she was sorry. Ellery told him that she had not been the same since her mother passed away. Sheldon explained to Ellery that he felt horrible about this and started to apologize. He asked her if there was anything she needed. She said no, that everyone had been so supportive and kind and that she could not impose on Sheldon.

She left his office and went to the break area. She made herself a cup of tea and then sat staring at her cup. People came into the break room to ask Ellery how she was. "Oh, I am okay," she would reply. They knew that she wasn't. At this point she started sharing what had happened with Sheldon and saying that he was so cold and mean towards her. She sat and shared what had happened and said that she felt like Sheldon was blaming her for not having made the copies, and that she thought she had told Sheldon about being out sick. She said, "I don't know what I did to him. When my mother passed away he never said anything and didn't even sign the card. I just don't know why he doesn't like me." She went on to say, "Today he knew that I was not feeling well and then he started yelling at me about the copies. It just simply slipped my mind and I did not mean not to get the copies to him. I had planned on getting the copies made but then I got sick." She went on to say that Sheldon had made her so upset that she got dizzy in his office and that she just didn't know what she had done wrong.

Bryan was listening to this and he thought that Sheldon was a bully. How could he be so mean to someone who was like a grandmother to everyone? Bryan went charging into Sheldon's office and confronted him about why he had been yelling at Ellery. Sheldon sat at his desk and said that he had no clue what Bryan was talking about. Sheldon went into detail about what had happened and what he had said to her. "Ellery has been through so much and we just have to be more understanding with her since she is going through a hard time." Bryan left the office and Sheldon was left wondering what had just happened. He replayed the events in his head over and over again to identify what he had said or done to make her so upset. Eventually, he thought he should apologize to Ellery. In reality, he felt as though she should apologize to him, but he was going to take the "high road" and tell her he was sorry for upsetting her. He knocked on her door and apologized for what had happened earlier that morning. "I am sorry if I upset you in any way. That was not my intention. I only wanted to understand where we might have a disconnect." Ellery looked at Sheldon and said she didn't know what he was talking about and that she was fine. She told him not to worry about her. Sheldon left the office confused and wondering what was going on.

After that event, things continued to go wrong with the relationship between Ellery and Sheldon. She continued to leave him out of important emails and to fail to provide him information when he needed it. He found that it was just easier to bypass Ellery and do the work himself. When she did complete work for him, it was usually done incorrectly and he ended up spending hours doing it himself or fixing the mistakes she had made. He realized that she created more work for him when he asked her for any assistance. It was just not worth the hassle. Eventually, Sheldon's boss asked him why he wasn't asking Ellery for assistance, Sheldon explained that it was just easier to do things himself and that he had a certain way of doing things. His boss then told him that Ellery was there to do a job and to support Sheldon and others in the department. Sheldon did not see it that way, but agreed to ask her for help. He only came to regret asking for help and found himself in a no-win situation.

Sheldon started avoiding Ellery at every opportunity. She continued to tell people how mean he was to her and they started to isolate Sheldon because Ellery was such a nice person. During his performance review, Sheldon was marked low in delegation and getting along with co-workers, especially as it related to Ellery. When Sheldon tried to defend himself, his boss said that he was aware that there were performance issues with Ellery, but she was going to retire eventually. They didn't want to fire her and she needed the job. Sheldon grew frustrated with the organization, and began to look for work elsewhere. At his going-away party, Ellery came up to him and hugged him in front of everyone and said that she had tried to get along with him, but he just didn't want to get to know her and she would try to forgive him.

The victim

Grace was a petite, doe-eyed woman. When people first met Grace, she came across as so very sweet and kind, and people were just naturally drawn to her. However, Grace was a person who always saw the negative, and thought that everything that happened to her was because of her fate in life. In her mind, fate had it out for her, as did everyone she came into contact with.

David came to the company and was excited about the new job. He was partnered with Grace. He liked her when he met her. On his first day, he was assigned to work with her and she showed him the ropes. At times she seemed negative about the company and some of the people they met, but Dave didn't think much of it. He was just excited for this new job opportunity. When it came time for lunch they went to the break room and Dave started to ask questions about the organization. Dave found that he had opened Pandora's box. Grace started to share the woes of her life. She began by discussing her personal life and sharing stories of how she was an only child and as a result she was expected to care for her aging parents. She said that it was difficult being an only child and how much she just didn't like having the responsibility of having to be the person that took care of her parents. On top of that she had just recently divorced from her husband, who had cheated on her and was now fighting for custody for her three children, who were a handful. She talked about how she suffered from severe dyslexia and a myriad of different health problems. Grace often called in sick because she was either taking care of her kids, her parents or because she was sick herself. She went on and on about her life and the problems that she experienced.

Dave listened and thought about how life could deal such a bad hand to just one person. It seemed like everything that could possibly go wrong had happened to this poor woman. Dave said that if there was anything he could help her with, she should just let him know. "No, that is okay. I will just do what I do every day: make it work," she said.

As the day continued with Dave's training, Grace continued to share the story of all the problems that were happening in her life. Dave felt his excitement about the job slowly drain from his body and instead he felt exhausted listening to Grace's problems. At the end of the day, Dave went home and his wife asked him how his first day had gone. She was expecting him to share a great day with her, and for him to tell her what he had learned and how excited he was. Instead he seemed exhausted and frustrated. He told her about Grace and how he felt so sorry for her.

The next day, Dave was partnered with a new person, Jill. She asked him how he was doing and he said, "Okay."

"Just okay? Let's see what you learned yesterday."

As they went through the information that was supposed to have been covered the day before, Jill grew frustrated that Dave didn't know it and was not as far along as he should have been. Dave sensed Jill's frustration and apologized, saying he was trying and that he would catch on. He was worried that he was not making a good impression and he worried that the job was starting out so badly.

At lunch, Dave sat quietly with Jill. She asked him if he was okay. He said he was fine. Grace came over to say hello and to tell them about her latest drama in her personal life. When she finally left, Jill just shook her head and said, "She is really something. Everything bad happens just to her. She never realizes that bad things happen to others and she always plays the victim." Dave said that he felt bad about what was happening in her life and he was impressed that she was dealing with it all and somehow managing to stay focused. Jill looked at him in a funny way and asked him how he had met Grace and found out about her problems.

"Well, she was my trainer yesterday, and at lunch and in the afternoon she shared some problems that she was having. I felt really bad for her."

Jill slammed her palm on the table and started laughing. "Oh, I get it now. I get why you don't know some of the things that we discussed this morning. Grace was your trainer. Let me guess, she told you about her recent divorce, about her illnesses, and taking care of her parents and kids."

"Yes!" exclaimed Dave.

"So instead of training you properly she shared her problems with you. I am so, so sorry. This makes complete sense now. She should never have been assigned to train you."

Dave said that Grace was very nice to him and that he thought that she had covered the material and that maybe he was a little slow learning the information.

Jill replied, "No, you have been doing a great job today. This is not your fault at all. She likes to pull people into her drama and play the role of the victim to anyone that will listen. You just happened to get caught up in the drama that was going on and I am sorry that you had to deal with those issues. No worries, we will get you back on track and hopefully get you off to a positive start."

As promised, Jill did get Dave off to a positive start. As he continued through his training he found his excitement about the job grow and he was once again excited about his future career with the company. Dave continued to do well in the position. On occasion he ran into Grace; he would be polite and she would share the latest drama.

One day in the break room she started to cry and say that she just couldn't take it anymore.

"The universe is out to get me. If I didn't have bad luck, I would have no luck at all," she said.

She went on to explain how she was struggling to get her work done and that there was a major project she just couldn't get any help with. Dave said that he had some time and could help her. Maybe he could give her project a look to see if he could help. Grace replied, "That would be great and I would love to have you help me with the project."

After lunch, Dave went to Grace's office to offer her some help. As they were working on the report, Grace continued to talk about the problems she was having. About an hour into the project Jim, Vice President of Marketing came in and asked Grace, "How is my star performer doing?"

"Oh, okay, I guess. Just so hard to concentrate on all this work that I have to do with everything that is going on."

"Well if anyone can do it, it would be you," he said. He then turned to Dave and asked how he was doing.

"Great."

Dave was interested in a position working with Jim on a new project, marketing a new line within the organization. It was a great fit for him and would allow him to use his social media expertise. When Jim left the office, Dave turned to Grace and said, "I would love to work on that new project he's launching. It's right up my alley with my expertise with social media. I would give anything to work on that project."

Grace said, "I don't know why you would be interested in that stuff. Social media makes absolutely no sense to me and I just don't have the time to learn it what with everything going on in my personal life. But I could put in a word for you with Jim if you want." She smiled at him and her big doe eyes shimmered.

"That would be great. Thank you."

They continued to work on the project and Dave noticed that Grace just kept going on and on about her problems and the lack of cooperation she found in the organization. Everyone was always blocking her and they just were not fair to her at all. Dave continued to focus on the project and found that he was doing most of the work and Grace was just talking. She was taking phone calls, getting something to eat or talking about a problem. At about 3:00 P.M. Grace said her back was killing her and she had to go the chiropractor, otherwise she was going to get a really bad migraine. She asked Dave if he minded if she left for the day. She then said that since he was so far along with the report, could he just finish it for her. Dave hesitated; he had his own work to do. He said that he really needed to get back to his office and work on some of his projects, but she had a good start on her project and should be able to finish it before the deadline.

Grace said, "I guess I can do that. Hopefully I can work on it tomorrow."

As she said this she stood up and swayed. Dave asked if she was okay.

"I'm fine," she responded.

But she was holding her head and rubbing her eyes. He could see that something was wrong. Suddenly, she reached for the garbage pail and started to look like she was going to vomit.

"Oh no, this is not a good sign. I'm getting a migraine and this will be a problem."

Dave went to get a cold towel for her as she put on some sunglasses to block the light.

"How will I ever get all these things done? I have to take care of my parents tonight, the kids have a program, and I have the start of a migraine and have to finish this report." She started to cry.

Dave said, "Look, I'm almost done, why don't I just finish it for you and you can look it over when you have time?"

Grace perked up. "I guess that would work, but I just don't know with my dyslexia if it might be difficult for me to understand it if I don't write it myself. You might have to meet with me to discuss the report."

"Okay," replied Dave. "I guess I can do that."

"Would you help me to my car?"

Dave helped to carry Grace's briefcase to the car and made sure she was okay. He asked her if she needed someone to drive her home.

"No, I will be fine. Don't worry about me. I do this all the time."

He watched her pull away and went back to the office to catch up on his work and to finish Grace's report. It was going to be a long night and he would have to miss his son's soccer game. It would be okay since Grace would surely put in a good word for him with Jim.

Dave went back to Grace's office and started pulling everything together. While he was doing that, Jim stopped in again.

"Grace around?" he asked.

"No, she wasn't feeling well and went to the doctor. She thought she was getting a migraine."

"Oh, that poor woman. I don't know how she does it, with everything going on and her health. I hope she is going to be okay."

Dave finished the report and sent it off to Grace, telling her he hoped she felt better. He did not hear back from her and the next day she called in sick. She called him later in the afternoon to go over the report and the findings. He went over it with her and asked her how she was doing.

"I am okay, I guess. Thanks for doing the report. I guess it will have to be good enough to turn in."

Dave was puzzled by the comment as he thought the report was pretty good. Two days later, Grace came into the office wearing dark glasses, no makeup and a neck brace. Several people asked her what happened and she shared the story that she had been in a car accident on the way to the chiropractic office. Dave was surprised as Grace had not mentioned anything about the accident. Jill came up to Dave and said, "If there was an Academy Award for the most dramatic co-worker, she would win hands down."

Jim came over and saw Grace in the neck brace. "Oh, you poor thing." He took her into his arms to hug her.

She started to cry. "I don't know why all these bad things happen to me all the time."

Jim seemed almost like a father comforting his daughter. "Poor kid. It will get better in time." Jim asked Grace if she was prepared to present her report to the marketing team.

"I think I can, but I am still a little shaky." She was trembling as she said it.

Jim said, "Now don't you worry. I read the report and it is excellent and I will jump in if needed. You don't worry at all."

Dave heard Jim's comment and was excited because this was his chance to have his report recognized, and he hoped that Grace would say something about his work since Jim was impressed with the report. Dave went to Grace and reminded her to put in a good word for him with Jim.

"I will try," she smiled weakly. Grace went into the meeting with her dark glasses still on and still looking shaky.

Later in the afternoon, Jim called everyone together for an announcement. Grace had taken off her dark glasses, was wearing fresh makeup and looked like a new woman. Everyone gathered around and Jim said that he was going to announce a new person to work on the new social media project for Marketing.

"I would like to thank everyone who worked on the report for the project. After today's meeting and the stellar work that was done on the report, I have decided to go ahead and name the person who will head up the new social media campaign."

Dave was surprised. Was this it? Jim had not even spoken to him about it, but Grace must have said something to Jim since she was not even interested in social media.

Jim smiled and said, "After all that this person has been through, they came forward and delivered an outstanding report. Please join me in congratulating Grace as the new director within the marketing team, heading up the whole social media effort of the group under my direction."

Dave stood there dumbfounded and speechless as he watched Grace stand and smile and thank Jim for the opportunity, the opportunity that Dave had wanted and Grace had said she had no interest in. What happened?

After the meeting disbanded, everyone was talking. Jill came up to Dave and asked him if he was okay.

"Yeah, I guess."

"That would have been a great job for you. I don't know why you didn't put in for it."

Dave smiled. "I did put in for it. I was the one who wrote the report for Grace and even prepared her for the meeting because she was sick."

He went on to share with Jill that he had asked Grace to put in a good word for him and she had said she would. He thought that she would have said something to Jim about the work he had done on the report.

Jill smiled, shook her head and said, "I am so, so sorry. You have been had by the best. We have all been pulled into her web at some point and as a result we have been burned by her."

"I felt sorry for her. I helped her and she said she would put in a good word for me. She said she didn't want the job and didn't understand social media."

Jill laughed and said, "I am sure that is true. She doesn't know her own area, let alone something new like this. We don't know what it is about Jim, but we think he feels like Grace is his daughter or something. She can do no wrong. He comes to her aid when things go wrong. She has moved up the ladder this whole time and Jim will do what he can to protect her. He knows that she struggles, but he rescues her every time."

Dave asked, "Should I say something to him about the report and the work I did on it?"

Jill shook her head. "Nope. Don't say a word. Next time she asks for help, don't give it to her. She will tell you something sad and she will make you feel horrible about what happened, but at the end of the day…do not help. Take this as your lesson."

Dave now understood why Grace had complained that no one helped her. It was because they had all been burned and so they left Grace on her own.

Grace continued to move up the ladder under the guidance and direction of Jim. She was protected by him and he learned to give her as little work as possible because people stopped helping her. When a new person came in, Grace sought them out and pulled them in. Dave was tapped for new responsibilities but never got the opportunity for the position he wanted. The only way he would get his dream job was if he moved to another organization, which he did eventually. He came to resent Grace and, even more, Jim. He lost respect for Jim for allowing Grace to get away with what she had done. Dave also resented himself for not speaking up, for allowing Grace to play the victim and for falling for the damsel-in-distress routine.

The gossip

In this particular organization, the leadership was not very transparent with what was happening within the organization. They kept information very tightly in the upper echelons and as a result the organization had a very active rumor mill. The rumor mill was built off information that people heard in passing. To further complicate matters, the information that circulated through the rumor mill was from employees who were very good at embellishing it to make it appear as the worst-case scenario.

One particular event was the catalyst for the rumor mill. The organization had experienced several quarters of loss. Because of these losses, upper leadership had started looking to cut certain products from their lines and to develop or increase product lines that were successful. This was reported to the employees. During one of the meetings, employees were told that, while product lines were being cut, they would do their best to keep employees on, but that it was inevitable that positions would have to be redesigned to fit the needs of the organization, or positions would be eliminated. The organization stated that they were looking to eliminate 10–15 jobs. While that seemed like a small number, it was still a large cut that would hurt the organization as well as the customers they served.

Meetings were held for months, but there was no communication other than that first meeting. A particular administrative assistant, Mary, loved to be the person who was in the know, or at least to give that impression. She would take information in and then twist it to her position herself accordingly. Organizational leadership did not share with the rest of the organization when the cuts were going to happen. Employees were told that they would hear something sometime in the first half of the year. There was no communication regarding what product lines were being cut, so employees had no choice but to advise customers based on the product lines that were available. There was utter confusion in regards to what was happening within the organization.

Employees started to talk and share information about what they each knew about the situation. In the center of these discussions was Mary. Any chance Mary had to put in her two cents about the events was her opportunity to feel important. Mary also loved to be the person who fueled the rumor mill. She started going to others and telling them that cuts had been made to certain departments. She always "had it on good authority" that there were cuts within particular departments. Nerves were on edge as it was, wondering when and where the cuts were coming. Now Mary had information about cuts within their department and they were left wondering when the hammer was going to hit and who was going to be eliminated.

Mary enjoyed going to different departments and spreading rumors about each of the departments in order to cause chaos and conflict within the team. She was extremely stealthy and strategic about her tactics. She would discuss what was said in one department and then embellish the truth and discuss what was being said in another. The departments found that they were pitted against each other. This conflict took place as everyone's nerves were raw from the layoffs.

Finally, the organization announced the cuts. It was found that many of the departments that Mary had said were going to experience cuts experienced no cuts. Other departments that had heard rumors about being safe were the ones that were targeted. Employees were fighting and angry with one another. Mary, on the other hand, continued to fuel the rumor mill and add to the frustration. The organization knew that Mary was at the center of the rumor mill, but they didn't do anything to address the behaviors. A culture was created that focused on dysfunction, fear and distrust. Because of how this issue was handled, employees did not trust leadership or one another.

The harasser

Laura was new to the department. When she interviewed, she talked about how she was going to bring new ideas to the organization. People who worked with Laura knew she had a challenging personality, but they were accepting of this because they thought that she would bring the department to another level. Immediately, Laura told her direct reports that she did not expect people to come to her with problems. Her expectations were that her team fix problems at their level and nothing should ever hit her desk. As a team, they needed to figure things out; she did not have time to deal with issues. If things were escalated to her, she would think her staff were incompetent and could not handle situations. The team was perplexed by this new approach. The previous leader had an open-door policy and they worked through situations together as a team, with the help of the former leader. Now they were expected not to escalate problems to their immediate director.

During her first few weeks, Laura set up time to meet with each of her staff members. She wanted to get to know them on a personal level and asked questions about their lives, including about their marriages, children and any other information that was personal in nature. Jay, who was openly gay, shared that he and his husband lived in the next town over. Laura blinked and pursed her lips when she heard that Jay was openly gay. She explained to him that she would prefer if he did not discuss his relationship with his husband with her or other staff members, as this might make other members of the team uncomfortable. Jay shared that everyone within the department knew that he was married and that he and his husband often attended social functions with the group. He also shared that every year they had the department over to their house for the annual holiday party, which they enjoyed hosting.

"Well, that will stop immediately. Holidays are traditional events for traditional families," she exclaimed.

She went on to say that she did not care about his sexuality, but if he would not talk openly about it that would be appreciated. At this point Jay felt that Laura might be homophobic, but he never called her out for it. He had no intention of hiding his sexuality, and he was legally married to his husband so he was going to live his life as he always had.

It was obvious to many within the department that Laura did not like Jay. It was pretty clear to everyone and she did not hide her feelings towards him. Laura piled work on Jay and he was overwhelmed. Eventually, Jay pushed back against Laura when she assigned him a project at the last minute as he was heading out the door for the weekend. He said he had plans with his husband and he was leaving town.

Laura responded, "I really don't care about your plans."

Jay was shocked, but kept pushing. "Can Liz take the project, since she has some time?"

"Nope." She smiled at Jay. "Well, I guess you will have to cancel your plans with your man."

Jay responded, "That would be with my husband."

She stopped smiling. "In your world, you recognize that you are married to your man, but in my world you will never be married." Then she walked out of his office and called back, "Oh, and the project must be completed and on my desk by Monday."

Jay felt that he had no choice but to work on the project and cancel his plans with his husband.

A few months later the team went to a meeting off site. At lunch Jay stopped to talk to a couple of people from another location. In the dining room there was a large table set up for the group. He came into the dining room and there was only one seat open, next to Laura. Jay was not excited about the prospect of sitting next to her for the next hour, but there was no other place to sit. Jay went over with his plate from the buffet and pulled out the chair. Laura quickly snatched the chair and placed her purse on it and said she didn't want him sitting next to her during lunch.

He said, "There is no other place to sit."

"Well, that is just too bad. I don't want your type sitting next to me while I am eating."

Jay looked at her angrily. He didn't know what she was talking about and why she didn't want him next to her. Others heard the exchange and said that they would make room for Jay and that he could sit with them. When Jay sat down, one of his team members asked him what she had meant by "his people". Jay responded that she had made it clear that she was uncomfortable with his sexuality. People around him were shocked by this comment; they knew Jay as a kind and talented individual. Susan said, "Well, she isn't going to like it when she meets my girl-friend". At this point everyone laughed and Laura looked at them angrily from the other end of the table.

After lunch Laura went over to Jay and told him that it was unprofessional of him to be laughing and joking at a company-sponsored luncheon. This was not a time for fun, but a time to be working and networking. She told him that his behavior at the luncheon was inappropriate.

He replied, "What was inappropriate was that you did not make room for me to sit down to join you for lunch."

"I don't share meals with people like you," she stated.

"What, are you afraid you're going to catch something from me?"

She replied, "Yes" and walked away.

Over the next several months Laura's behavior continued to get more and more harassing. She often went up behind Jay with a Lysol can and sprayed down things that he had touched. The secretary in the office was ordered to wipe anything that Jay touched with a sanitizing wipe. "We can never be too careful," Laura would say. Jay just assumed that Laura had issues with germs, but when others came into the office sick with a cold she did not wipe down anything they touched. The only time was when Jay touched something. Still, Jay just shrugged it off as Laura's ignor-ance and thought that it was her problem if she could not accept him.

When the holidays came around, Jay was looking forward to his three-week vac-ation and going to Europe to visit his husband's family. He was looking forward to the break because of the tension Laura caused. It was during this time that Jay had a feeling that he was going to be let go. He shared his fears with others and they told him he was being paranoid. There was a process that the organization followed before terminating employment. They asked him if he had even received a warning. He replied that he had not. He was asked if Laura had talked to him about his per-formance. He responded that she had not said anything positive or negative about his performance. There was nothing to worry about, they told him. He figured that they were right and he was just being tense and paranoid. Nothing happened and he went off for vacation. During this time, he completely unplugged from work and started to feel the tension leaving his body. He had been suffering from headaches and found that he felt better during his vacation. When he returned, he felt energized and did not experience any of the physical or emotional symptoms he had been experiencing for the previous several months. Instead he felt like his old self.

That Monday when he came back to work he said hello to everyone and shared some chocolates he had purchased from Europe for the team. Everyone dived in to the chocolates, except for Laura. Jay went to his desk and opened up his calendar. His resolution for the new year was not to let Laura bother him. She had her beliefs and he had his and that was okay. They both needed to focus on what was best for the customer and the organization, and that is what he was going to do. Everything else was just noise, as far as he was concerned. When he looked at his calendar he noticed that he had a 9:00 A.M. meeting with Laura. He was surprised at the calendar invite, since it was last minute. Jay figured that the meeting was to go over everything that he had missed while he was gone. He was ready to meet with her with a new attitude.

When 9:00 A.M. arrived, he went to Laura's office and was surprised to find Bonnie from Human Resources in there too. He figured it was a meeting to discuss some of the issues that had happened while he was away. Jay took a seat and made himself comfortable. He smiled at Bonnie, but she looked down at the pad of paper in front of her. Laura handed him a letter and told him to read it. The letter informed him that he was being terminated and that he was to leave the building immediately. Jay said he didn't understand; he had not received any notification that his performance was lacking in any way. There was a process that needed to be followed, according to the employee handbook. Laura responded that he did not deserve a warning and that he served at the pleasure of the CEO. He was to leave immediately. He kept saying that he wanted an explanation, but none was given to him.

When he opened the door, he saw that security was standing outside the office and they were there to escort him out of the building. Jay turned to Laura and asked what this was about. She said it was standard procedure. He said that was not the case, it was something they only did if there was legal issue, and there was only one time where an employee had been escorted out and that was when Charlie was let go for presumed embezzlement. Laura shrugged and went back into her office and closed the door. Jay was escorted out of the building by security and HR. He was told that he had to come in at a designated time to pick up the items in his office and he would have to be accompanied by a security guard and someone from HR. He looked over at Bonnie and asked her, "What is this about?" She said she had never seen anything like this. She had tears in her eyes and said that the only thing she would say was that it was clear that Laura did not like him, and she asked him what he had done to Laura for her to hate him so much. Jay said, "I guess because she doesn't believe in my lifestyle." Bonnie just shook her head. As Jay walked out he noticed various people from other departments watching him. He felt humiliated and ashamed, but he kept reminding himself that he had done nothing wrong.

Jay contacted corporate headquarters and they had no knowledge of the termination. They told him they would investigate. While investigating, Laura started spreading rumors that Jay had been let go because of wrongdoing, but nothing had been documented. People were forbidden to talk to Jay and he was ostracized by the organization as well as his former co-workers. Jay was contacted by corporate HR and they agreed that his employment would be extended for three months, but he was forbidden to step on site. Essentially, he would collect a paycheck and benefits during this time but do no work. Human Resources said this would give him time to find a job. Jay asked for an explanation of what he had done to be terminated and they said it was due to his performance. He said there was a process and it was not followed. Human Resources stated that they had given him a warning effective the day of his termination.

Jay recognized that the process was not being followed and he contacted an attorney. The attorney agreed to take the case and asked for Jay's personal files. While the organization dragged out the wait time to get the files to Jay's attorney, the three-month employment time was running out. When the file was sent to his attorney it was not complete and past performance reviews were missing, except for Laura's review which she had never given him. This was the first time he had seen the review. Jay tried to reach out to his friends from work, but he found he was ostracized by co-workers and the community he lived in. Laura was relentless and attacked him personally and professionally. When applying for jobs, he could not find anything because he was now blacklisted in his professional community, and Laura was not subtle in implying that his performance was not strong. Laura worked hard to leak lies about Jay to professional networks. Jay finally landed a job, but it was two steps down and paid significantly less. He was forced to leave the community and friends that he had loved.

The ordeal put a strain on every aspect of Jay's life. His marriage suffered and he is still trying to get things back on track with his husband. They had hoped to adopt a child before this whole mess started, but that has been put on hold until they can work things out. Financially, they have suffered by having to go into their savings, and then their 401k plan in order to pay for health insurance. When Jay finally found a job, he took a pay cut and relocated, but they had a hard time selling their house and ended up taking a loss because they could not afford to pay for rent and a mortgage. In addition, Jay's physical health was compromised and he ended up spending money on medications to alleviate his headaches and on endless tests to find out what was wrong with him. Jay has a hard time emotionally; he doesn't trust people with information about his personal life and does not share that he is married. To this day, he struggles with the idea that someone could hate another person so much based on their lifestyle. He is waiting patiently as his lawyer continues to fight for his rights, but the organization has been very good at tying up the process in red tape. There are times when he wants to just give up the lawsuit and move on, but he also wants to fight the injustice of the situation.

The self-promoter

Lexi interviewed so well. She came across as strong yet humble, a down-to-earth individual. She was a great fit for the organization; she matched their values and seemed to be someone who was good at what she did. She did not come across as bragging or aggressive in any way and she was very likeable. After the interview, people flocked to the hiring manager's office and encouraged him to hire her as she was the best candidate they had interviewed. Lexi was hired and reached out to individuals through social media to meet with them before she even started. She met with people individually to get to know those in the department. Lexi stated that she wanted to understand the culture of the organization and the department through meeting with individuals.

On her first day Lexi was quiet and people took her under their wing to show her the ropes. During the first week, Lexi went to Shannon's office and asked for help with the technology platform that the department used. Shannon started to explain how to use the technology platform, but when she shared that the technology platform was limited in its capabilities, Lexi's frustration became clear. She was flushed, redness crept up her neck to her face and it was evident that she was agitated. Shannon recognized the frustration, apologized to Lexi and promised she would teach her the work-around for the limitations. She told Lexi that when she ran into problems she should come and find Shannon or another person in the department and they would help her. Lexi continued to look agitated, but didn't say anything. When Shannon got up to leave she told Lexi to hang in there and said it wasn't too bad. Lexi didn't say anything to Shannon and just turned her back. Shannon wrote this behavior off as a new employee being nervous during their first week, though she was surprised by Lexi's reaction.

A few weeks went by and Lexi was starting to meld into the department, but she spent most of her free time getting to know different departments and making connections. She said she wanted to get to know the culture and the other departments. During these meetings Lexi was brilliant at networking and finding people she could "partner" with; however, she did not network within her own team. Individuals made efforts to invite Lexi to lunch or coffee and she would turn them down. Shannon had to share news with the team that there was a change to a process that would impact the customers they worked with. While it was not a positive change, Shannon was just sharing the information with the people in the department. When Shannon got to Lexi's office and told her about the new change, Lexi's neck started to flush and the redness crept up to her face, just like the first time Shannon had met with her. It was clear she was angry and she started yelling. Shannon stood there dazed and looking at Lexi. She raised her hands up in an "I surrender" movement and said, "Look, don't shoot the messenger. I'm the one that was asked to communicate this change. Let's talk about this in more detail when you've cooled off." Lexi did not like this at all, and when Shannon turned to leave Lexi grabbed her arm and yelled at her, "How dare you walk off. I am not done with you." Shannon told Lexi to release her arm and that they could talk when Lexi was in a better frame of mind. Shannon walked out of the office, shocked at her behavior. This was the second time that Lexi had lashed out at her and, frankly, she was tired of the unprofessional behavior that Lexi was displaying.

A few minutes later, Lexi came in to Shannon's office and said she didn't appreciate the comment she had made in regards to "shooting the messenger". She said she was not angry with Shannon and that she shouldn't take it personally. Shannon looked at her and said, "This is the second time I have felt uncomfortable with your temper. It is clear that we are not going to be able to work together." Lexi shrugged her shoulders and said, "Everyone likes me. You are the one with the problem. Maybe you are just too sensitive and have a problem with assertive women." She turned and walked out of the office.

Shannon went to talk to the director to give her a heads-up about what had happened. Of course, the director was surprised, since Lexi had shown herself to be nothing but humble, kind, quiet and open to others around her. Shannon shared the outburst with others and they all looked at Shannon as though she was crazy. "Not Lexi, surely you just misunderstood her reaction," they said. Shannon knew that she had to tread lightly and just said, "Fine," and told people that when they saw this side of Lexi then they should come and talk to her. Lexi's true colors would show eventually, but in the meantime Shannon opted to avoid Lexi at work. Shannon was cordial with Lexi, but she only worked with her when things had to be done and the rest of the time she stayed away.

Shannon sat back and observed. Lexi was a pro at getting her agenda out to others. She worked hard at making sure everyone knew what was happening and what she was working on. Even with the smallest of initiatives she made everyone aware of what was happening. Lexi made sure that she was at all the right events; if the president of the company was at an event, Lexi was there, and when pictures were taken Lexi made sure she was in the center. In the meantime, people saw Lexi as a high performer. Shannon was also a high performer but did not believe in self-promoting. She believed that your character and work should speak for itself. But Lexi was the opposite and started to share with others around her how much she was focused on putting everyone else's needs first, while in reality she was putting her own needs first. Lexi had the canny ability to get others to do the work for her while she managed to take the credit. In meetings Lexi always reported what she was working on and highlighted her efforts. Lexi was the first to share her accomplishments. Lexi started to do events that received a great deal of press and she was always front and center to receive credit.

When Shannon grew frustrated and spoke to others about what was happening, they did not know what the problem was; Shannon seemed jealous of Lexi. But in reality Shannon knew what Lexi was doing: getting under her skin. Shannon decided to just let things go with Lexi. She figured it was not worth her effort or energy. Shannon went about doing her own work and focusing on her own accomplishments. In the meantime, Lexi was able to become friendly with the vice president of the department. She met with him on a weekly basis and was able to befriend him. She started telling him how things should be run. She focused on Shannon's work and what Shannon should be doing. Lexi was quick to take ownership of work that Shannon was already doing. During meetings she would take ideas that Shannon presented and write them down, or she would challenge them. After the meeting she would run with the ideas and make them her own. She wanted the credit for coming up with innovative ideas. When she went around telling others about the new direction that the vice president was taking, they started to notice how Lexi was positioning herself and taking credit for the work of others. Lexi never got her hands dirty. When a fundraiser was implemented, Lexi made sure that she was front and center, but at the end of the day it was others doing the work. She had a knack for being at the events that involved her and always looking busy in front of senior leadership, but she really wasn't doing much other than taking credit. Meanwhile, others who had completed the actual work waited to get credit, but nothing was said to them and they started to become bitter. During meetings the team would listen to the vice president exclaim Lexi's virtues and the great things she was doing, and that was the only praise he gave out to the department. He ignored all other efforts and the accomplishments of others on the team were diminished. A few months later Shannon won an award for a project that she had been focused on; it was an organization recognition. A reception was held to honor the work of Shannon and other team members. Lexi came to Shannon and said it was just a matter of time until she would also be the recipient of the award. She warned Shannon to be worried because she was going to give her a run for her money. Shannon took this as a threat, but others viewed it as a joking and harmless comment.

Eventually, Lexi was given bigger projects and more responsibility. However, her networking was not keeping up and she was unable to get enough people to support her efforts. One could easily see the tension building in Lexi and it was also obvious that she was not as competent as she had portrayed herself to be. As a result of the pressure she was experiencing, Lexi started to lash out at others. One day Devon, a long-term employee who was well respected, asked Lexi why she was edging him out. She said she didn't understand and he was being too "sensitive". Devon was correct, Lexi was edging him out. He told her that if this behavior kept up then he would take his customers and leave the organization. He didn't need this from Lexi or the organization that he had been with for the last 30 plus years. Lexi started to panic because Devon was a moneymaker in the organization and if he left then her department would fall apart. After all, people came to Devon as the person they wanted to work with. Everyone knew that she wanted to be the next Devon, but she never could be as he had his own unique style that was difficult for anyone to emulate. The only one close enough to possibly take Devon's position was Shannon and Lexi was not about to let that happen.

The pressure continued and Lexi started lashing out. She was quickly losing her network of people and now she was expected to do the work. She stepped up to participate in presentations to customers, but on the day of the presentations she would call in sick. Shannon picked up the slack at the last minute. Lexi thought that by calling in sick she could kill two birds with one stone, getting out of the presentation and setting Shannon up for failure, since she had never shared with Shannon any of the information for the presentation. However, to Lexi's surprise Shannon always stepped up and made things happen. Shannon knew the game that Lexi was playing.

Unfortunately, others could not accept that Lexi was a self-promoter who was not capable of the work she was doing. People continued to step in for Lexi, letting the vice president know what they were doing, but Lexi somehow still got the credit for the work being done. People started to see Lexi for who she really was and often said things to Shannon about her being right about Lexi. The only one who did not see what was happening was the vice president, but he was very much like Lexi—also a self-promoter—and Lexi did everything in her power to make him look good, while making herself look good as well. In turn, he was focusing on Lexi. Meanwhile, his high performers were becoming disengaged and were looking to leave the organization. In many cases they went to other places where they were respected and their work was rewarded.

The narcissist and the bully all in one

The department had been in turmoil for months. There had been a change in leadership and the director had been asked to step down. As a result, a new position was created. This department needed a heavy hitter, someone who could come in, make it all come together and take it to the next level. The organization thought they had the right person when they hired Kelly. She came from a major manufacturer in the pharmaceutical industry and they thought for sure she would shake things up. During her recruitment she highlighted how she had brought in the best talent to her old organization, as well as innovative thinking, leadership and change. She was impressive and said all the right things. When her hiring announcement was made, she helped to create it. The wording the vice president of the division stated that Kelly was one of the best hires they had made in a long time and that she was going to be the ace they had been looking for. After the announcement was made the vice president met with the units that Kelly was going to oversee and told them about Kelly, including her talent and the skills that she brought to the organization. It was evident that everyone was excited for her to take the lead.

The team waited in anticipation for Kelly to start. In her first week Kelly never made it down to the unit to meet her new direct reports. The following week she traveled to the three different site locations to meet the people who would be working with her. She introduced herself to the remote locations, but had yet to meet the people she would be working side by side each day. The unit thought it was odd but didn't really pay much attention; they were just excited to meet with her. When Kelly came back from her road trip, the team waited in anticipation for their turn to meet with her. But that didn't happen, as Kelly had negotiated a two-week vacation with her husband to Europe. The team had to wait another two weeks to meet with Kelly. During the wait, they listened to other areas sing her praises and talk about how wonderful they thought she was. The local team could not respond because they had yet to meet her. One person commented that they would not know who she was even if she walked into the department at that moment. They didn't even know what she looked like. Patrick, the former director who had stepped down to make room for Kelly, was angry that she had left them hanging. Word made its way to the vice president and he promised that as soon as Kelly returned the team would meet her.

The day arrived when Kelly came back from Europe. It was exactly one month after she had started that she finally met her primary team. Kelly came into the office area and everyone was excited to meet with her. Instead of talking about work, she discussed her trip. Someone commented on the beautiful silk skirt that Kelly was wearing and she said that she had had a fantastic shopping trip on a stopover in Paris with her very nice sign-on bonus. Members of the team looked at each other. A sign-on bonus? They had not received a pay increase in two years and this rubbed them the wrong way. She twirled in her silk skirt and talked about the fabulous trip. Finally it was time for Kelly to leave. After she left, the team felt underwhelmed. Here they had waited and anticipated some sort of guidance, vision, strategy or direction. All they had learned from her was about her trip to Europe and what a great time she had. They were disappointed and hoped that the next time they met it would be different.

Kelly decided to meet with individuals one on one. The team members met with Kelly and were asked not to share information from their meeting with other team members. During lunch one afternoon, Carl spoke up.

"What's up with women who constantly play with their hair and look in the mirror during meetings? I mean, I get it if you want to check your mirror *before* a meeting, but *during*?"

Some of the women at the table smirked or giggled.

"*What*?" Carl asked.

Donna spoke up first. "Well, why don't you explain your experience and we can put it into context."

Carl said that in his one-on-one meeting with Kelly she had kept looking into a mirror that was propped on her desk. She was checking for lipstick on her teeth, pulling her hair and playing with her clothes. The whole time they were talking she was distracted by her appearance and the way she looked.

He then asked, "Is this something that women do when they are nervous?"

Donna chimed in, "It is what they do when they are self-absorbed and just rude."

She admitted that she had had the same thing happen to her and that Kelly had kept talking about her clothes and how she was appalled at the way the women in the office dressed. Kelly had commented, "They should not dress for the job they have, but for the job they want." Kelly explained that she always dressed for her next job, which in this case was the vice president's position.

Several team members shared that they had had odd experiences with Kelly as well. They mentioned that most of their one-on-one meetings had been focused on getting to know all about Kelly and the great things that she had done. When Kelly did speak about the work they were going to do, she kept saying it was going to be cutting edge and innovative and that she was looking forward to being invited to be a keynote speaker at leadership conferences because she was the person to take the organization to new levels.

Patrick sat back and listened to everything. He had been invited to be a part of the hiring team and, frankly, Kelly had not been his first choice. Patrick thought another candidate was a better fit for the department.

Word got back to Kelly that Patrick did not agree with her hire and that he did not want her for the position. Kelly started to invite Patrick to meetings where she would ask him about the past and his leadership of the team. He shared some of his decision-making processes with her and slowly she started to pick his decisions apart. Work began to roll out of the group, but it was nothing earth-shattering. When things went well Kelly took credit for it, and when things went wrong she pointed to Patrick's past leadership and how his decisions had led to the mistakes that were happening now. Patrick started to feel the pressure from Kelly and any time something went wrong, which it often did, he took the brunt of the negative fallout.

During this time, Patrick stopped sleeping; he lost his appetite and just was not interested in work. He had been humiliated by being asked to step down from the leadership role because the vice president wanted someone newer and better. Patrick felt he was a good soldier, but he stepped down and took a pay cut for the good of the department and the organization. He had hoped he would learn from Kelly, but that was not the case. Instead, he was the fall person for her mistakes. Patrick made the decision to apply for a position outside the division. Other leaders in the organization respected him. Whenever Patrick interviewed, the other leaders let Kelly know out of courtesy. Once Kelly found out about the interviews, she blocked his movement out of the unit. "The only place Patrick is moving to is out the door," was a comment that she made often. Patrick started to fear that his job and career were going to be derailed by Kelly.

In the meantime, Kelly surrounded herself with individuals who were termed the "minion crew". The crew was an army of individuals that Kelly had handpicked; they were yes-people, new to the unit; they didn't know the full history and they did what Kelly wanted. Their role was to spy on the unit and report back to Kelly about who was cooperating, who was causing problems and who Kelly had to watch out for. She painted the picture that there were individuals who still supported Patrick and were sabotaging her. Members of the crew constantly praised Kelly and supported her vision. They were rewarded with leadership positions on her team. If any members of her leadership team pushed back, Kelly would shove back. Her crew learned not to question her. Those who did challenge her were eventually pushed out and quickly replaced by people that Kelly wanted. The atmosphere in the team became cut-throat and backstabbing. Kelly began speaking at conferences about the work the team was doing, but it was really Patrick's work that was being presented. Kelly took Patrick's former ideas, repackaged them and rolled them out to the organization.

Kelly did a complete reorganization within the team. Each area was renamed and employees were identified who were subject-matter experts in these particular areas. However, that was not the case. People were placed into these centers not for what they knew and could contribute, but based on their loyalties to Kelly. In the meantime, Kelly created so many layers between the units and the locations that everything filtered up, but never got to Kelly. Essentially, she did not lead the team but made her directors, managers and supervisors do it while she went around networking and building relationships with other vice presidents and the CEO. Kelly took credit for industry work and often explained that she had come up with these same ideas years ago and under her leadership her team had been practicing them long before they became popular through the research. Because Kelly was so charming, people believed this to be true—all except her own people.

It was clear to her followers that Kelly was a narcissist, or at least to those who did not worship her. It was also clear to these individuals that Kelly was a bully. As quickly as she came to like you, she would turn on you, especially if anyone threatened her or questioned her. Angelo was one of her favorite targets. Angelo was new to the organization and did not know the history of the unit. Therefore, when listening to Kelly share her vision and direction, Angelo thought that these ideas were Kelly's and he was impressed. Eventually, though, Angelo learned that these ideas were not Kelly's ideas, but were really Patrick's or other people's. Kelly spent a great deal of time networking and took ideas and concepts from the people she met with and spun them to her advantage. She vetted these newly packaged ideas through the "minion crew" and got feedback. Nothing that Kelly came up with was an original idea of her own. Eventually, Angelo came to realize this and he said something to Kelly. She ignored the pushback and started to give Angelo the jobs that no one wanted. Nicknamed the "hatchet man", Angelo was responsible for cutting programs, finding alternative solutions and implementing change. The team became resentful towards Angelo because he was doing these things. Angelo was viewed as the villain, while Kelly came across as untouchable.

When Angelo had to have major surgery, Kelly came into the hospital room shortly after, while he was recovering. Angelo was heavily medicated and Kelly asked him to submit several job requisitions for positions desperately needed in the department. Human Resources wanted these done immediately and they had to come through Angelo's emails. Angelo asked Kelly why she could not do it since she was the head of the unit. Kelly said she had tried to do it herself but that it had to be done by Angelo since these positions were for his area. Angelo was happy that he was finally getting these resources. He knew the team had been begging for these new positions. So Angelo agreed to work on the requisitions. While in pain and under medication, Angelo submitted the job requisitions, which required new job descriptions. The whole time that Angelo worked on these from his hospital bed, Kelly did her nails, waiting for Angelo to finish. When it took Angelo more time than anticipated, Kelly became frustrated. She kept saying that she needed these requisitions before the next morning otherwise the positions would not be filled. Angelo was in tears because he was so uncomfortable and the nurses kept coming into the room and saying that he needed to rest and his blood pressure was elevated. Kelly dismissed the nurses and said this was an emergency.

Finally, after three hours, the job requisitions were completed and emailed to Kelly's account. Kelly stood up and commented, "Well, it is about time. I can't believe it took you so long to finish a simple task." Kelly left. Angelo was in pain and called for the nurse. The nurses came into the room and tried to help Angelo get comfortable, but he was exhausted. The nurses shared with Angelo that they could not believe what they had just seen; they had never seen a boss come into a patient's room to demand work from them.

Angelo left the hospital and went home to recuperate. During this time, Kelly's "minion crew" began to call him at home about anything and everything, from small things to major things. Angelo finally stopped answering calls and emails, especially when the doctor said that he was not healing as he should. When word got to Kelly that Angelo had stopped answering calls and emails and was claiming that he was out on medical leave, she went to Angelo's house under the guise of dropping off a get-well gift. When Kelly got to Angelo's house she began telling him that he was expected to answer any requests from the staff. Kelly had bigger and more important things to do than deal with any of these issues and it was Angelo's responsibility to deal with them. He either had to learn to deal with them or look for another job. Angelo said that he was on medical leave and was not supposed to work while on short-term disability. Kelly told him she did not care and said that he had to "suck it up".

Angelo received another visitor, Patrick. Angelo was surprised to see Patrick since Patrick had disliked Angelo because one of his jobs was to cancel and revamp any projects that Patrick had worked on. Patrick came to Angelo's home and sat down to tell Angelo that Kelly was using him and that what had happened to Patrick was now happening to him. In the meantime, Dave, another team member, was back at the office playing the confidant to Kelly and throwing Angelo under the bus. Patrick warned Angelo that Kelly was out for blood and that Dave was helping her get information to take Angelo down. Angelo could not believe it. He told Patrick that Kelly was working to ramp up his area with new hires and that he had just worked on some emergency job requisitions. Patrick laughed and said, "You are not going to get your staffing. Kelly is giving those heads to Dave. You have been had by her." Patrick wished Angelo a speedy recovery and reminded him that he was out on short-term disability and should not do any work during this time. He told Angelo to see if he could get extra time off and to come back strong because he had to get ready for a fight. When Patrick left, Angelo had mixed feelings. Who was out to get who? Was Patrick out to destroy Kelly and was he using Angelo to fight his battles? Or was Kelly out to get Angelo and was Patrick being a friend and warning him? He didn't know.

Angelo waited a week and then emailed Kelly to ask when they could start the process of recruiting for the new positions. Kelly did not respond. Angelo called but his phone calls went unanswered. The more Angelo was ignored, the more paranoid he became. Angelo did not take Patrick's advice and went back to work as soon as possible. He had to get back in the game. He set up a meeting with Kelly, and when they met she said she was so very sorry but she had gone home that night from visiting Angelo in the hospital and forgotten about the job requisitions. She had not remembered for two weeks and at that point a hiring freeze had been put in place. Angelo was not getting his positions filled. Kelly said, "I need you to carry the workload and figure out how to get things done. It is so good to have you back." Angelo went back to his office and Patrick stopped by to ask him what he was doing back so soon. Angelo had no words to respond. Patrick asked him if he had come into recruit for his new positions, but Angelo told him simply, "No." Patrick said, "Well, Dave has been busy getting his two new positions filled. I warned you." Angelo sat in his office, closed the door and knew that things were taking a turn for the worse.

As the months went by, Kelly shifted the blame game from Patrick to Angelo. Dave was in Kelly's office on a daily basis and Angelo felt himself being put in cold storage. He was excluded from meetings and decisions made in regards to his unit. The stress was affecting Angelo and he was gaining weight, losing sleep and not healing as quickly from his surgery. His blood pressure was through the roof. Eventually he relapsed from his surgery and ended up back in the hospital. During his stay in the hospital, the doctor could not find the reason for the relapse. Eventually the doctor sat down on Angelo's bed and said, "You are still young. But whatever is happening in your workplace is causing you to become sick. You have two choices: either you quit or you die. The choice is yours." He got up and walked out of the room. Angelo knew what he had to do.

After Angelo was released and went back to work, Kelly continued her efforts to go after him. Angelo quietly looked for work behind the scenes and used his short-term disability time to look for work. He found a job and waited to tell Kelly. Eventually Kelly called Angelo into the office and told him that she was very disappointed in him. Angelo was a good worker but did not have the stamina to be in a leadership position. She was demoting him.

This was Angelo's time. He replied, "I quit." Kelly was dumbfounded as that was not what she wanted. She wanted to control Angelo and get him to do the dirty work and take a pay cut. Angelo said that he needed a few weeks to find something and then he would leave. Angelo wanted to collect his paycheck and his health insurance until his new job started. Kelly told Angelo that he owed her because she was the one who had brought him into her inner circle. Angelo left the organization as planned, but did so on his terms.

Kelly was emboldened and continued to go after what she wanted and her sights were now on the vice president's position. She was focused on getting the VP out of his position and she politicked herself for that position. She was more than qualified for the position and she was getting it. The person who had brought her into the organization was now the target. In the end, Kelly was successful in getting the vice president removed from the organization.

Angelo came forward to share his experiences with Kelly and he focused on sharing information about what had happened during his time working for Kelly. He knew that he would never go back to work there, but he was not going to let Kelly get off without a fight. Several people came forward, both within the organization and outside it. Kelly knew her days were numbered and she left, stating that she was over-qualified for the mess that was this organization. Patrick survived and ended up being happy in his role, out of the aim of Kelly. They filled the vice president's role with someone who understood the role and felt that Kelly's position should not be filled. The team was strong and the new vice president asked people to help determine who should lead the organization forward. The team chose the right individuals and they were excited about the direction in which the department was going. Since that time the department has written about best practice and they truly have become the centers of best practice within the industry. It was not due to Kelly, but through what they learned not to do.

The "queen bee" syndrome

Staines, Jayaratne and Tavris first identified the queen bee syndrome in 1973 (Cooper, 1997). The concept of the queen bee syndrome is that women in authority often treat other women more critically. Gabriel et al. (2018) explained the phenomenon as women essentially discriminating against one another in the workplace. As women move into levels of higher authority or seniority, they are able to flex their power. In recent studies, it has been reported that women tend to file more complaints against other women than against their male counterparts. Research also shows that women who are more assertive and dominate in the workplace are more likely to be the ones targeted by other females (Gabriel et al., 2018). Because of this behavior, women tend to hold back other women and prevent them from moving forward within the organization. It is essentially a form of bullying. The following provides an example of this type of behavior.

Alisha was the head female of the organization. She was considered to be the person who broke glass ceilings. She moved up through the organization quickly based on her competency. She started as a manager, moved to director and eventually to vice president. She was the only female on the senior leadership team, which consisted of five men and Alisha. For several years, she was a woman that many either looked up to or feared. She endured criticism from males within the organization who thought that she should not be on the executive leadership team. There were women who viewed Alisha as a role model and those who saw her as someone who made women look bad. Alisha didn't really care how people saw her. She viewed herself as a woman who was capable and able to run with the guys. She ran her division like a well-tuned machine. Her division never ran in a deficit; she had over 300 people reporting to her and she knew each one by name; and there was little to no staff turnover in her departments. Alisha was well respected in her field and often contacted to consult with organizations on her subject-matter expertise. She made her rounds and would not hold back on her feedback, which was constructive and candid; she would tell it like it was. There were times when she was known to make men cry, but at the end of the day everyone respected Alisha. Her direct reports always knew where they stood with her.

Richard, the president, announced his retirement for that spring. The organization had to name an interim president during the search for Richard's replacement. Alisha thought that this was her opportunity to step forward and she stepped up to the leadership role as acting president. She was the first female president of the organization; more than cracking the glass ceiling, she had shattered it. She was in position as the acting president when a new president was named. Alisha helped to transition the new president and gracefully stepped down.

The new president, Alex, was not as competent as Richard, but Alisha gave him the benefit of the doubt. He hired Toni to head up the information technology department, and one of the negotiation tactics she used was to be named vice president, so she would now be a member of the senior leadership team. It was clear to many people from the start that Toni did not know her area of IT. However, she loved to position herself as knowing everything about everyone else's areas of expertise. Toni did not spend much time discussing her own area, even though there were problems. Instead, she spent a great deal of time focusing on Alisha's areas and pointing out faults that just did not exist at all. In senior leadership meetings, whenever Alisha had spoken about something happening in her division, Toni was quick to criticize or offer advice on how to do things differently. Alisha was not softly spoken and would often call Toni out for some of the criticism and point out why certain recommendations would not work because of the nature of the organizational structure. Alex noticed the conflict between Alisha and Toni. He liked conflict and thought that positive and negative forms of conflict were good for promoting synergy in the group. Alex did not step in and address the problems with the two women.

Alex hired Janie as the Director of Communications and Public Relations. Janie was attractive and she and Alex enjoyed playful and harmless flirtations. Eventually, Alex asked Janie to sit in on the senior leadership team meetings. Within just a few months of being hired, Janie was sitting on the executive team, which was now six men and three women. Alex sat back and watched the conflict escalate between Alisha and Toni. Janie came to Alisha to ask her for mentoring, as she admired Alisha for being a strong female leader within the organization. Alisha agreed to mentor Janie and eventually word got to Toni about this mentorship. Toni didn't like that Alisha had been tapped to mentor Janie and said she would work with her instead. Alisha suggested that they both mentor Janie from two different perspectives. Toni told Janie that Alisha was old and behind the times. If Janie wanted to get ahead, she should stick with Toni. Janie moved over to Toni to be mentored, but neglected to say anything to Alisha about the move. Janie would just decline meeting notices for mentorship meetings with Alisha or tell her that something else had come up. A few months later Alex made the announcement that, under the mentorship of Toni, Janie was now the new Vice President of Communications and Public Relations. With the move Janie received a pay increase; she now made more money than Alisha, who had been with the organization over 20 years and had more responsibility and direct reports. Alisha spoke to Alex about the issue and he said that it would be worked out eventually and that Alisha should be a team member and wait for a few months.

Time went by and Alisha started to dread executive leadership meetings. These meetings were long, boring and full of negative conflict. When Alisha pushed back, she was called out either by Toni, Janie or Alex. After one very heated meeting Alex asked Alisha to stay behind. Alisha thought this was the time for her to speak up about the toxic relationship that was brewing with Toni and Janie. Alex sat down and said that he was disappointed that Alisha had not mentored Janie. As the senior woman, he would have thought she would have welcomed Janie and taken her under her guidance. Alisha said that she had and that Janie had often canceled meetings or simply not shown up. He explained that Janie had come to him to complain about Alisha and that Janie was not comfortable with her. Alex stated that he was impressed that Toni was the one who had come forward to mentor Janie. Alex then stated that, because of Alisha's unfair treatment of Janie, he had promoted Toni to vice president because she had demonstrated her loyalty to Alex and the organization. Alisha was devastated and shocked at what she had just heard. She had never been accused of blocking another woman, or anyone for that matter. Alisha believed in promoting women. Alex then went on to say that he did not appreciate the conflict between Toni and Alisha and that it had to stop. She agreed and said she welcomed a conversation in which she and Toni could set some expectations. Alex stated that he thought the relationship was too volatile and he would mediate the meeting. Alisha stated that she did not think they needed a mediator and could talk through it civilly. Alex said he did not think that was possible. Toni had already come to Alex to complain about her interactions with Alisha and to say that she did not feel comfortable meeting one on one with her. Alisha was again surprised.

"This is the first time I have heard that she has a problem with me," she exclaimed. "I knew we had problems and conflict, but I thought we could be professional about this and that she, as a professional, would come to talk to me if there was a problem so that we could work it out, rather than going over my head."

Alex said that Alisha was being too sensitive and he understood that women were sometimes overly emotional when it came to these situations, but he was happy to mediate and get things settled.

The mediation meeting took place a week later. At the meeting were Alex, Alisha and Toni. Alex also invited Norman from Human Resources. Alisha asked why HR was there and whether there was a disciplinary action taking place. Alex said no, that was not the case, but that in his experience of mediation HR should be available. Alisha just shrugged and said, "Fine."

The mediation was not a mediation, in Alisha's mind. It was an attack. Toni came out blaming Alisha for everything that was going wrong. By the end of the meeting, Alex, who was the mediator, had labeled Alisha an "obstructionist". When asked for examples, Alex could not provide any. He went on to say that he did not appreciate the conflict that Alisha was brewing up. He blamed Alisha for the tension and obstruction because he thought she wanted his job. After all, she had once been acting president and it was clear that she liked that position and wanted it for herself. Alisha said that was not true.

Shortly after the comment was made, there was a knock at the door. Janie walked in to the meeting. She reported that early on in her mentoring conversations with Alisha, a comment had been made that Alex should never have been hired. Janie said that she was uncomfortable with what Alisha thought of Alex; that was the reason why she went to Toni for mentoring. Alisha knew when she looked at Toni, who smirked at her, that she was being set up. At the end of the meeting Alex asked Alisha to stay back. He stated that he didn't need negativity on his team. Alisha said that the comment was never said and he shared with her the signed statement of both Toni and Janie that claimed Alisha had said it. He said that he respected Alisha's service to the organization but that it was not a good fit for her to stay on his leadership team or in the organization. She was given a severance package that Norman had drafted up. Alisha knew that this had all been orchestrated as a witch hunt. She left the office and the building.

A few weeks later they had a going-away party for Alisha. She had said that she did not want one, but Alex felt that it should take place so as not to reflect poorly on him. "Be a good team player just one more time," he said to her. She agreed and sat at the going-away party, listening to people making speeches, thanking Alisha and recognizing her for the good work she had done. Alex sat off to the side with Janie and Toni. One thing that Alex knew was that Alisha was loved by the organization and he was happy to be rid of her. Toni was also happy to see Alisha gone because she knew that she was now the go-to woman. Janie was happy to see Alisha gone because she thought she would be the person that Alex would rely on.

Upon leaving, Toni went to shake hands with Alisha, who refused. Toni said to her, "No hard feelings, it wasn't personal, it was just business. A girl has to do what a girl has to do in this man's world." Alisha left the organization. From a distance, she heard news about what was happening there. As time went by, Janie developed issues with Toni as they battled for power. Janie left the organization and tried to contact Alisha to apologize for her role in her firing. Alisha said she had nothing to say to Janie and wished her all the best. Janie asked if she could be mentored by Alisha, who started to laugh and hung up the phone. Toni was able to get Alisha, Janie and two other females out of the organization. One could classify Toni as the queen bee of the hive, having successfully eliminated any competition from other females in the organization. She is still at the top of the organization and still in Alex's favor.

Conclusion

This chapter has highlighted many of the dark side behaviors that we have covered in this book. These stories all rely on experiences of other individuals who have reported these behaviors. Again, these stories are real, and although they may have had some information added, for the most part they are actual demonstrations of these types of dark behaviors, which describe the act as well as the impact on the organization and on the individuals involved.

References

Cooper, V. 1997. Homophily or the Queen Bee Syndrome. *Sage Journals*, 28(4), 483–499.
Gabriel, A., Butts, M., Yuan. Z., Rosen, R., & Sliter, M. 2018. Further understanding incivility in the workplace: The effects of gender, agency and communion. *Journal of Applied Psychology*, 103(4): 362–382.

INDEX

active-passive aggression 6
age: bullying based on 44
aggressive behavior: categories 6–8; types
    6–7; *see also* passive-aggressive behavior
anonymity: social media 10–11, 20
anxiety: impact of dark behaviors 101–102
avoidance: impact of dark behaviors 102

backstabbers 58–59
body language 47, 79, 82, 128
bullying/bullies 36–50; blaming others
    43; bystanders stand against 136; case
    study 158–164; critical 46–47; definition
    37–39; derailment 45; destructive
    criticism/feedback 42; direct 45–46;
    emotional harassment 81; exclusion
    tactic 41–42; friendly 47–48; hoarder
    48–49; hostile work environment 42;
    indirect 46; invasion of personal space
    42; isolation tactic 41–42; name-calling
    42–43; opportunistic 49–50; personal
    characteristics, based on 44–45; physical
    characteristics, based on 44–45; physical
    threats 44; psychopath behavior
    72–73; public 45–46; responsibility
    shifting 43; rules and policies applied
    inconsistently 43–44; rumor or gossip
    spreading 44; silent 46; tactics 41–45;
    threats to job or personal security 44;
    types 45–50; unfair criticism/feedback
    42; verbal and non-verbal threats 44;
    workplace 37
bystanders: reaction to dysfunctional or
    uncivil behavior 13, 106–107, 135–136

cell phones and incivility 20
civility: definition 16–17
coaching on civility 122
code of conduct for employees 116–117
communication: online etiquette 119;
    organizations 118–119, 125
control: behavior tactic 31; loss caused by
    dark behaviors 103
corporate psychopaths *see* psychopaths
corporations: deviant behavior 66–68
costs of incivility 12–13; emotional costs
    112–113; organizations 108–111
crime: corporate deviances 67–68;
    violence 93
criticism: unfair or destructive 42
culture: organizations 33, 110–111, 118,
    124–125
customers: reactions to incivility 33
cyberspace: cell phones and incivility 20;
    emails 119; incivility 23–24; technology
    10–11, 20

dark side: meaning 5–6; *see also* aggressive
    behavior; deviant behavior; dysfunctional
    behavior; incivility
deception 90
depression: impact of dark behaviors 101
derailment: bullying 45
deviant behavior 66–96; corporate
    deviances 66–68; definition 66;
    definition of corporate deviance 67;
    employees, by 68–80; evil 89–92;
    extreme 89–92; identification 68–69;
    impact on individuals 99–107; incivility

10; indicators 95–96; meaning 6;
organizational impact 107–113;
prevention 95–96; theft 70; triggers
69–70; types of individual 70–80; *see also*
emotional harassment; psychopaths;
sexual harassment/harassers; violence
direct-indirect aggression 6
disability: bullying based on 44
disciplinary actions against employees 117
discrimination 87, 135, 136
documents: conversations with leader on
dysfunction 135
domestic violence 93
dysfunctional behavior 36–63; backstabbers
58–59; business impact 109–111;
bystanders reaction 13, 106–107, 135–136;
causes 8–9; economic impact 105–106;
educating organizations to address
117–126; emotional costs 112–113;
financial impact 105–106, 111–112; impact
on individuals 99–107; incivility becoming
10, 33; interventions 120–121; leadership
133–135; meaning 6; organizational impact
107–113; paranoia 50–51; physical distress
caused by 104–105; psychological distress
100–104, 112–113; ruined careers 106;
the target 127–130; teams 109, 123–124;
see also bullying/bullies; emotionally
abusive behavior; manipulation/master
manipulators; narcissism/narcissist

education: civility and behaviors 122; online
etiquette 119
EEOC *see* Equal Employment Opportunity
Commission
egotists *see* narcissism/narcissist
emails: online etiquette 119
emotional harassment 81–83; bullying
81; characteristics 81–83; dominating
behavior 83; intentional behavior
82; jealousy 83; non-physical 81–82;
recurring behavior 82; use of power 82;
verbal 82–83; *see also* sexual harassment/
harassers
emotionally abusive behavior: definition 81;
examples 62–63; gaslighting 61–62, 78;
harassment 81–83
employees: accountability 123; as bystanders
reacting to dysfunctional or uncivil
behavior 13, 106–107, 135–136; code of
conduct 116–117; deviant behaviors by
68–80; disciplinary actions against 117;
employee-to-employee violence 93–94;
exit interviews 123; feedback 122; impact
of dark behaviors on 12–13, 33, 99–107,

109–110, 112; informal meetings 120;
interviewing 114–116, 122; manager's
behavior towards 121; morale 109;
onboarding process 116–117; peer
relationships 123; screening 114–116;
shifting within organization 123; staff
turnover costs 110; violence 93
employment discrimination 136
Equal Employment Opportunity
Commission (EEOC) 85–86, 87,
136, 137
evil behavior: examples 90–92
exclusion behavior tactic 31, 41–42, 127
exit interviews 123

family conflict: impact of dark
behaviors 100
feedback: managers, from 122; unfair or
destructive 42
financial performance: dark behaviors,
impact of 109

gaslighting 61–62, 78
gender: bullying 44; interpretation
differences 9
generation: interpretation differences 9
gossip: bullying 44; case study 149–150;
consequences 27–28, 129; organizational
29; participants 28–29; reaction to 29

harassment: case study 150–155;
investigations 125–126; women, by 89;
see also emotional harassment; sexual
harassment/harassers
human resources: dysfunctional behavior
issues 135, 136–137
humiliation: impact of dark behaviors 102

incivility 16–34; business impact
109–111; bystanders reaction 13,
106–107, 135–136; case study on
society/workplace 138–141; causes in
the workplace 26–27; costs 12–13,
108–111; customer reactions 33;
cyberspace 24; definition 17–18;
definition in the workplace 22;
dysfunctional behavior, into 10, 33;
economic impact 105–106; emotional
costs 112–113; employee reactions 33;
example 26; financial impact
105–106, 111–112; impact on
individuals 99–107; increased perception
of 21–22; interpersonal 23; leadership
133–135; manager's intervention
121–123; meaning 5–6; organizational

impact 32–33, 107–113; overt 25; physical distress caused by 104–105; psychological distress 100–104, 112–113; reactions in the workplace 33; research in the United States 18–20; road rage 10; ruined careers 106; society 10–11, 18–21; subtle 24–25; target of 127–130; types in the workplace 23–24, 27–32; victimless 24; workplace 11–12, 22–32; *see also* gossip; passive-aggressive behavior

internet *see* emails; social media

interviews: employees 114–116, 122; exit of employee 123

investigations: organizational harassment 125–126; retaliation 126

isolation: behavior tactic 31, 41–42, 81–82, 127; impact of dark behaviors 102

jealousy 83

leaders/leadership: dark behaviors, impact of 109; dealing with incivility and dysfunction from 133–135; development plan 118; expectations contributing to dark behavior 8–9; organizational culture 125; *see also* managers

Madoff, Bernie 75–77

managers: behavior towards employees 121; feedback to 122; interventions on incivility 121–123; self-awareness 121; stress 121

manipulation/master manipulators: distortion of relationships 59; gaslighting 61–62, 78; honing in on flaws and insecurities 60–61; lack of respect 59–60; psychopaths 74

name-calling 42–43

narcissism/narcissist 51–58; case study 158–164; characteristics 54–58; corporate 52–53; definition 52; distrusting of others 57–58; emotionally challenged 57; extreme 53; inability to maintain relationships 55; lack of empathy 54–55; minions 56; not a team player 57; one-sided decision making 55; positioning 56; productive 53; quiet 53–54; self-focus 55; taking credit 56–57; threat of challenge 56; types 53–54; unable to show gratitude 57; visioning 55

non-deviant behavior: meaning 5–6

non-verbal threats 44, 128–129

online etiquette 119

organizations: addressing dysfunctional behavior 117–126; business impact of incivility 109–111; communication 118–119, 125; corporate narcissism 52–53; costs of incivility 108–111; culture 33, 110–111, 118, 124–125; dark behaviors, impact of 107–113; gossip 29; impact of incivility 32–33; interventions to address dysfunctional behavior 120–121; investigations into harassment 125–126; proactive 120–121; *see also* corporations

paranoia 50–51

passive-aggressive behavior 30–32; backhanded compliments 31; case study 141–144; control 31; dishonesty 30–31; exclusion tactic 31; isolation tactic 31; leaving tasks undone 32; silence 31; wishful thinking 32

physical-verbal aggression 6

politics: social media 11–12, 22

post-traumatic stress disorder (PTSD) 103

psychological distress 100–104, 112–113

psychopaths 70–80; arrogance 74; bullying behavior 72–73; chameleon-like behavior 72, 75; charm 74; example 75–77, 79–80; leadership role 77–78; looking down 74–75; manipulation 74; pathology 73–80; recognition of behavior 78–80; relationships 73–74; lack of remorse 73; tactics 71–72, 73–75, 78; thrill-seeking 75, 78; traits 71–72, 74–75

race: bullying based on 44

racial discrimination 136

records: conversations with leader on dysfunction 135

recruitment: checking references 115–116; screening 114–116; *see also* interviews

road rage 10; case study 138–141

rumors 27, 44; case study 149–150

sabotage 46, 92, 110; derailment 45

screening employees 114–116

self-harm 103–104

self-promotion 53; case study 155–158

sexual discrimination 87; bystanders stand against 135

sexual harassment/harassers 83–89; definition 85–86, 87; dominance 88; history 84–85; impact 88–89; key facts 86–87; predatory 88; private 87; public 87; reporting to HR 136; strategic 88;

street 88; territorial 88; types 86–87;
United States 84–85
sexuality: bullying based on 44
silence behavior tactic 31–32, 82
social isolation tactic 42, 82, 127
social media; anonymity 10–11, 20; politics
11–12, 22
society: incivility 10–11, 18–21
stress: deviant behavior and 70; manager's
121; physical 104–105; psychological
100–104, 112–113

target of incivility: addressing the situation
130–135, 136–137; case study 144–149;
choice of 128–130; indicators 127–128;
speaking up 89, 126, 135–136
teams: accountability 123, 124; cohesion
118; dysfunctional 109, 123–124
technology: cell phones and incivility 20;
dark behavior, contribution to 8; emails
119; social media 10–11, 20; societal
incivility and 20–21
theft 70
Trump, Donald 11, 22, 84

uncivil behavior *see* incivility
United States: research on incivility 18–20;
sexual harassment 84–85

verbal aggression 6, 44, 82–83
victim *see* target of incivility
violence: categories 93; criminal 93;
customer/client 93; domestic 93;
employee-to-employee 93–94;
ideological 93; physical 92–94

weight: bullying based on 44–45
women: case study on the
"queen bee" syndrome 164–167;
harassment by 88, 89